The book explores the factors that contributed to the definition of a 'European identity' with special regard to the role played by the interaction between national Constitutional Courts and European Courts.

There is no doubt that the Courts have been key actors in the progressive establishing of this identity over the years by defining elements of homogeneity and affirming or reaffirming essential values, such as human dignity, in respect of that pluralism which represents a distinctive feature of Europe; nevertheless, this 'circular movement' has not failed to reveal contradictions and concerns that are still unresolved over time.

Thanks to the reflections developed by the group of authors collaborating to this publication, the book delves into the theme with a variety of approaches and perspectives. More specifically, it is structured in three main parts: *i*) the historical roots of a common European heritage, emphasizing its role in shaping what is currently called the 'European way of life'; *ii*) 'lights and shadows' of constructing the European identity through the instruments of multilevel and inter-court relationships, by critically analysing the propulsive and homogenising tendencies coming in particular from the CJEU; *iii*) the so-called 'dialogue between Courts', by addressing some significant jurisprudential trends of supranational and national Courts and relevant cases in recent years, offering new insights into the 'model' of multilevel protection of rights.

Maria Grazia Rodomonte (PhD) is Associate Professor of Constitutional Law at the Department of Political Science (DISP), Sapienza University of Rome. She is Director of the Sapienza-CIVIS (Europe's Civic University Alliance) Advanced Training Course in *Rights and Democracy: the Multilevel Protection of Fundamental Rights and the Role of Constitutional and European Courts*. She is the author of more than 70 essays related to several issues in Italian Constitutional Law and Political Institutions, including gender equality, regionalism, constitutional justice, multilevel protection of rights, democracy and populisms in Europe. Among the monographies: *L'eguaglianza senza distinzioni di sesso in Italia. Evoluzioni di un principio a settant'anni dalla nascita della Costituzione* (Giappichelli 2018); *Il bicameralismo incompiuto. Democrazia e rappresentanza del pluralismo territoriale in Italia* (Padova 2020).

Ludovica Durst (PhD) is Assistant Professor of Constitutional and Public Law at the Department of Political Science (DISP), Sapienza University of Rome, and Associate Researcher at the CNR-CID Ethics. She is Scientific coordinator of the Sapienza-CIVIS (Europe's Civic University Alliance) Advanced Training Course on *Rights and Democracy: The Multilevel Protection of Fundamental Rights and the Role of the Constitutional and European Courts* and PI of the project *The judicial protection of rights in the virtual ecosystem. Challenges, critical issues and opportunities for a 'digital constitutionalism'* (Sapienza 2022). She's author of a monography titled *Introduzione al ruolo della 'sicurezza' nel sistema dei diritti costituzionali* (Aracne 2019) and of scientific publications mainly focusing on protection of fundamental rights, new technologies, constitutional justice.

Judicial Review, Fundamental Rights and Rule of Law: The Construction of the European Constitutional Identity

Judicial Review, Fundamental Rights and Rule of Law: The Construction of the European Constitutional Identity

Edited by

Maria Grazia Rodomonte and Ludovica Durst

Routledge
Taylor & Francis Group
LONDON AND NEW YORK

G. Giappichelli Editore

First published 2025
by Routledge
4 Park Square, Milton Park, Abingdon, Oxon OX14 4RN

and by Routledge
605 Third Avenue, New York, NY 10158

Routledge is an imprint of the Taylor & Francis Group, an informa business

and by G. Giappichelli Editore
Via Po 21, Torino – Italia

British Library Cataloguing-in-Publication Data
A catalogue record for this book is available from the British Library

Library of Congress Cataloging-in-Publication Data
A catalog record has been requested for this book

ISBN: 978-10-328-8840-8 (hbk-Routledge)
ISBN: 978-10-034-9389-1 (ebk-Routledge)
ISBN: 978-10-327-9797-7 (pbk-Routledge)
ISBN: 979-12-211-0786-9 (pbk-Giappichelli)

Typeset in Simoncini Garamond
by G. Giappichelli Editore, Turin, Italy

The manuscript has been subjected to a peer review process prior to publication and has been subject to linguistic revision.

The publication is supported by the Department of Political Science-Sapienza University of Rome, and by the research project PRIN2017 CUP B88D19002540001 "The essential and competitive role of specialised courts and alternative dispute resolution mechanisms in financial law as a precondition for the attainment of social desirable levels of public and private enforcement. Lessons from history in administrative and business law and the future of judicial review in European financial law in light of European and national fundamental rights" (Sapienza Research Unit, on Forms of protection of fundamental rights in the economic-financial sphere between European constitutional tradition and prospects for innovation, Scientific Coordinator Prof. Roberto Nania).

CONTENTS

CONTRIBUTORS

Francesco Battaglia, Associate Professor of EU Law, Sapienza University of Rome.

Antonio López Castillo, Professor of Constitutional Law, UAM – Autonomous University of Madrid.

Adriana Ciancio, Professor of Constitutional and Public Law, University of Catania.

Athina Dimopoulou, Professor of Legal History, National and Kapodistrian University of Athens.

Raphaël Déchaux, Maître de conferences, Public Law, University of Lorraine.

Ludovica Durst, Assistant Professor of Constitutional and Public Law, Sapienza University of Rome; Associate Researcher, National Research Council (CNR) - CID Ethics.

Cristina Fasone, Associate Professor of Comparative Public Law, LUISS University.

Maria Cristina Marchetti, Professor of Political Sociology, Sapienza University of Rome.

Daniele Mattiangeli, Senior Scientist of History of Law, Paris Lodron University of Salzburg.

Martin Nettesheim, Professor of Public Law and European Law, Eberhard Karls University of Tübingen.

Giovanni Pitruzzella, Professor of Constitutional and Public Law, University of Palermo; Judge of the Italian Constitutional Court; former Advocate General of the CJEU.

Maria Grazia Rodomonte, Associate Professor of Constitutional and Public Law, Sapienza University of Rome.

Giulia Santomauro, Post-doc Resarcher of Constitutional Law, Sant'Anna School of Advanced Studies, Pisa; Associated reasercher in the 'Human Rights Discourse in Migration Societies (MeDiMi)' project.

Federico Savastano, Assistant Professor of Constitutional and Public Law, Sapienza University of Rome.

Elena-Simina Tănăsescu, Professor of Constitutional Law and European Law, University of Bucharest; Judge of the Romanian Constitutional Court.

Giulia Vasino, Assistant Professor of Constitutional and Public Law, Carlo Bo University of Urbino.

Foreword

IDENTITY OF THE EUROPEAN UNION AND IDENTITIES OF THE MEMBER STATES: WHAT IS THE RELATIONSHIP?

Giovanni Pitruzzella *

There are two different ways of conceiving the relationship between the identity of the Union and the constitutional identity of the Member States: the first sees them in opposition, the second in a relationship of cooperation and mutual learning.

The notion of 'identity' itself has an inherent ambiguity. On one hand, identity is used to distinguish oneself from others and requires protection against those who have been marked by a different identity and have the power to destroy and assimilate the former.

Today we speak of the *politics of identity* specifically to indicate the urge of groups with a distinct identity to demand to be recognised as such, rather than be assimilated into the dominant identity and even to obtain forms of redress for abuses committed against them.

At the same time, cultural rights, which precisely signify the recognition and guarantee of cultural identities that are juxtaposed and in no way assimilated to the identity considered dominant are becoming more prominent. In this case, identity is used to erect barriers to protect the identities of very specific groups identified on the basis of certain cultural factors.

Cultural identity can also be non-exclusive, but open to confrontation and dialogue. In this case, several identities may overlap and bridges are built between them thus connecting them, although they remain distinct. In contrast to the first version of identity, belonging to an identity is not exclusive, so that the same subject can belong to different groups, each with its own identity.

This relationship between different but complementary identities is at the core of the European Union. Article 4 TEU, which recognises national identities, must be read in conjunction with Article 2, which sets out the fundamental values of the European Union. They form the basis of what Article 2 itself configures as a single society: respect for human dignity,

---

* Judge of the Italian Constitutional Court. The opinions expressed are of a personal nature and do not reproach the administration in any way.

freedom, democracy, equality, the rule of law and respect for human rights, including the rights of persons belonging to minorities. These values are common to the Member States in a society in which pluralism, non-discrimination, tolerance, justice, solidarity and equality between women and men prevail. Member States are equal parts of this European society, according to Article 4(2) TEU, which mentions equality between Member States before national identities. Common values, a European society, equality between Member States and then the guarantee of national constitutional identities are the foundation of the Union.

In the historic judgment of the Court of Justice of 27 February 2018, the *Portuguese Judges' Association* case,[1] as it is known, considered it of "primary importance" to preserve the independence of judges in order to guarantee the principle of effective judicial protection of the rights that individuals derive from Union law. The Court linked this principle to the value of the rule of law enshrined in Article 2 TEU, stressing that the Union is founded on certain values common to the Member States, including the rule of law.

This judgment marked a turning point in the constitutional structure of the Union, as it focused the constitutional identity of the Union on the common values listed in Article 2 TEU.

More recently, in the judgments adopted by the Grand Chamber on 16 February 2022, the so-called *conditionality judgments*, the Court stated that "Article 2 is not merely a statement of political guidelines or intentions, but contains the values which ... are an integral part of the identity of the EU as a common legal order, these are values which find concrete expression in principles, including binding obligations on the States".[2]

As the President of the Court of Justice, Koen Lenaerts, observed in an extrajudicial context, the Union is "first and foremost a Union of values". This is not just the value of the rule of law, but all the values listed in Article 2.

This view of the Union has important consequences. First, values – but mind you, values, not legal principles – express a particularly strong form of integration. To share the values listed in Article 2 is not simply to be part of an internal market or an international organisation looking after com-

[1] ECJ, judgment of 27 February 2018, Associação Sindical dos Juízes Portugueses, C-64/16, EU:C:2018:117.

[2] K. Lenaerts, "On Checks and Balances: the Rule of Law within the EU", *Columbia Journal of European Law*, Special Issue, 2023, p. 1, and also K. Lenaerts, *National Identity, the Equality of Member States before the Treaties and the Primacy of EU law, Bilateral meeting between the Court of Justice of the European Union and the Italian Constitutional Court: celebrating the 70th Anniversary of the Court of Justice of the European Union*, Rome, 5 and 6 September 2022.

mon interests. It means being part of a European society. Von Bogdandy argues explicitly that Article 2 and the European public law based on it are at the origin of a European society.[3]

Member States freely joined this society and agreed to share these values. Values, unlike principles, do not provide for trade-offs or allow themselves to be sacrificed for the sake of another value, such as a State's cultural identity.

The jurisprudence of the Court of Justice on the rule of law, which does not tolerate violations by a State in the name of its specific cultural identity, but also the jurisprudence on the prohibition of regression in the realisation of a value, fits into this perspective. Values, by virtue of their universality require a gradual process of realisation. A State cannot move backwards to the level of realising a value and thereby weaken it. That is why, according to the Court, no illiberal and anti-democratic tendency can be allowed in the Union.[4]

One of these values is equality between Member States. Equality means that Union law must have the same meaning for everyone. Hence the role of the Court of Justice in ensuring the uniform interpretation of Union law.

The national courts, and particularly the constitutional courts, have the interpretation of national constitutions reserved to them, but the interpretation of Union law from the Treaties for everyone is the responsibility of the Court of Justice.

The same requirement of equality and of a law applied in the same way in all States grounds the two principles of the supremacy of Union law and direct effect, but also the essentiality for the Union's legal order of the preliminary reference, which prevents as the Court of Justice has stated, the power of the individual national court to refer a question to the Court for a preliminary ruling from being limited.

The binding and uncompromising nature of the values is coupled with their generality, which comprises of different forms of realisation. This is where the constitutional autonomy of the Member States comes into play, in the face of which the Union comes to a halt, except in the case of a specific conflict with the rules of European law.

Thus, the Court of Justice recognises that the value of the rule of law underpins the inviolable principle of the independence of judges, but recognises that each State may define its judicial order differently in accordance with its own constitutional principles,[5] or that the prohibition of discrimination in

---

[3] A. Von Bogdandy, *Strukturwandel des öffentlichen Rechts*, Berlin 2022.

[4] ECJ, judgment of 20 April 2021, Repubblika, C-896/19, EU:C:2021:311.

[5] ECJ, judgment of 21 December 2021, Euro Box Promotion and Others, C-357/19, C-379/19, C-547/19, C-811/19 and C-840/19, EU:C:2021:1034; ECJ, judgment of 22

labour relations applies to all States, as laid down in the relevant directives, but that since states follow different constitutional principles regarding the place of religion in the public sphere, they will regulate in accordance with their constitutional principles the possibility of wearing the Islamic headscarf by a civil servant in a public administration, even to the extent of justifying the ban.[6] In Boris Cilevičs and Others,[7] the Court of Justice held that it was legitimate for a member State to protect its national identities by adopting measures that sought to promote and develop the use of the official language in higher education. Such a policy, according to the Court, constitutes a manifestation of national identity for the purpose of Article 4(2) TEU.

But if values are generic and are specified in the principles that are then detailed in more stringent rules, in this process of specification comes the dialogue between the Courts, between the Court of Justice and the Constitutional Courts. In this way, a process takes place that is not top-down, but is circular. The Constitutional Courts question the Court of Justice on the meaning of the Union law, also of the Union constitutional law, and the Court's answer influences the national living constitution, because the Constitutional Courts in their judgments use the case law of the Court of Justice (a frequent occurrence in the case law of the Italian Constitutional Court). At the same time, the Court of Justice takes its cue from the indications contained in the preliminary references from the constitutional courts to interpret EU law, which is thus animated by what the Court of Justice has long called the "constitutional traditions common to the Member States". The Court of Justice and the Constitutional Courts also make references to the Jurisprudence of the Court of Strasbourg, when dealing with fundamental rights. The community of the European supreme courts (Court of Justice, Strasbourg Court, Constitutional Courts) thus forms, through a process of mutual learning, the European constitutional heritage, which is and must remain essentially pluralistic, cohesive around common values while safeguarding national constitutional specificities.

This complex framework forms the basis of this volume, edited by Maria Grazia Rodomonte and Ludovica Durst. By retracing some of the main threads of the European integration process, it has the merit of providing the reader with a broad overview of the problematic definition and construction of a European constitutional identity. This is a crucial issue that imposes itself on the reflection not only of jurists in relation to future developments of participation in the common European project.

February 2022, RS (Effect of the decisions of a constitutional court), C-430/21, EU:C:2022:99.

[6] ECJ, judgment of 28 November 2023, Commune d'Ans, C-148/22, EU:C:2023:924.

[7] ECJ, judgment of 7 September 2022, Cilevičs and Others, C-391/20, EU:C:2022:638.

PREFACE

The construction of a common European identity is not a novel issue: it is at the core of the long-lasting process, which prompted the move from a European Economic Community set up in the aftermath of the second-world war to a new worldwide-known entity, the European Union (EU). Actually, the EU is much more than just a wide common market and is regarded as a genuine political actor, a key global player as well as a regulatory power both with regard to its Member States and, on the basis of the "Brussels effect", in the international sphere.

Nevertheless, far from having completed or reached a definitive point on this journey, the EU is still undergoing crucial transformations, questioning the very fundamental goals and principles of its political project and facing the challenges brought by its federalizing tendencies and institutional organisation, sharpened by enlargement dynamics or even exiting procedures of former Member States (such as 'Brexit').

At the same time, at Member States' level, democracies seem to be grappling with a crisis of identity and values that even challenge the rule of law in Europe in some cases.

How to deal with the complex issue of building a common European identity in the context of the current crisis of democracies and political representation? Moreover, how can the need to respect the 'national identity' of each member state, also stipulated in Article 4 of the Treaty of the Union, be reconciled with the need to proceed along the path of building a constitutional identity for the Union itself? And besides this, what does the concept of 'European constitutional identity' refer to? Indeed, it not only derives from the EU Treaties and the rulings of the Court of Justice (CJEU), but it also comprises a nucleus which can be considered as a sort of European 'material constitution', built on common history, cultural heritage and values, including the protection of fundamental rights, expanding towards a wider dimension fostered by the European Court of Human Rights (ECtHR).

Within this complex framework, this book explores the factors that contributed to the definition of a 'European identity' with special regard to the role that can be played by the interaction between national Constitutional Courts and European Courts, and thus tries to investigate whether through this way it might be possible to follow paths of a political and democratic 'revitalization'. There is no doubt that the Courts have been key actors in the progressive establishing of this identity over the years by defining elements of homogeneity and affirming or reaffirming essential values; nevertheless, this 'circular movement' has not failed to reveal contradictions and concerns that are still unresolved over time.

In this regard, the question remains open whether the construction of this identity can be delegated to the prevailing role of the Courts compared to that of the political process: a theme that is part of the broader issue of the relationship between the juridical and the political power as well as the crisis of democracy, even in its pluralistic essence.

Thanks to the reflections developed by the group of authors collaborating to this publication, consisting of highly experienced academics in the fields of Constitutional, European and Comparative Public Law, but also in Legal History and Sociology, as well as young scholars, fascinated by this challenging research topic, the book delves into the theme with a variety of approaches and perspectives.

More specifically, the book is structured in three main parts: *i)* the historical roots of a common European heritage, emphasizing its role in shaping what is currently called the 'European way of life'; *ii)* 'lights and shadows' of constructing the European identity through the instruments of inter-court relationships, by critically analysing the propulsive and homogenising tendencies coming in particular from the CJEU; *iii)* the so-called 'dialogue between Courts', by addressing some significant jurisprudential trends of supranational and national Courts and relevant cases in recent years, offering new insights into the 'model' of multilevel protection of rights.

The hope is that this work can contribute to enrich the analysis and debate on the actual phase of the European project, by deepening the comprehension both of its origins and present dynamics, and to provide further perspectives to reflecting on the future trajectories of democracy and of the EU as a space of dialogue between multilevel subjects and of non-waivable guarantees for fundamental rights.

Indeed, the nature of Europe is characterized by cultural and legal pluralism. This is one of its main values and assets. Therefore, strengthening unity while guaranteeing difference is still the real challenge of a united Europe today.

Maria Grazia Rodomonte and Ludovica Durst

Part I

IN SEARCH OF 'A EUROPEAN WAY OF LIFE'. IDENTITY AND FUNDAMENTAL RIGHTS: LESSONS FROM THE PAST AND FUTURE PERSPECTIVES

Chapter 1

'FUNDAMENTAL RIGHTS' AND THE RULE OF LAW IN ANCIENT GREECE AND ROME

Athina Dimopoulou

ABSTRACT: *The paper discusses whether the concept of fundamental rights, such as included in modern legal texts, can be found in the legal orders of ancient Greece and Rome. It is argued that although the concept of individual rights is a modern construction, and when one speaks about rights in antiquity one should beware of anachronisms, the equivalent of many modern rights can be identified in both ancient Greece and Rome, forming their early precursors. Despite the fact that the notion of natural law came close to recognizing an intrinsic value to human beings, rights in antiquity were always connected to citizen status. Broad categories of persons, including women, foreigners, and slaves, were deprived of basic rights. However, for those entitled to citizenship, rights recognized and protected by law included the right to life, liberty, equality before the law, political rights, freedom of movement, the protection of children and the elderly, the protection of property, freedom of association, access to health services and many others. In both ancient Greece and Rome access to a judicial system was essential for the protection of such rights.*

SUMMARY: 1. 'Rights': a modern concept with ancient roots? – 2. The birth of rights connected with the written law. – 3. Rights and natural law. – 4. *Humanitas* and other concepts connected to rights. – 5. Rights limited to male citizens. – 6. Fundamental citizen 'rights' in ancient Greece and Rome.

1. 'Rights': a modern concept with ancient roots?

In the Preamble of the EU Charter of Fundamental Rights, the Union declares that it is conscious of its spiritual and moral heritage, and describes itself as an area of freedom, security, and justice, to be founded on the common values of the peoples of Europe, including human dignity, freedom, equality and solidarity, the principles of democracy and the rule of law. Within the spiritual and moral heritage of the European continent, the ancient Greek and Roman civilizations and their respective achievements hold central stage. The Greeks' contributions to the modern world included the foundations of democracy, philosophy, art, politics, and science, while the Romans distinguished themselves in public administration and the creation of the legal system that forms the core of the civil law legal tradition to this day. To what extent, however, can we speak of a contribution of both civilizations to the principles recognized today as 'fundamental rights'?

The starting point of many historians' discussion of the subject is the constatation that 'rights' in the modern sense is not an ancient concept.[1] The question of whether the idea of rights did exist in antiquity, or can even be approached in historical terms, is open to debate and inspires contrary scholarly views.[2] The notion of 'fundamental rights' of the individual, which are universal and inalienable, is generally considered a concept that begins to take shape from the Enlightenment onwards, in the late 17th and mainly in the 18th century, with the American and French Bills of Rights, before reaching its peak in the 20th and 21st century. Modern approaches to ancient societies are sometimes accompanied by criticism precisely regarding the lack of 'fundamental rights', which is connected to our own understanding thereof. Any attempt to evaluate the past according to our own criteria of what constitutes a 'right' entails the risk of anachronisms. In ancient societies any notion akin to 'individual rights' was depending first and foremost on one's personal status as a free person or a slave, then to the possession of a specific citizenship and then to gender. Ancient Greek and Roman societies were male dominated and did not recognize an intrinsic value to all human beings regardless of status, citizenship, gender, or race. Slavery for example was considered a universal norm that formed the basis of ancient economies.

The term 'right' itself, in the modern sense, did not exist in ancient Greek, which makes its use problematic even when discussing ancient realities. Instead, among others, the adjective "*δίκαιον*" (just) was used to signify a right, which derives from *Δίκη*, the personification of Justice, who in Greek mythology was the daughter of Zeus and Themis (the personification of justice) and the sister of Εὐνομία (Order) and Εἰρήνη (Peace). This semantically rich term denoted an act of right, a duty, the amendment of a wrong, hence also a judgement or penalty, but also the pleadings or documents in court. *Δίκαιον* was the opposite of "*ἀδίκημα*", meaning offence, and all its different meanings converge around the idea that rights are synonymous with and based upon the rule of law. The same concept is evident in Latin, where the equally semantically rich term "*ius*" meant the law in

---

[1] See M. Ostwald, "Shares and rights: 'Citizenship' Greek and American style", in J. Ober, Ch. Hedrick (eds.), *Demokratia. A conversation on democracies, ancient and modern*, Princeton 1996, pp. 49-61.

[2] See J. Giltaij, K. Tuori, "Human rights in Antiquity? Revisiting anachronism and Roman law", in P. Slotte, M. Halme-Tuomisaari (eds.), *Revisiting the Origins of Human Rights*, Cambridge 2015, pp. 39-63, citing previous works on the debate.

general, a particular law, the place where justice is rendered (*iuris-dictio*), a set of possibilities to act (*jus est facultas agendi*, "law is a license to act") and the rights (*iura*) of an individual citizen or of a group of persons.

It is however important to acknowledge that approaching ancient societies with a modern mindset which focuses on the individual differs fundamentally from the approach of the ancients, who viewed the individual with much less importance that the collectivity. Securing rights did not focus on individual persons, but on groups of persons of similar interests, namely the citizens. We must also remember that some modern aspects of human rights, such as the legal equality of all regardless of gender, are very recent historical achievements. While the projection of our modern moral concepts and our own understanding of "rights" into the past would be a pointless exercise,[3] trying to identify whether the Greco-Roman cultural heritage recognized some "rights" worthy of protection, offers the legal historian food for thought on a variety of questions related to the long historical process leading to the recognition of such rights. What is considered a right in the legal sense? How were rights first born and acknowledged by a given state? If rights are not codified, do they exist? What is the relation between social strife and the recognition of rights? What are the moral principles fueling the quest for rights? What are the sources attesting their existence and to what extent do they depend upon an efficient system of administration of justice and access to impartial courts of law? The experience of ancient Greece and Rome, as two civilizations in which the notion of the citizen as holder of a series of rights guaranteed by the law was first formulated, both within the context of the Athenian democracy and the Roman Republic and then throughout the Roman Empire, allows us to study the process of the birth of rights.

Several caveats must be considered. Specific rights are always connected to a historical period, geographical area, and its socio-political context. In the context of a very short article, only a basic outline of some aspects related to the question of rights in antiquity can be briefly discussed. The ancient Greek and Roman civilizations, from their beginning to their merger in later antiquity form an historical spectrum which is too broad, complex, and ever changing to allow for generalizations, and this is without even taking into account the fragmentary state of the sources. With no 'bill of rights' or written constitutions existing in either society, to find the equivalent of modern rights we must therefore search an enormous corpus of dif-

---

[3] See G. Crifo, "Per una prospettiva romanistica dei diritti dell'uomo", in K.M. Girardet, U. Nortmann (eds.), *Menschenrechte und europäische Identität: Die antiken Grundlagen,* Stuttgart 2005, pp. 245-247.

fuse information in literary sources, such as the writings of philosophers and historians, theater plays and other literary works, the various legal sources of ancient Greek cities and the Roman Empire, including laws and other legal enactments, the *ius honorarium*, the jurists' works and Justinian's codification. This wide range of sources shows however that both civilizations shared a common understanding that their citizens should enjoy certain rights, although their formulation was the result of a long process.

2. The birth of rights connected with the written law

The birth of rights in ancient Greece and Rome was intrinsically connected to the establishment of the principle of the rule of law. An important milestone for the recognition of individual rights was the cultural revolution that consisted in the introduction of writing, first in the form of the Greek alphabet around the 8th century BC, later to be adapted into the Latin alphabet, and the phenomenon, recorded in Greece from the 7th century onwards, of the local societies' transition from oral to written law.[4] This revolutionary passage from an unwritten, customary, oral law, known to few, to the keeping of written records of the rules of law and publishing these same laws in public spaces, allowed everyone to understand and claim their rights.

In ancient Greek societies, written laws that guaranteed some fundamental rights were often enacted as a response to and as a means of resolving civil strife. A pattern of civil unrest was recorded throughout the ancient Greek world, involving conflicts among factions of the nobility, the establishment of tyrants and the murder, exile, and confiscation of the property of citizens. Such bloody conflicts gave rise to a process of recording of the law in writing by charismatic lawgivers, such as Draco and Solon in Athens, Lycurgus in Sparta, Zaleucus of Epyzephyrian Locris, Charondas of Catana, and Pittacus of Mytilene, which confirmed some basic citizens' rights. This process marked a long transition, leading from the predominance of aristocracy and tyrannies to oligarchy and finally to the birth of democracy in classical Athens, which was founded on the recognition of equal rights for citizens and on the development of institutional safeguards against the abuse of authority.

The first written laws are in fact the first recordings of fundamental individual rights, such as the right to life, human dignity, property, and fair trial, which had to be safeguarded by the authorities. Infringement of these laws brought some form of punishment and that entailed a right to access

[4] On this process see M. Gagarin, *Writing Greek Law,* Cambridge-New York 2008.

the justice system for protection. Such rights are reflected for example in the famous 'Law Code' of Gortyn, the longest surviving set of legal inscriptions from ancient Crete, dating from the mid 5th century BC. The law fixing the financial penalties to be paid for certain crimes meant that it was the legislation and not the judge that determined the sentence, guaranteeing the right to fair trial. A parallel process took place in the Roman Republic in the mid-5th century BC, with the recording of the law in the Twelve Tables as a response to plebeian unrest, which included all the actionable citizen rights of the time. [5]

3. Rights and natural law

Today rights are considered universal and connected to the intrinsic value of the human being and the individual. The concept of inherent 'human rights' did not exist in antiquity. The closest ancient equivalent is the notion of 'natural law', as a law which derives from nature or from divine law, first appearing in Greek philosophy and later further developed by the Roman jurists. [6] Socrates viewed true justice as something that may or may not coincide with human justice. The principle of natural law was considered by Aristotle (*Rhetoric*, 1373b6-1373b11) to have made one of its first appearances in Sophocles' tragedy *Antigone* (450-61), as an argument justifying her disobedience to a ruling of her uncle Creon, who forbade her from burying her brother Polyneices. The underlying principle is that there are some rules, inherent to human dignity, proper to the gods and to human nature, which transcend time and space and apply to all, regardless of the laws of a particular state.

A philosophical consideration about the possible existence of 'human rights' could be detected behind the ideas of the Stoics on fundamental virtues aiming to protect human dignity. As a result of Stoic influence, the philosopher Seneca pleaded in favor of the humane treatment of slaves and the respect of their dignity. The Roman jurists adopted and adapted Greek philosophical concepts to Roman law, including the teachings of Stoicism on cardinal virtues. Stoicism formed the theoretical background of the Roman concept of 'natural law' (*ius naturale*), [7] the laws common to all be-

---

[5] On the content of the Twelve Tables see M. Humbert, *La Loi des XII tables, Édition et commentaire*, Paris, 2018.

[6] See R.U.S. Prasad, *The Origins of Human Rights. Ancient Indian and Greco-Roman Perspectives*, New York 2022, pp. 111-154, pp. 157-200.

[7] See R. Bett, "Did the Stoics Invent Human Rights?", *Oxford Studies in Ancient Philosophy*, 2012, pp. 149-169.

ings. According to the Institutes of Justinian (1.1.11), "*Natural laws, which are equally observed among all the nations and constituted by some divine providence, remain immutable and stable*", as opposed to human laws, that are prone to change. The Roman jurists understood natural law as a kind of moral code, which every person – regardless of nationality – could approach intuitively through logic. It was, in short, the ideal of the law, although its relation to the *ius gentium* (international law) and *ius civile* (national law) is not always clear. [8] The Roman jurist Ulpian considered natural law as "what nature teaches to all living things" (D.1.1.3.), such as the institutions of marriage or childbearing. The Roman jurists recognize that the institution of slavery, which was an established practice of the ancient world (part of the *ius gentium*), whereby someone is made subject to another's authority, was contrary to nature (D.1.5.4.pr.), where all men are born equal. However, natural law has little practical value for Roman jurists. They do not consider that, in spite of being morally superior and timeless, it could take precedence over civil law. Nor did they recognize the existence of fundamental 'individual rights' common to all men.

4. *Humanitas* and other concepts connected to rights

In the later Roman Empire and under the influence of Christianism, the concept of *humanitas* [9] developed into a major legal principle, appearing in legal texts and in imperial decrees as a concept dictating a more humane treatment in certain situations as opposed to the strict application of the law. It expresses the idea that concern for the welfare of the people should be at the heart of legislation. Christian emperors referred to "*humanitas nostra*" as their main concern. Under the influence of Christianism, the idea emerged of humans being worthy of protection, which dictated certain rules, while related concepts such as *pietas* (piety), *caritas* (diligence), *benignitas* (benevolence), *clementia* (charity) also emerged and enriched Roman law, particularly with regard to the family, inheritance, and criminal law. However, this did not extend to the point of questioning the institution of slavery.

---

[8] See M.P. Zuckert, "'Bringing Philosophy down from the Heavens': Natural Right in the Roman Law", *Review of Politics*, 51.1, Winter, 1989, pp. 70-85.

[9] See R. Bauman, *Human Rights in Ancient Rome*, London 2012, p. 20 ff.

5. Rights limited to male citizens

Full rights in ancient Greek cities were limited to male, adult citizens, who formed a small percentage of the overall population. Political rights were recognized only to citizens, while the vast majority of a city's population, which included metics (i.e. the permanent foreign residents), women and children, only had limited rights. Foreigners could be granted specific rights, usually as a personal privilege due to important favours offered to a city, such as the right to possess land withing the city's borders or to intermarry with a local citizen in a marriage that would be considered legally valid and produce legitimate heirs. No individual rights were recognized to slaves who did however have limited legal capacity, since they could act on behalf of their masters. Although the Athenians followed an 'open city' policy (contrary to Spartan society which was suspicious of foreigners as potential spies of their military know-how), keeping their city accessible to all, visitors and metics alike, they strongly safeguarded Athenian citizenship and the rights connected to it to those descending directly from citizens,[10] as a valuable asset, precisely because of the fundamental rights which citizenship entailed as well as practical considerations.[11]

Among the ancient Greeks, the strongest indication that being a citizen entailed specific rights was the penalty of ἀτιμία, a form of disenfranchisement applied by the courts in classical Athens.[12] Atimia literally means "lack of honor" and was used to denote the legal penalty by which one was deprived of right of access to the honor of holding public functions (τιμαὶ), normally open to all citizens, thus becoming synonymous to a "deprivation of rights". The penalty could be imposed for various crimes and offenses connected with citizenship ideology and the good behaviour expected from citizens, such as bribery, embezzlement, false witness, and breach of duty as a public officer. Ἀτιμία could partially or fully limit the political functions of a citizen, including his right to attend

[10] See J. Blok, *Citizenship in classical Athens*, Cambridge 2017, pp. 1-46.

[11] Practical considerations connected to the direct democracy operating in Athens involved the number of citizens participating in all the city's bodies and the salaries paid by the Athenian state to magistrates, judges and citizens voting in the Assembly. Limitations to the number of those having full access to all rights were connected to the economic viability of the state, its limited resources, and the importance attached to limiting the participation in decision-making process to those sharing the same cultural values and the risks of over-population.

[12] See M.S. Youni, "Outlawry in classical Athens: Nothing to do with Atimia", in G. Thür, U. Yiftach-Firanko, R. Zelnick-Abramovitz (eds.), *Symposion 2017*, Wien 2018, pp. 137-155.

the Agora (marketplace), to participate and vote in the assembly, or serve as juror in the public courts.

In Rome, only free male Roman citizens by birth, called *cives Romani optimo iure*, had full political and legal rights, as long as they did not hold certain convictions (*capitis deminutio*). In Roman Law, only the male head of the family (*pater familias*) has full legal capacity. Non-Roman citizens living in the Roman empire (*peregrini*) lived according to the law of their state, however, some rights could be conferred to them (such as the right to marry a Roman or conclude agreements in Roman Law). Roman citizenship was highly sought after, as it conferred important rights and privileges. The importance of being a Roman citizen is summed up in the phrase "*civis Romanus sum*". Cicero quotes it in his speech against the corrupt governor of Sicily Verres (2.5.161), as the cry for help of a citizen that was illegally flogged. It became proverbial as a synonym for the guarantee, within the borders of the Roman Empire, of basic procedural and substantive rights and of the protection from abuse that every Roman citizen should enjoy. Rights such as the right to receive a trial according to Roman Law was claimed by the Apostle Paul when he was arrested in Philippi (*Acts of the Apostles* 16:37, 25:11). The expression is still used today as a motto of individual rights in a State of Law.

6. Fundamental citizen 'rights' in ancient Greece and Rome

The Universal Declaration of Human Rights adopted by the United Nations in 1948, in Articles 2-29, recognizes a series of rights, including the right to life, liberty, security of person, equality before the law, fair trial, asylum, freedom from torture and inhuman punishment, the right to privacy, reputation, opinions, religion, mobility, nationality, the right to marry, own property, take part in government, choose one's occupation, and receive an education. To what extent can similar rights be identified in the Greek and Roman world?

Human rights are generally closely linked with liberty and democracy. Democracy was born in ancient Athens, where equal citizen rights were recognized for the first time in history. In Rome, although the *Res Publica* was not a democracy, citizen rights were also considered the foundation of the Roman state. In Greek and Roman antiquity, some principles were considered fundamental attributes that all citizens should enjoy.[13] In classical

[13] See J. Gaudemet, "Des "droits de l'homme" dans l'Antiquité?", in R. Feenstra *et al.* (eds.), *Collatio iuris romani: études dédiées à Hans Ankum à l'occasion de son 65e anniversaire*, vol. I, Amsterdam 1995, pp. 105-114; Id., J. Gaudemet, "Le monde antique

Athens, Pericles in the Funeral Oration, included in Thucydides' *History of the Peloponnesian war*, a speech delivered by the Athenian politician in 431 BC in praise of the soldiers lost to Athens during the first year of the war, made a eulogy to Athenian Democracy by stressing the liberties that made Athens an open society guaranteeing fundamental rights to all its citizens, including equality before the law and freedom of speech, as opposed to the Spartan controlling regime. The Oration reflects the Athenians' self-consciousness of the fundamental rights connected to their democratic institutions, which is a precious indicator that citizen rights were understood and valued as unique and "exemplary" (in Pericles' words) among the Greeks. Such 'rights' in classical and Hellenistic Athens included, among others:

Right to life. Homicide was considered the most serious offense, being also connected with the metaphysical belief of pollution (*miasma*). However, the death penalty was applied by the courts for the most serious crimes, including treason and religious offenses. Fathers had the right to expose undesirable newborn children (in which case, if they survived, they were often brought up as slaves by those who saved them), although if they accepted them in the family, they could no longer have a claim on their life.

Liberty. Although, other than being born into slavery, becoming a slave at some point was a risk inherent to ancient life (due to piracy or warfare), the status of citizen entailed and supposed the right of personal freedom. Solon, with his political reforms, was the first to abolish slavery for indebtment. In Athens, freedom, being defined by Aristotle (*Politics*, 1317a40) as the right to live as one wishes, was at the very heart of democracy. Personal freedom stopped though where the law began (Herodotus 3.83.3, Thucydides 2.37.3). The respect for the rule of law, both written and unwritten, formed the basis of all liberties (Thucydides 2.37.3).

Right of equal participation in political life. In ancient Athens the term ἰσονομία, meaning equality of all citizens before the law, and implying an equality of their rights and obligations, is it term older than 'democracy'. According to Pericles, under a democracy (Thucydides 2.37.1.4), "*all citizens are equal before the law in their private disputes. For public offices, preference is given to those who are able and deserving, not to those who belong to a certain class*". Laws afforded equal justice to all in their private differ-

---

et les droits de l'homme: Quelques observations", in H. Jones (ed.), *Le monde antique et les droits de l'homme: Actes de la 50ème Session de la Société internationale Fernand De Visscher pour l'histoire des droits de l'Antiquité*, Bruxelles 1998, pp. 174-183; T. Honoré, *Ulpian: Pioneer of Human Rights*, 2nd ed., Oxford 2002.

ences, while advancement in public life did not depend on social standing, nor did poverty ban anyone from serving the state if he was deserving (Thucydides 2.37.1). In application of this principle, magistrates in most offices of the Athenian Democracy were selected by lot, under certain conditions.

Right to asylum. Asylum is a Greek word deriving from the practice established under ancient Greek law of recognizing to a city or place exception from the right of reprisals, usually through a bilateral agreement.[14] The gods' temples were considered a place of asylum for all and arresting or killing a supplicant to the gods equalled sacrilege.

Freedom from torture. In Athens, the decree of Scamandrius ordered that no free Athenian could be tortured (Andocides, *On the Mysteries* 43). Torture of slaves was allowed only for the purpose of extracting a confession in a legal dispute, although whether it occurred in practice is disputed by legal historians.[15] Inhuman punishment did exist in the form of torturous execution of the death penalty.

Right to privacy, reputation and opinions. In Athens, according to Pericles, "*we live not only free in the administration of the state but also one with another void of jealousy touching each other's daily course of life, not offended at any man for following his own humour, nor casting on any man censorious looks, which though they be no punishment, yet they grieve*" (Thucydides 2.37.2), and "*we live exactly as we please*" (Thucydides 2.39.1), with citizens enjoying a right to personal development (Thucydides 2.40.2).

Right to fair trial. The right to fair trial was guaranteed in Athens by a complex judicial system, allowing every citizen access to justice in large popular courts, made up of jurors drawn by lot among the citizen body, who swore an oath to abide by a series of principles guaranteeing individual rights (Demosthenes, *Against Timocrates,* 149-151).

Family and other rights. Pericles introduced in Athens a limitation of the right to contract a legitimate marriage, the outsprings of which would be considered legitimate heirs only when both the groom and the bride had Athenian origins. Women were referred to as citizens and could pass on citizenship to their children but had no political rights. As adults, they lived

---

[14] See B. Bravo, "*Sylan*. Représailles et justice privée contre des étrangers dans les cités grecques. Étude du vocabulaire et des institutions", *ASNP* 10, 1980, pp. 675-987.

[15] See M. Gagarin, "The Torture of Slaves in Athenian Law", *Classical Philology* 91.1, 1996, pp. 1-18.

under the constant guardianship of a male and laws sometimes regulated their behaviour in the public sphere. A father was expected to pay for his children's proper education, manage their property, and not leave his fortune to third parties, with all males inheriting equal shares after his death. Public education became available in Hellenistic times through the institution of the Gymnasium. Children were obliged to take care of their elderly parents and if not, could suffer disenfranchisement (*atimia*). Widows and orphans were under the custody of a magistrate (Demosthenes, *Against Macartatus* 75), and any citizen could make an accusation against anyone who abused his parents, orphans, unmarried girls or the mentally insane. Persons with disabilities who could not work were entitled to a daily allowance of food at public expense. Healthcare was provided at religious healing centers such as Epidaurus or through the institution of the public physicians. Access to the theatre, which was considered to contribute to the citizen's education, was subsidized by the state in Athens. Participation in athletic training and competitions in the public structures included in every Greek city were an important part of daily life in ancient Greece.

Freedom of trade and right to work. Freedom of trade in Athens, whose port, Piraeus, was an important commercial hub for imports and exports, was praised by Pericles as a by-product of democracy (Thucydides 2.38.2). Special magistrates (*agoranomoi*) oversaw fair trade conditions for consumers and (*metronomoi*) the use of standard weights and measures, as well as the affordable price of basic commodities such as grain. Rather than a right to work, the law in ancient Greek cities prescribed the obligation not to remain idle, since inactivity was considered suspicious, leading to crime and loss of fortune. Trade and other associations of people pursuing common interests were very common among the Greeks.

Religion. Religion was considered a state affair and priesthoods were public magistracies. Foreigners could worship their own gods and sometimes foreign deities were imported. However, sacrilege and any attempt to corrupt state religion was punishable by death, the sentence imposed on Socrates in Athens for this alleged crime.

The right to own property. The possession of immobile property was restricted to Athenian citizens. Magistrates and jurors had to take an oath they would not harm citizens' property, which was considered the mark of a tyrannical regime. Laws protected private and public property from theft and damage. For serious offenses, the penalty of confiscation of property was applied, while land and movable property were also subject to confiscation for debts.

Rome on the other hand was did not value the principle of democratic equality, although the Roman state was deemed to guarantee some basic rights for all. Citizens belonged to a predetermined social class, patrician or plebeian, based on their wealth and origin. The claim of equal access to elected offices by plebeians and the granting of other rights marked the long struggle of the classes under the Roman Republic, which lasted several centuries. Such rights were granted through legislative reform, although Roman society never became egalitarian, with the patricians having the upper hand in all aspects of life. However, in principle, Roman citizens enjoyed rights such as the following:

Right to life. No Roman citizen, under normal circumstances, could be put to death without trial by a Roman court. Capital punishment against Roman citizens was practically discontinued under the later Roman Republic, although the phenomenon of proscriptions by political opponents, in the last century BC, led to many victims in turbulent times. [16] The head of the Roman family, the *pater familias,* maintained the right of life and death over the children under his authority through their life, although being actually used was rarely recorded in the sources.

Liberty. For Roman citizens *libertas* (also worshipped as a Goddess) was the supreme value, the legal status of a citizen being the opposite of slavery. As defined by Florentinus in the Digest (D.1.5.4 pr.), "*Freedom is one's natural power to do what one pleases, but for the things prohibited by force or law*", whereas slavery, although recognized as an institution of the law of nations, (D.1.5.4.1) "*by means of which anyone may subject one man to the control of another*", was considered to be "*contrary to nature*". As the foundation of all other rights and a highly politicized notion under the Republic, liberty was also understood as freedom from tyranny, and was always equated with freedom from foreign rule. Later, the Roman Emperors would use the slogan *libertas Augusta* to present themselves as guarantors of public freedom. [17]

Freedom from torture. Freedom from torture was a privilege of Roman citizens. In the (extremely rare) *poena cullei* reserved for parricides, the condemned were thrown to the Tiber tied in a sack with wild animals [18]

---

[16] See W. McAllen Green, "An Ancient Debate on Capital Punishment", *The Classical Journal* 24.4, 1929, pp. 269-275.

[17] See R. Syme, "Human Rights and Social Status in Ancient Rome", *The Classical Outlook* 64, 2, 1986-7, pp. 37-41.

[18] See S. Radin, "The Lex Pompeia and the Poena Cullei", *The Journal of Roman Studies* 10, 1920, pp. 119-130.

Execution of non-Roman citizens could be performed by crucifixion and the *damnatio ad bestias,* where the condemned was killed by wild animals, which was used frequently against the Christians, considered guilty of high treason for refusing to sacrifice to the deified Emperor. Progressively, rules limiting cruelty towards slaves were established (Justinian, *Institutes* 1.8.2).

Political rights. Being a citizen under the Roman Republic implied the right to vote (*ius suffragium*) and the right to be elected (*ius honorum*) to the various offices of Rome, although actual access to power, through elections, was narrowly connected to status, with the patricians having a much better chance of success than the plebeians. The unique magistracy of the *Tribuni Plebis* and legal instruments such as the *sacrosanctitas* (personal inviolability which could be extended to citizen protection), *ius provocationis* and the *auxilium* (right of appeal and assistance offered to all citizens) guaranteed citizens' rights against the risk of illegal execution or seizure by a magistrate.[19] Under the Principate all political powers will concentrate around the Emperor's figure and citizen participation in elections will disappear.

Religion. Keeping the *pax deorum*, peace with the gods, was considered of outmost importance for the survival of the Roman state, hence any threat to public religion was akin to treason. In spite of the Roman state being generally tolerant to foreign religions, Christians were severely persecuted, until Constantine the Great established religious toleration for Christianity with his edict (313 AD).

Right to fair trial. For the Romans, access to a justice system guaranteeing substantive and procedural rights was considered of primordial importance. Roman Law eventually developed into the most sophisticated and accomplished legal system of the ancient world, the essence of which is still included in all the modern civil codes. Other than the magisterial work of the Roman jurists, the Praetors, in their role as magistrates giving access to justice by granting legal actions to litigants under the formulary procedure of the Roman Republic, were instrumental in the recognition of new rights which translated into new legal tools. For the Romans, no right could exist in practice if an efficient legal remedy of redress was not available to the litigants. Access to a judicial system that was impartial, accessible, and efficient, open to foreigners as well as to citizens, was considered an essential part of the state's duty to guarantee the Rule of Law, even if in practice the system often proved dysfunctional due to corruption.

---

[19] These rights are considered the precursor of the *habeas corpus* principle of modern Common Law, according to which a prisoner can complain to the court about his unlawful arrest and imprisonment.

Family and other rights. Roman citizens were entitled to several personal rights regulated by Roman Law, such as the right to contract marriage (*ius conubii*), with any children born of that marriage becoming legitimate heirs. The emperor Augustus reformed family law, making marriage for all compulsory, in an attempt to raise the birth rate of Roman citizens. Women had no political rights and were subject to a man's tutorship for life, except for mothers of three children to whom Augustus granted a special privilege making them legally independent. Women, who could freely divorce their husbands and remarry, did however enjoy a higher level of independence than in most subsequent societies.

Freedom of trade and protection of property. The Romans had the right to participate in economic life and conclude contracts under Roman law (*ius commercii*). Special magistrates, the *Aediles curules*, oversaw the proper regulation of markets, the correctness of weights and measures and took care of public buildings. Grain was regularly distributed to poor citizens. Property rights under Roman Law were considered of the outmost importance, could be transferred by specific legal tools and were protected by a wide array of legal remedies.

Mobility and welfare. The *Pax Romana* lasting approximatively throughout the two first centuries AD was the longest period of peace and prosperity recorded in European history. Throughout the Empire, the Romans provided universal access to fresh water by building aqueducts, and enhanced daily life and hygiene by the construction of public thermal baths which were open to all. Freedom of movement across the Roman Empire was secured both by the extensive network of roads built and by policing the seas across the Mediterranean against pirate raids. According to Aelius Aristides in his oration "Regarding Rome" (224-225) "*Only those who remain outside your hegemony, if there are any, are worthy of pity, because they lack similar goods. You have proved perfectly what everyone says, that the earth is the mother of all and the common home of all. Now it is now possible for Greeks and barbarians to go wherever they want, with or without their possessions, easily and simply, as if they were going from home to home… To enjoy security, it is enough to be a Roman, or rather, one of your subjects*".

Roman law adopted the principle of personality according to which the law of the state applied only to its citizens. Following the granting of Roman citizenship to almost all the inhabitants of the Roman Empire by Emperor Caracalla in 212 AD, the rights recognized under Roman Law extended to all the new Roman citizens. Long before the European Union, the Roman Empire became the first European state where people of different ethnic backgrounds living within its borders could freely move, live and enjoy some fundamental rights guaranteed and protected by a State of Law.

In conclusion, the respect and protection of what we today call 'rights' was among the main duties of the magistrates, rulers and judges in both ancient Greece and Rome. All legislation produced, and all the refinement of the Roman jurists' legal analysis, aimed to define and offer the best possible protection to specific 'rights' recognized by law, as they developed through many centuries of practice of private exchanges, within different forms of public rule. However, always keeping the risks of anachronism in mind, as in most pre-modern societies, we can only speak of preliminary forms of rights or expressions of rights, which remained non codified. Taking into consideration this limitation, it is still possible to argue that in the Greco-Roman world there is recorded evidence of the *de facto* and *de iure* recognition of some fundamental values connected to citizen status or to special categories of people, which the modern world later elevated to the status of 'human rights'. What we can search for in antiquity are seeds of thought and early examples of such rights. These are rights that did exist, although they were not considered in practice universal or unconditional, and therefore were not the same as our modern legal concept of 'human rights'. They offered, however, the prime material upon which the modern era would elaborate the notion of fundamental rights, and this is a valuable precedent, even if incomplete.

Chapter 2

CIVITAS ROMANA AND *CIVITAS EUROPEA* – A JOURNEY THROUGH HISTORY AND POLITICS IN SEARCH OF A LEGAL IDENTITY

Daniele Mattiangeli

ABSTRACT: *This contribution aims to draw a historical line between Roman civitas and European citizenship, highlighting both important features of historical evolution and fundamental points, such as the building of a state's political and social identity and the importance of citizenship itself for its construction.*

SUMMARY: 1. General Introduction. – 2. Historical background in Rome and Greece. – 3. The Roman way of integration and 'legal-political' identity from an historical perspective.

1. General Introduction

Media coverage reflects the importance attached to the issues of citizenship and the integration of migrants of different origins within Europe. The topic is at the centre of current political and social debates and features in the election campaigns of many parties.[1] This can be seen as an indication that the issue is characterized by a certain degree of complexity and certainly holds potential for socio-political conflict. As a logical consequence, the issue has been taken up by political parties that are promoting their respective political solutions in the course of their election campaigns across Europe. Just as the problems of managing migration vary greatly from country to country, the solutions also differ from one EU Member State to another. The problems themselves are of a social, economic and legislative nature and do not appear to be improving, which in turn is of interest to populists and anti-European movements. It is problems such as these that have the potential to cause radical change in the European Union over the next ten years.

The difference between the individual legislative solutions of the Union

---

[1] See G. Cotturri, "Cittadinanza attiva/populismo: fare politica con la Costituzione", *Questione Giustizia,* 1, 2019, p. 142 ff.

members and the predominance of national interests over those of the Union actually seem to be the biggest barriers to solving this crisis.[2] On the other hand, it should not be forgotten that the majority of European countries are now characterized less by emigration than by immigration. This is actually facilitated by the freedom of movement within the European Union. With the exception of some European countries, such as Germany, the United Kingdom of Great Britain and Northern Ireland (which left the EU in 2020) and France, which already faced massive immigration flows after the Second World War (in the case of France and the United Kingdom, immigrants from former colonies; in the case of Germany, mainly so-called 'guest workers' from countries such as Turkey), this situation is a new one for most European countries[3] and in particular for Eastern European countries.[4]

For the first time since the founding of the European Community, large numbers of people from different ethnic and cultural groups have reached the Union, creating mass immigration over the last twenty years[5]. In the Treaties of Rome, drawn up in the post-war context, no one could have foreseen and provided for such a phenomenon. Moreover, 20 years ago, a renewal was undertaken: the introduction of European citizenship[6], which applies to all citizens of the European Member States and encompasses the individual citizenships of all European countries.[7] This was a decision with social, economic and political implications, for example on labour relations within the Union, political ideas, social positions of groups of people, etc., especially in connection with intra-European migration. In social, economic and legislative matters, it is difficult to find a common consensus on how to deal with migrants arriving in Europe. The difficulty of this situation lies, on the one hand, in the lack of previous experience and legislative models and, on the other

---

[2] See P. Serra, *Europa e Mondo. Temi per un pensiero politico europeo*, Roma 2004, p. 12 ff.; D. Grimm, *The Constitution of European Democracy*, Oxford 2017, p. 5 ff.

[3] See A. Künnecke, *Türkei und EU: Perspektiven einer Partnerschaft nach dem gescheiterten Putsch*, Norderstedt 2017, p. 4 ff.

[4] G. Moro, *Cittadini in Europa. L'attivismo civico e l'esperimento democratico comunitario*, Roma 2009, p. 32 ff.

[5] On the problem of immigration in the legal-political sense, see: G. Cotturri, "Cittadinanza attiva/populismo: fare politica con la Costituzione", *Questione giustizia* 1, 2019, pp. 147-148.

[6] G. Moro, *op. cit.*, p. 41 ff.

[7] See E. Koops, "Masters and Freemen: Junian Latins and the Struggle for Citizenship", in G. De Kleijn, P. Benoist (eds.), *Integration in Rome and in the Roman World*, Leiden-Boston 2014, p. 106.

hand, in the lack of a uniform solution for citizenship and integration at European level. [8]

However, these two weaknesses can be countered by looking at the historical past on a different level. We are not referring to more recent history, however, but rather to the history of the Roman Empire in the period from the 7th century BC to the fall of the Western Roman Empire. Roman law, of all things, which is seemingly outdated and sometimes considered obsolete in academia, can offer interesting models for far-reaching solutions with regard to citizenship and integration. [9]

2. Historical Background in Rome and Greece

In fact, the Romans had been dealing with citizenship and integration problems since the founding of Rome. [10] They were the first to develop a model of citizenship that was completely independent of the modern idea of nationality and nation and worked for a very large territory made up of peoples with different languages, cultures, customs, laws and ethnicities. [11]

Thanks to a special system based on flexible solutions and different forms of citizenship, the Romans were able to integrate numerous different peoples and cultures within the Roman Empire, thus extending *romanitas* [12] to large parts of Europe, North Africa and the Middle East.

Roman expansion and the associated integration of immigrant populations was achieved to some extent by 212 AD through measures including the conclusion of various *foedera* (international treaties) with cities and the concession of Latin or Roman citizenship, *cum* or *sine suffragio* [13], the

[8] See P. Luft, P. Shimany (eds.), *Integration von Zuwanderern: Erfahrungen, Konzepte, Perspektiven*, Bielefeld 2010, p. 327 ff.

[9] J.M. Rainer, "Minima sur la citoyenneté romaine", in J. Bouineau (éd.), *L'environnement méditerranéen. De l'Antiquité vécue à l'Antiquité réinventée*, Paris 2019, p. 125 ff.

[10] See E. Koops, "Masters and Freemen: Junian Latins and the Struggle for Citizenship", in G. De Kleijn. P. Benoist (eds.), *Integration in Rome and in the Roman World*, cit., p. 105.

[11] See A. Mirabelli, *Storia del pensiero romano da Romolo a Constantino*, IV, Napoli 1882, p. 334 f.

[12] For an explanation of the difficult and complex concept of *romanitas*, see for example D. Mattiangeli, *Romanistas, Latinitas, Peregrinitas*, Città del Vaticano 2010, p. 35 ff.; D. Mattiangeli, *Vorteile der Romanitas im Bereich des Vertragsrechts aus einer historisch-vergleichenden Perspektive*, Frankfurt 2009, p. 47 ff.

[13] For a simple explanation of the concept of *civitas romana cum* or *sine suffragio*, see M. Sordi, *I rapporti romano-ceriti e l'origine della civitas sine suffragio*, Roma 1960,

founding of a colony or a Latin or Roman *municipium*[14], and the introduction of laws and decrees that created new classes of citizens, such as the *Latini Iuniani*[15] and *Aeliani.*[16]

A radical change in Roman citizenship and integration policy came with the decree of Caracalla, when Roman citizenship was extended universally and to the entire empire. This resulted in a type of citizenship that was no longer characterized by treaties or the principle of recognition, but by financial aspects such as taxes, universal duties and rights, but which did not (as before) place special demands on the population to be integrated. The result was a shift from integration based on multiculturalism and legal characteristics to integration that was directly linked to real factors, such as universal rights and obligations.[17]

The integration factors of *Caracalla's erga omnes* Roman citizenship consisted of Roman taxes, the military system and the Roman legal system, three factors that every new citizen (apart from the *dediticii*) had to deal with without distinction or exception. This represented a development from an individual regulation to a generally applicable regulation, which can also be traced by looking at the history of the terms *civis* and *civitas* in contrast to *polis* and *polites*[18]. This development can also be tracked through the course of history, beginning with the integration of the Etruscans[19] and ending with the settlement of the Germanic peoples within the empire.[20]

The *civis* is the citizen and fellow citizen and around him arises the *civi-*

---

p. 109 ff.; M. Humbert, *Municipium et civitas sine suffragio: l'organisation de la conquête jusqu'à la guerre sociale*, Roma 1978, p. 41 f.

[14] For the *municipes latini* see in general: G. Mancini, *Cives romani municipes latini*, I, Milano 1997, p. 14 ff.; C. Soraci, "Diritto Latino, cittadinanza romana e municipalizzazione", *Dialogues d'histoire ancienne*, 44/1, 2018, pp. 37–58.

[15] For the *latini Iuniani* in general and the *Lex Iunia Norbana*, see: B. Sirks, "Informal Manumission and the Lex Iunia", *RIDA,* 28, 1981, pp. 247-276; B. Sirks, "The Lex Iunia and the Effects of Informal Manumission and Iteration", *RIDA,* 30, 1983, pp. 211-292.

[16] On the *Latini Aeliani* see C. Masi Doria, "La Latinitas Iuniana. Aspetti patrimoniali", Gerión, *Revista de Historia antigua*, 36 (2), 2018, pp. 555-571.

[17] Lastly, in general, about Roman citizenship: A. Calore, *Cittadinanze nell'antica Roma*, I, Torino 2018, p. 7 ff.

[18] G. Crifò, *Civis. La cittadinanza tra antico e moderno*, Bari 2000, p. 23 f.

[19] See in general L. Aigner-Foresti, *Die Integration der Etrusker und das Weiterwirken etruskischen Kulturgutes im republikanischen und kaiserzeitlichen Rom*, Wien 1998, p. 5 ff.

[20] Regarding the Germanic tribes in Italy, see U. Roberto, "I Germani e l'impero universale", *Diritto@Storia,* 17, 2019, pp. 10-18.

tas,[21] which on the one hand means citizenship itself, and on the other hand the set of all citizens as an abstract term encompassing citizenship in its entirety.[22]

The *civitas romana* is therefore on the one hand an individual characteristic and on the other hand a term that with *cives* means all citizens in their entirety,[23] just as the *municipes* represent the *municipium* (without *municipes* there is no *municipium*).[24] The citizens are the city, regardless of where it is located. The right of citizenship is the right of the citizens of that city.[25] In contrast, *res publica* refers to the Roman state as such.[26] Consequently, the Roman state is the *res publica*,[27] and not the totality of Roman citizens. This is an abstract conceptual construct, in contrast to the Greek terms *polites* and *polis*,[28] which are based on the idea of personal alliances.

On the basis of this abstract conceptual construct of the *civitas romana*, expansion outside Roman territory is possible, which was not the case of Greece.[29] Roman citizenship was the first modern structure in which different peoples and territories within a state legal system could be endowed with a set of rights and duties on a large scale, independent of pre-existing relationships between citizens in individual cities. The system went beyond the particularities of individual cities and their citizenship regimes, as it included certain rights and duties (applicable to all) that were established within a multicultural, multireligious, multi-ethnic and pluralistic system, where national characteristics in the modern sense were not decisive. In this way, the integration of peoples was made possible in an effective way. Roman *civitas was* independent of ethnic or national circumstances and was only linked to birth, territory, merit and wealth.[30] This citizenship could be

---

[21] E. Benveniste, "Deux Modèles linguistiques de la cité", *in Échanges et communications. Mélanges Lévi-Strauss I*, The Hague-Paris 1970, p. 589 ff.

[22] G. Crifò, *op. cit.*, p. 26.

[23] D. Roussel, *Tribu et Cité, études sur les groupes sociaux dans les cités grecques aux époques archaïque et Classique*, Paris 1976, p. 10.

[24] G. Mancini, *Cives romani municipes latini*, I, Milano 1997, p. 96 f.

[25] It is the difference between city citizenship and nationality: R. Grawert, "Staatsangehörigkeit und Staatsbürgerschaft", *Der Staat*, 23, 1984, p. 179 ff.

[26] Cicero, *De Re publica*, 1.25.39.

[27] *Ibidem.*

[28] E. Meyer, "Vom Griechischen und römischen Staasgedanken", in R. Klein (ed.), *Das Staatsdenken der Römer-Wege der Forschung*, XLVI, Darmstadt 1966, p. 80.

[29] G. Crifò, *op. cit.*, p. 28.

[30] See E. Koops, "*Masters and Freemen: Junian Latins and the Struggle for Citizenship*", in G. De Kleijn, P. Benoist (eds.), *Integration in Rome and in the Roman World*, Leiden-Boston 2014, pp. 109, 123.

granted to different cities, municipalities, colonies and even entire peoples, both during the Republic and the Empire.[31] There are numerous cases of such concessions, such as the granting of citizenship to all Italians by virtue of *the lex Plautia Papiria* from 89 BC after the *bellum sociale*[32], or the granting of citizenship by Caesar to the Gallic nobles, which was followed by a concession to all Cisalpine Gauls, or Hadrian's concession to various cities in the Near East (for example Smyrna).[33]

It was after 212 AD that this system of concessions developed further, Romanising the entire empire into a single *civitas* based on comparatively few clear criteria. Accordingly, anyone who had paid taxes to the Roman state and served in the military became a Roman citizen and could thus enjoy all the benefits that the *civitas* brought to the imperial system of public and private law.[34] Roman law, the system of administration of justice and judicial procedure, as well as the whole public imperial service system were the main incentives for foreigners to integrate into Rome and the *civitas.* A system of *civitas* which, as *Sherwin-White* describes in his work *Roman Citizenship*, was not only applied to a large area, but was also imitated by other peoples.[35] One example in this context are the so-called barbarians, who basically had few points of contact with Rome, but wanted to copy this system even after the fall of the Roman Empire (especially Theodoric the Great in the case of the Ostrogoths). But why was this *'spread'*of the *civitas* so successful and why did it exert such an *'appeal'*[36] on other peoples inside and outside the empire?

---

[31] A.N. Sherwin White, *The Roman Citizenship*, Oxford 1973, p. 221 ff.

[32] On the civil war, see most recently: C. Hermenio Chimeno, "The social war as a civil war: an initial step in the analysis of its nature", *De Rebus Antiquis,* 7, VII/2017, pp. 18-34.

[33] See G. Salmeri, A. Raggi, A. Baroni, *Colonie Romane nel Mondo greco*, Roma 2004, p. 255 ff.; M. Guidetti, *Vivere tra i barbari, Vivere con i romani germani e arabi nella società tardoantica, IV-VI secolo*, Milano 2007, p. 145 ff.

[34] In general: P. Günther, *Vectigalia nervos esse rei publicae: die indirekten Steuern in der Römischen Kaiserzeit von Augustus bis Diokletian*, Wiesbaden 2008, p. 164 ff.

[35] A.N. Sherwin White, *op. cit.*, p. 222 ff.

[36] See also: E. Chrysos, "Legal Concepts and Patterns for the Barbarian's Settlement on Roman Soil", in E. Chrysos, A. Schwarcz (eds.), *Das Reich und die Barbaren*, Wien 1989, pp. 13-23; D. Claude, "Zur Ansiedlung barbarischer Föderaten in der ersten Hälfte des 5. Jahrhunderts", in H. Wolfram, A. Schwarcz (eds.), *Anerkennung und Integration: Zu den wirtschaftlichen Grundlagen der Völkenwanderungszeit 400-600*, Wien 1988, pp. 13-16; R. MacMullen, "Barbarian Enclaves in the Northern Roman Empire", *Antiquité Classique,* 32, 1963, pp. 552-561; L. Okamura, "Roman Withdrawals from Three Transfluvial Frontiers", in R. Mathisen, H. Sivan (eds.), *Shifting Frontiers in late antiquity*, Aldershot 1996, pp. 11-19; P. Garnsey, "Roman Citizenship and Roman Law in the Later Empire", in P. Swain, M. Edwards (eds.), *Approaching Late Antiquity: The Transformation from Early to Later Empire*, Oxford 2004, pp. 133-155.

3. The Roman way of integration and the 'legal-political' identity from an historical perspective

One possible explanation for the success of integration and cohesion is provided by the admittedly controversial political scientist *Alexandre del Valle*[37] in his book *Le complexe occidental.*[38] He hypothesises that the Roman Empire was the first[39] multiculturally successful empire because it was based on a principle that he calls "patriotisme intégrateur"[40] – a form of integrative patriotism: as we already know, Rome limited the freedom of many peoples, but pursued an effective and lasting integration policy based on the unification of Roman values with those different peoples. Rome had given its 'immigrants' the opportunity to become Romans and to be proud of it, but without denying their own roots. This mechanism is described by *Alexandre del Valle* as "patriotisme intégrateur".[41]

Within Roman history, there are numerous examples of the term "patriotisme intégrateur" from the very beginning. Important representatives of Latin literature were foreigners, for example *Livius Andronicus*, a Greek who translated the Odyssey into Latin, or *Quintus Ennius*, from Rudiae, who proudly claimed "Nos sumus Romani qui fuimus ante Rudini". One could also think of *Julius Caesar*, who integrated many people from Gaul into the Roman army and appointed some Celtic peoples as a senator. Other famous examples of Roman integration from the time of the Empire are characterized by the fact that they came from the Jewish world. The Jewish province

[37] A. Del Valle, *La mondialisation dangereuse*, Paris 2021, p. 33 ff.

[38] A. Del Valle, *Le Complexe occidental: petit traité de déculpabilization*, Paris 2014.

[39] There have been other examples in history, such as the Persian Empire or the Hellenistic Empire of Alexander the Great. On this point, I would like to disagree with Del Valle's considerations, as these two great ancient empires were also multicultural and successful, comparable to the Roman Empire. This is particularly true of the Hellenistic Empire under Alexander the Great: although torn apart by different political events, a single language was spoken there for a long time and a special culture developed in certain areas, which even outlasted the Roman Empire. The best example of this is today's Turkey and the former region around Constantinople, where the main language was still Greek even during the time of the Eastern Roman Empire, and where Greek culture continued to have a formative influence. The same was also true for some parts of Egypt (then Alexandria), which were still considered 'Hellenistic' at the time of the Romans. In the case of Persia, the circumstances were different, as multiculturalism and integration were the norm in the Persian army, but there was no uniform culture that could have survived the centuries.

[40] A. Del Valle, *Le Complexe occidental: petit traité de déculpabilization*, Paris 2014, p. 49 ff.

[41] *Ivi*, p. 53 ff.

was one of the most turbulent areas of the empire, otherwise *Vespasian* (and his then general *Titus*) and later *Hadrian* would not have made decisions of such drastic proportions for Jerusalem. It should be noted that Roman hostility towards the Jewish world was not related to the religion itself or to "somatic-origin-related" characteristics, but was rather based on the hostility of the Western, religiously tolerant world towards supposed fundamentalism of a religious nature.[42] From a cultural and religious perspective, Rome's approach made perfect sense: forms of religious terrorism first emerged during the Judean Revolt of 66-70 AD, carried out by the Zealot sect. Rome's response to the revolt was the destruction of Jerusalem by *Titus* in 70 AD.[43]

---

[42] The Romans had had a lot of problems with some so-called 'sects' of Judaism during their rule in Palestine due to their radicalism. The best example of this is the so-called Zealot sect, which played an important role during the Jewish war.

[43] In 68 AD, Vespasian was ready to begin the siege of the city of Jerusalem when he received the sudden news of the death of Emperor Nero. The general decided to halt all military action until he learned that the proconsul of Hispania Tarraconensis, Servius Sulpicius Galba, had been elected successor to the principality. He then sent his son Titus to Rome to pay homage to the new emperor, inform him of the Jewish campaign and ask him for instructions on how to proceed. When Titus reached Corinth on the coast of Achaia in January 69 AD and learned that Galba had been killed and Oton had taken his place, he decided to return to Syria to meet his father and decide together how he should act in order to avoid being a hostage in the hands of the new emperor, and because it was pointless to continue a conflict against foreigners when his own people were engaged in civil war. Vespasian learned that Vitellius had taken Oton's place by defeating him in battle and was very upset by this new situation, as he did not consider Vitellius capable of ruling the empire. He therefore thought of returning to Rome and claiming the throne for himself, but as the season was not yet favorable, he first went to Antioch and, at the urging of his soldiers, decided to claim the purple mantle anyway. In Italy, troops loyal to Vespasian under the leadership of his son Domitian conquered Rome and killed Vitellius while the new emperor was still in Alexandria. Vespasian was received there by numerous ambassadors from cities and peoples who congratulated him on the conquest of the empire, but as winter had already set in, he decided to stay in Egypt. Vespasian and Titus were appointed consuls for the year 70 AD, and both took office while away from Rome. Vespasian was still in Egypt, while Titus had been sent back to Judea with a selected part of the army and arrived in Caesarea after a week-long march. In the following year, Jerusalem was plundered, the temple destroyed and a large part of the population killed or forced to flee. During his stay in Jerusalem, Titus had an affair with Berenice of Cilicia, the daughter of Herod Agrippa I. All the events surrounding the revolt and the fall of Jerusalem are described by the Jewish historian Flavius Josephus whose work, *Jewish War*, is the main source on the war itself. The merits of Titus in the Jewish War are difficult to assess as Flavius Josephus was the Jewish commander of the fortress of Iotapata (besieged and conquered by Titus in 67) and later a supporter of the Flavian dynasty. In Josephus' descriptions, Titus is the heroic commander who besieged and conquered five enemy centers, but, after considering the author's viewpoint, it becomes clear that Titus, who had no previous experience as a commander, had not excelled at the beginning of the campaign. For the history of the

There are also other famous cases of "patriotisme intégrateur" in this context. The best-known case is that of the apostle *Paul,* a Hebrew from Tarsus and a Pharisee who was also a Roman citizen. [44] Paul is particularly well known for his imperial appeal before the governor *Festus* (Acts 25) which he was entitled to as a Roman citizen, even though he was a Jew by birth and therefore not a Roman. *Festus* replied the following to the apostle's request: "You have appealed to Caesar, you should go to Caesar". [45] Another case is that of the contemporary witness *Flavius Josephus,* who witnessed the destruction of Jerusalem by *Titus* in 70 AD. This Jewish writer was adopted by the imperial family *gens Flavia* (to which *Vespasian*, *Titus* and *Domitian* also belonged). [46] He wrote *Antiquitates Judaicae* and *The History of the Jewish Wars* in Greek. *Flavius Josephus* remained a

---

Jewish war, see: Flavius Josephus, *Jüdischer Krieg 5*, p. 446 ff; 5, p. 491 ff; 5, p. 567 ff, 6, p. 420; Tacitus, *Historiae*, 4,51; 5,13; In general about Titus: C. Weikert, "Nach der Tempelzerstörung. Die gens Flavia und die Juden", in G.K. Hasselhoff, M. Strothmann (eds.), *'Religio Licita?' Rom und die Juden*, Berlin 2017, pp. 159-174; V. Croce, *Tito: l'imperatore che distrusse Gerusalemme*, Roma 2007, p. 31 ff.

[44] With the introduction of the papacy, Paul even became the patron saint of Rome.

[45] Acts 25, 11.12 (Elberfelder 1905).

[46] Flavius Josephus was an ancient Jewish writer and historian with Roman citizenship. Also known as Josephus Flavius or simply Josephus, he wrote his works in Greek and, unusually for classical literature, the corpus of Josephus' works has been almost completely preserved. Josephus was born between 37 and 38 AD, in the first year of Emperor Caligula's reign, in Jerusalem in Roman Judea into a family of Israelite priestly nobility related to the Hasmonean dynasty. Josephus received a traditional Jewish education with a strong influence from Greek and Latin culture. In his youth, he held political positions close to the Pharisaic movement. He strictly adhered to the Torah, but was hostile to the Jewish nationalists and the Zealots in particular. During the First Jewish War, which began in 66 AD, he was appointed military leader of the rebellious forces in Galilee. When the rebels, forced by the Romans to barricade themselves in Iotapata, realized that defeat was imminent, they immediately thought of suicide to avoid falling into the hands of the enemy as prisoners, but Josephus convinced them of the immorality of such an act and suggested as an alternative that each of them would take the life of the other. Through a special and complicated ruse (now known in mathematical circles as Josephus' problem) concerning the order of this death cycle, he managed to be the last person of the rebel group to remain alive and, instead of killing himself, spontaneously surrendered himself to the Romans. On Flavius Josephus in general, see: H. Schreckenberg, *Bibliographie zu Flavius Josephus* (= Arbeiten zur Literatur und Geschichte des hellenistischen Judentums. Band 14), Leiden 1979, p. 45 ff.; H. Schreckenberg, "Josephus (Flavius Josephus)", in *Reallexikon für Antike und Christentum*, vol. 18, Stuttgart 1998, pp. 761-801; I. Wandrey, "*Iosephos (4) I. Flavios*", in *Der Neue Pauly*, vol. 5, Stuttgart 1998, pp. 1089-1091; L.H. Feldman, "Flavius Josephus Revisited: The Man, His Writings, and His Significance", in W. Haase (ed.), *Aufstieg und Niedergang der römischen Welt (ANRW)*, vol. 21/2: *Hellenistic Judaism in Roman Times: Philon and Josephus (cont.)*, Berlin-New York 1984, ISBN 3-11-009522-X (retrieved via De Gruyter Online).

Jew but was also a loyal Roman citizen and even a member of the imperial family. [47]

There are also countless examples of Romans who, although born outside Rome, had a successful career within the empire. Examples include *Tiberius Julius Alexander*, a Jew from Alexandria, who was prefect in Egypt and governor of Judea, or emperors such as *Septimius Severus*, from Leptis Magna in Libya, and his son *Caracalla*, who granted citizenship to all inhabitants of the empire with the '*Constitutio Antoniana*'. Other examples include *Philippus Arabs,* who is assumed to have been a Christian of Arab descent, and *Maximinus* from Tracia, as well as *Trajan* and *Hadrian*, who were both born on Spanish territory, and the philosopher *Seneca* from Cordóba, who was an imperial preceptor. [48]

A closer look at post-Roman history, reveals that no other empire had such a strong power of integration. The Ottoman Empire, which is often cited as a role model for integration, was not characterized by racist traits but there was discrimination on the basis of religious background, which the Roman Empire did not have in this form. [49]

In the Ottoman Empire, Christians and Jews (*Ahl al-Kitab*, the People of the Book) had the status of *dhimmi*, a kind of second-class citizen. After the Pact of Omar[50], they were forced to dress differently to distinguish themselves from Muslims (for example, a yellow stripe for Jews and a pink stripe for Christians). [51] The wearing of religious symbols was forbidden at the time.

Of course, it can be argued that Rome was also merciless towards Christians for a long time. However, this can only be affirmed for certain periods

---

[47] H. Schreckenberg, *op. cit.*, p. 21 ff.

[48] K. Christ, *Geschichte der römischen Kaiserzeit*, 6th ed., Munich 2009, p. 260 ff.

[49] The persecution of Christians was also not justified by the different nature of the religion, but by the denial of imperial primacy. Whether the state's primacy over the religious beliefs of individuals also constitutes a violation of religious freedom is a question that has only arisen in modern times. At the time of the Roman Empire, the question of religious freedom was not really discussed. The fact that several religions could exist within a state and be tolerated was not a problem as long as they did not interfere in 'state' business. The Romans were indifferent to 'theological' problems or the question of which was the 'only true religion', as they only had a practical interest in the administration of the conquered territories. See J. Scheid, *La religione a Roma*, Bari 1993, p. 18 ff.

[50] N.E. Pasachoff, R.J. Littman, *A Concise History of the Jewish People*, Lanham (Maryland) 2005, p. 45 ff; M. Cohen, *Under Crescent and Cross: the Jews in the Middle Ages*, Princeton, NJ 1994, p. 52 ff; A.P. Tritton, *Caliphs and Their Non-Muslim Subjects: A Critical Study of the Covenant of Umar*, London 2008, pp. 5-6.

[51] A.P. Tritton, *op. cit.*, p. 5 ff.

of time[52] and is rather due to the Romans' ignorance around other religions, as well as one of the most inhumane facets of Rome: statolatry.

Another example of an empire in the post-Roman period that included many foreigners and managed to ensure that they became a well-integrated part of society is the Habsburg Empire.[53] It even managed to create a kind of admiration for the monarchy among its citizens, regardless of which crown land they came from, just as the Romans had previously succeeded in doing with their "patriotisme intégrateur".[54] With thirteen different languages and multiple different peoples and ethnicities within a much smaller territory than the Roman Empire, the Habsburg Empire was a model of statehood offering citizenship endowed with certain rights and duties which could only be revoked with imperial permission .[55] On the one hand, the empire obligated its citizens to pay taxes and embark on compulsory military service; on the other, it gave all citizens access to all state services and political careers. The Austrian land register, laws and the courts, together with the great employment and economic opportunities within the empire, meant that in the period from the 17th century to 1824, or at least until the time of *Metternich's* restrictive policies[56], the different populations in the subject territories were sometimes happy to be citizens.

Many notaries, lawyers and jurists held the imperial Austrian legal system in high esteem, especially in Lombardo-Venezia.[57] Many were citizens of the empire who – although not born in Austria – had nevertheless followed successful careers within the empire. Among the most famous were Karl-Anton von Martini (born in Trento), one of the fathers of the ABGB,

---

[52] Not all emperors were persecutors: the great persecutions were carried out under Nero, Domitian, Trajan, Marcus Aurelius, Septimius Severus, Maximinus of Thrace, Decius and Diocletian. Among these, there were three major waves of persecution that had a legal basis. See also: K. Christ, *Geschichte der römischen Kaiserzeit*, 6th ed., Munich 2009, p. 78 ff.

[53] See in general E.J. Görlich, *Grundzüge der Geschichte der Habsburgermonarchie und Österreichs*, Darmstadt 1988, p. 48 ff.

[54] In the case of Hungary, for example, this integration was not without difficulties and met with resistance. See G. Pálfy, "Die Länder der ungarischen Krone im grossen Krieg Europas: Forschungsresultate und- desiderata", in K. Keller, M. Scheutz (eds.), *Die Habsburgermonarchie und der Dreißigjährige Krieg*, Wien 2020, p. 75 ff.

[55] R. Sieghart, *Die letzten Jahrzehnte einer Großmacht: Menschen, Völker, Probleme des Habsburger-reichs*, Berlin 1932, p. 265 ff.

[56] On Metternich's policy, see: K. Kraus, *Politisches Gleichgewicht und Europagedanke bei Metternich*, Frankfurt 1993, p. 7 ff.

[57] D. Mattiangeli, *Die Anwendung des ABGB in Nord Italien*, Frankfurt 2012, p. 63 ff.; p. 77 ff.

and Johann Joseph Wenzel Anton Franz Karl Graf Radetzky (born in Třebnice, Bohemia), probably the most famous general of the Austrian empire.[58] After the Roman period, the Habsburg Empire was an ideal European example of "patriotisme intégrateur", until it came to an end following *Metternich's* policy of reprisals, which was probably also the real reason for the fall of the Austrian Empire and the cause of the revolutions of the crown lands, with the exception of Austria itself.

While the social, political and economic decline of the Austrian Empire can probably be traced back to *Metternich's* reprisals against other ethnic groups, which were regarded as subjugated peoples,[59] other reasons can be found in the nationalism that emerged throughout Europe, together with the technical and bureaucratic impossibility of integrating new classes of citizens as nationals (as could already be observed among the Romans from the end of the 3th and the 4th century AD). At the same time – as in Rome at the time of *Caracalla* – a progressive standardization of citizenship policy was observed; it was no longer regarded as a privilege, but as a matter of course and a duty. It was precisely this standardization that led to a reduction in the appreciation of the imperial ideal and the individual citizen's sense of belonging. The fact that this phenomenon is linked to the fact that citizenship is seen less as a privilege and more as a duty can also be observed within the European Union.[60]

In Rome, after the universal granting of citizenship in the 3rd century AD by *Caracalla,* it was no longer possible to use citizenship as a means of integrating foreigners into the *civitas.* While citizenship had previously been perceived as a privilege, *Caracalla's* decree turned it into a purely fiscal and military obligation, without patriotic ideas of any kind and without consideration for the individual cultural characteristics of certain population groups who did not want to become part of a Roman ideology.[61] This is comparable to the situation in the European Union, which lacks a Euro-

---

[58] For Karl Anton von Martini, see the book by G. Kleinheyer, J. Schröder (ed.), *Deutsche und europäische Juristen aus neun Jahrhunderten*, Tübingen 2017, p. 289 ff.; for Radetzky, see: F. Herre, *Radetzky: Eine Biographie*, Cologne 2017, p. 36 ff.

[59] One need only think of the replacement of all Italian officers in the Empire by Austrian or Hungarian officers in Lombardy and Veneto, for details see Maria Rosa Di Simone: M.R. Di Simone, "Il diritto austriaco e la società veneta", in *Venezia e l'Austria*, Venezia 1999, p. 134 ff.

[60] See A. Strüber, *Europäische Union, Geschlecht und Wohlfahrtsstaat: Eine Untersuchung der Europäischen Beschäftigungsstrategie 2003 unter besonderer Berücksichtigung ihrer gleichstellungspolitischen Konsequenzen*, Norderstedt 2004, p. 24 ff.

[61] R.W. Mathisen, "Peregrini, Barbari and Cives Romani: Concepts of citizenship and the legal identity of barbarians in the later Roman empire", *American Historical Review,* 111/4, 2006, p. 1011 ff.

pean identity[62], which in turn makes integration within the Union more difficult and the integration of external immigrants almost impossible.[63] One example of this is the fact that the individual population groups of the European Union, with the exception of certain higher social circles, do not see themselves as 'European', but define themselves by nationality (Italian, French, German, etc.). Conversely, the peoples of the Roman State (during the Republic before and after during the empire) saw themselves as Romans as long as they possessed the *civitas romana. At the* time of the *civitas romana,* this applied to all inhabitants of the empire, regardless of their origin.[64] They not only called themselves Romans, they also aspired to this status which was desired, not imposed. It is precisely this voluntary nature of being or becoming a citizen that deserves a discourse within the European Union, in which the flexible solutions of the *civitas romana* from the time of the Republic and the first Empire could serve as inspiration, with the aim of enabling the European population of the near future *to* live under the umbrella of a *civitas europea.* Nowadays, it is possible to see a parallelism with the current European citizenship, which complements national citizenships; as well as a parallelism in the state formation in Italy during the XIX century as an example of the acquisition of a new and trans-regional 'citizenship'.[65]

---

[62] For a summary of the term 'European identity' see: P. Ciaglia, C. Fuest, F. Heinemann, "What a feeling?! How to promote European Identity", *EconPol Policy Report*, 9, October 2018.

[63] L. Hooghe, P. Verhaegen, "The Effect of Political Trust in European Citizens on European Identity", *European Political Science Review*, 9, 2017, H. 2, p. 163.

[64] A.N. Sherwin-White, *The Roman Citizenship*, Oxford 1973, p. 221 ff.

[65] R. Lill, *Geschichte Italiens in der Neuzeit*, Darmstadt 1988, p. 45 ff.

Chapter 3

IDENTITY AND VALUES IN THE EUROPEAN UNION: THE ROLE OF THE 'RULE OF LAW' IN THE CONSTRUCTION OF A EUROPEAN IDENTITY

Maria Cristina Marchetti

ABSTRACT: *The reference to values has assumed an increasing role in the construction of European identity. The values enshrined by the article 2 of the Lisbon Treaty establish an internal and external conditionality principle that guides the political action of the European Institutions and the definition of the "European way of life". Among the values set out in Article 2, the institutions have paid particular attention to the principle of the rule of law, certainly one of the most controversial values in the recent experience of the European Union. Over the last three years, the European Commission has published a Report on the Rule of Law, with the aim of monitoring of positions taken by some Member States. In an attempt to address such violations, as of 2021, the EU budget has an additional layer of protection in cases where violations of the principles of the rule of law affect or risk affecting the EU's financial interests.*

The paper will focus on the analysis of the data provided by the Special Eurobarometer 508, Values and Identities of EU citizens (2021), trying to highlight the role of the "rule of law" in the definition of European identity.

SUMMARY: 1. 'United in diversity': European identity in the language of the European institutions. – 2. Is the rule of law a value for European citizens? – 3. Conclusions.

1. 'United in diversity': European identity in the language of the European institutions

The topic of European identity has been a constant in the debate on the European integration process. The desire to create a supranational institution has generated an implicit confrontation with the dimension of statehood, which constitutes the reference point of the institutional systems of Western modernity and which unites, in the formula of the nation-state, the legal-institutional dimension of the state with the identity dimension of the nation. Starting from this basic assumption, the European Union was faced with the need to identify a founding element of aggregation that would go beyond the unifying principle of the market.

More recently, the project of a Constitution for Europe, signed in Rome in 2004, but then vetoed by the referendums in France and the Netherlands, has further stimulated reflection on the issue, starting from the idea that a constitutional text requires the existence of a people, endowed with an identity. The debate that arose on that occasion resonated throughout the 1990s up to the Lisbon Treaty.

In the past, European institutions have repeatedly tried to contribute to the definition of a European identity. Beginning with the Declaration on European Identity, signed in Copenhagen on 14 December 1973 by the nine Foreign Ministers, emphasis was on the diversity of cultures within the framework of a common European civilisation. In an attempt to define the content of European identity, it was stated:

The Nine wish to ensure that the cherished values of their legal, political and moral order are respected, and to preserve the rich variety of their national cultures. Sharing as they do the same attitudes to life, based on a determination to build a society which measures up to the needs of the individual, they are determined to defend the principles of representative democracy, of the rule of law, of social justice – which is the ultimate goal of economic progress – and of respect for human rights. All of these are fundamental elements of the European Identity.

In these terms, the topic of European identity is closely related to that of Europe's founding 'values' or 'principles' and to Europe's role in the world and its foreign policy ambitions, to which the Declaration devotes considerable attention.

The reference to 'common values' appears for the first time in the Maastricht Treaty which refers to the "defence of the common values, fundamental interests and independence of the Union" (Article J.1). Article 128 states that:

The Community shall contribute to the flowering of the cultures of the Member States, while respecting their national and regional diversity and at the same time bringing the common cultural heritage to the fore.

Since 2000, the European institutions have adopted the motto "united in diversity", which in turn risks being reductive with respect to the complexity on which it is based. [1] As Delanty assesses:

---

[1] "It signifies how Europeans have come together, in the form of the EU, to work for peace and prosperity, while at the same time being enriched by the continent's many different cultures, traditions and languages". https://european-union.europa.eu/principles-countries-history/symbols/eu-motto_en.

The notion of unity in diversity, while appealing in itself, fails to capture the fact that the units in question interact with each other and, as they do so, they undergo change. My central analytical argument is that the specificity of the European dimension of culture is in the entanglement of these cultures. The cultures of Europe are not separated but have been shaped in close interaction with each other and with the non-European world– Furthermore, Europe is not only shaped by its nations but also by relations with the rest of the world. Nations are not therefore unique, exceptional, or fundamentally different from each other. The outcome of such intermingling is a multiplicity of ideas of Europe that serve as shared cultural reference points. The plurality of Europe and should not also be mistaken for divisions.[2]

The motto also takes for granted the existence of European citizens and their ability to participate in public debate and act as a single body. An attempt to overcome this thesis is the notion of *demoicracy* introduced by Kalypso Nikolaïdis:

The idea of European demoicracy is seductively simple: a Union of peoples who govern together, but not as one. However much shared κράτος or power to govern, we must contend with the plurality of δήμοι; but also crucially, however many *demoi*, we need a common *kratos* to define and deliver, through mutually agreed disciplines, the responsibilities we owe to one another.[3]

In the wake of the Maastricht Treaty, the Treaty of Nice, with regard to enhanced cooperation, refers to the objective of aiming "at safeguarding the values and serving the interests of the Union as a whole by asserting its identity as a coherent force on the international scene" (Article 27/a). A further institutional step forward was the approval by the European Council in Nice of the Charter of Fundamental Rights of the European Union, which came into force with the Lisbon Treaty. The Charter does not introduce any new rights, but merely brings together in a single text the civil, political, economic and social rights of European citizens and all persons living on the territory of the Union. Internally, the Charter addresses the topics of dignity, freedom, equality, solidarity, citizenship and justice.

---

[2] G. Delanty, *The European Heritage. A Cultural Re-Interpretation*, London 2008, pp. XI-XII.

[3] K. Nikolaïdis, "European Demoicracy and Its Crisis", *Journal of Common Market Studies* 51, 2, 2012, pp. 351-352. On the political-institutional level, the author considers the notion of demoicracy as the third way compared to the thesis that theorises the existence of a single European demos with a supranational character and to that which denies its existence in favour of individual national demos.

The reference to common values becomes more explicit with the Lisbon Treaty. In the Preamble, the introductory formula is better specified, with the addition of a paragraph "drawing inspiration from the cultural, religious and humanist inheritance of Europe, from which have developed the universal values of the inviolable and inalienable rights of the human person, freedom, democracy, equality and the rule of law".

However, it is in Article 2 that the reference to the founding values of the Union takes centre stage:

> The Union is founded on the values of respect for human dignity, freedom, democracy, equality, the rule of law and respect for human rights, including the rights of persons belonging to minorities. These values are common to the Member States in a society in which pluralism, non-discrimination, tolerance, justice, solidarity and equality between women and men prevail.

In addition to Article 2, in the Lisbon Treaty the reference to values is expressly present in Article 7 (concerning the procedures provided for in case of "clear risk of a serious breach by a Member State of the values referred to in Article 2" and in Articles 8, 13, 21, 32, 42, 49 (the latter concerning the accession of a new Member State).

In Article 3, para. 5, it is specified that:

> In its relations with the wider world, the Union shall uphold and promote its values and interests and contribute to the protection of its citizens. It shall contribute to peace, security, the sustainable development of the Earth, solidarity and mutual respect among peoples, free and fair trade, eradication of poverty and the protection of human rights, in particular the rights of the child, as well as to the strict observance and the development of international law, including respect for the principles of the United Nations Charter.

With regard to the external action of the Union, the Lisbon Treaty reaffirms that:

> The Union's action on the international scene shall be guided by the principles which have inspired its own creation, development and enlargement, and which it seeks to advance in the wider fundamental freedoms, respect for human dignity, the principles of equality and solidarity, and respect for the principles of the United Nations Charter and international law (Article 21).

With the Commission chaired by Ursula von der Leyen, this issue has entered the European agenda through a new formulation of the European identity in terms of a 'European way of life'. In choosing the composition of the new Commission, the President has in fact entrusted the Commissioner for Migration Policy and Vice-President of the Commission, Margaritis Schinas, with the task of promoting the 'European Way of Life'.

The juxtaposition of migration policies and the promotion of the 'European way of life' did not fail to arouse controversy,[4] which led the Commission to revise, at least formally, the approach given in the first formulation.[5] Protection of the 'European way of life' also returns in the Commission's Six Priorities Policy Paper 2019-2024, presented in July 2019. Finally, in a tweet of 12 September 2019, President von der Leyen returned to the topic, identifying the content of the notion of a 'European way of life' in Article 2 of the Lisbon Treaty.

Interpreted in this way, European values are configured as a true principle of conditionality, contributing to the process of building the identity of the Union as a 'community of shared values', which define the way in which the Union positions itself on the international scene,[6] but also internally as a 'value entrepreneur', at a time when the Union's political purpose is no longer only economic integration, but also that of shaping European society.[7] It thus emerges that, as understood by the European institutions, the values contained in Article 2 of the Lisbon Treaty can be traced back to the catego-

---

[4] A. Tidey, "What's the 'European way of life'? EU chief's new Commission portfolio draws criticism", *EuroNews*, 12 September 2019.

[5] In the first draft of the text the Commission used the term "protect" and subsequently replaced it with "promote". The letter of assignment states: "The European way of life is built around solidarity, peace of mind and security. We must address and allay legitimate fears and concerns about the impact of irregular migration on our economy and society. This will require us to work together to find common solutions which are grounded in our values and our responsibilities. We must also work more closely together on security, notably on new and emerging threats that cut across borders and policies. You will chair the Commissioners' Group on Promoting our European Way of Life".

[6] P. Akaliyski, "United in Diversity? the Convergence of Cultural Values among EU Member States and Candidates", *European Journal of Political Research*, 58, 2019, pp. 388-411; G.N. Toggenburg, J. Grimheden, "Upholding Shared Values in the EU: What Role for the EU Agency for Fundamental Rights?", *Journal of Common Market Studies*, 54, 2016, pp. 1093-1104; O. Oshri, T. Sheafer, T. Shenhav S.R., "A Community of Values: Democratic Identity Formation in the European Union", *European Union Politics*, 17, 2016, pp. 114-137.

[7] J. Gerhards, "Non-Discrimination towards Homosexuality. The European Union's Policy and Citizens' Attitudes towards Homosexuality in 27 European Countries", *International Sociology*, 25, 2010, p. 6. See also J. Gerhards, *Cultural Overstretch? The Enlargement of the European Union and the Cultural Differences between Old and New Member States and Turkey*, London-New York 2007.

ry of 'emancipative values', and are a distinctive feature of modern Western culture, which in turn finds its foundation in the Enlightenment.[8]

2. Is the rule of law a value for European citizens?

Among the values set out in Article 2, the principle of the rule of law is one of the pillars of European constitutional tradition. It is not possible to dwell here on the historical genesis of this notion, nor on the differences with the German notion of *Rechtsstaat*, or the French notion of *État de droit* and the Italian notion of *Stato di diritto*,[9] which are often considered synonymous. Instead, it is important to clarify that the European institutions have devoted special attention to it, providing specific instruments for its protection. This centrality can be traced back to the events that in recent years have affected two Member States, Poland and Hungary, which have approved internal reforms that seriously challenge the rule of law.[10]

In response to these reforms, the European institutions have put in place a number of instruments to safeguard respect for the rule of law. Since 2020, the European Commission has engaged in the publication of the *Rule of Law Report*, part of a broader 'rule of law mechanism' aimed at the annual monitoring of the state of application of the rule of law in the various Member States.

In addition to these measures, in January 2021, the so-called 'conditionality regulation' came into force, effectively tying the budget to compliance with the rule of law.[11] The adoption of the regulation provoked protests from Poland and Hungary, which were directly affected by the measure adopted and lodged an appeal with the European Court of Justice, which was rejected by the Court.[12] These legal instruments are undoubtedly a deterrent against

---

[8] P. Akaliyski, C. Welzel, "Clashing Values: Supranational Identities, Geopolitical Rivalry and Europe's Growing Cultural Divide", *Journal of Cross-Cultural Psychology*, 51, 2020, pp. 740-762.

[9] G. Amato, B. Barbisan, C. Pinelli, *Rule of Law vs Majoritarian Democracy*, Oxford-New York 2021; P. Costa, D. Zolo (ed.), *Lo stato di diritto. Storia, teoria, critica*, Milano 2002.

[10] A. Pin, *Il rule of law come problema. Le sfide dell'Europa centro-orientale della Brexit e del Medio Oriente*, Napoli 2021; N. Neuwahl, C. Kovacs, "Hungary and the EU's rule of law protection", *Journal of European Integration*, 43, 1, 2021, pp. 17-32.

[11] Regulation (EU, Euratom) 2020/2092 of the European Parliament and of the Council of 16 December 2020 on a general regime of conditionality for the protection of the Union budget.

[12] European Court of Justice C-156/21 and C-157/21 16.2. 2022. Further insights in: C. Curti Gialdino, "La 'legge bavaglio' polacca viola l'indipendenza, l'imparzialità e la

threats of violation of the rule of law by Member States, but they have little effect on the real rooting of this principle among European citizens and Member States.[13] From this point of view, it is not so much decisive to arrive at an abstract definition of the notion of the rule of law, as at an operational notion that allows for a sort of breakdown of the principle into its constituent elements. In practice, it is a question of implementing a sort of operationalisation of the concept, aimed at verifying its rootedness in the daily practices of European citizens and within the institutions of the Member States.

In the social sciences, in fact, the value system taken as a whole can be further broken down into its constituent components. These elements, considered from the point of view of the individual social agent or actor, can be named as follows: the *belief*, the *model*, the *interest* and the "*image of the world*" (*Weltbild*).[14] The process through which individual subjects make values their own and accept them is not easy to define. These in fact, as shared meanings, are sedimented through a series of stratifications that then have the capacity to guide individual and collective action. The motivational dimension can take on different connotations ranging from actual sharing to material interest, feelings, and customs, identifying a different degree of adherence to them that can also give rise to internal contradictions within the subject.

If the principle of the rule of law is to be analysed as a value capable of orienting individual and collective actors, it must therefore be broken down into its individual elements to verify its rootedness in the practices of daily life and in the life of institutions. From this point of view, in fact, the assumption contained in the European Commission's 2020 *Rule of Law Report* ("The rule of law is a well-established principle. While Member States have different national identities, legal systems and traditions, the core meaning of the rule of law is the same across the EU") risks remaining confined to a level of generality that does not account for the principle's real rooting within the EU. If this were to be the case, the EU would be faced with increasing threats to the rule of law within its own Member States or with the rise of parties that aspire in their programmes to question all or part of the principles underpinning the rule of law. The same report states that:

Under the rule of law, all public powers always act within the constraints set out by law, in accordance with the values of democracy and fundamental rights, and under the control of independent and impartial

vita privata dei giudici ed è incompatibile con principi fondamentali del diritto dell'Unione europea", *Federalismi*, 12 July 2023.

[13] M. Blauberger, V. van Hüllen, "Conditionality of EU funds: an instrument to enforce EU fundamental values?", *Journal of European Integration*, 43:1, 2021, pp. 1-16,

[14] G. Pollini, "Dalla Wertrationalität all'indagine empirica dei valori: problemi e prospettive", *Quaderni di Sociologia*, 68, 2015.

courts. The rule of law includes principles such as legality, implying a transparent, accountable, democratic and pluralistic process for enacting laws; legal certainty; prohibiting the arbitrary exercise of executive power; effective judicial protection by independent and impartial courts, effective judicial review including respect for fundamental rights; separation of powers; and equality before the law. [15]

The principle as a whole encompasses a series of closely interrelated aspects, which in turn refer to systems of checks and balances, implemented by different institutions, but also by the citizens themselves. The rule of law thus becomes the backbone of democracy, and not simply one of its elements.

The European institutions themselves, in various documents, have made an attempt to operationalise the concept, which is particularly useful if we want to measure in some way the respect (or otherwise) of the principle by the Member States. The *Special Eurobarometer 489, Rule of Law* identifies a list of 17 indicators, grouped in three thematic areas: 1) Legality, legal certainty, equality before the law and separation of powers; 2).Prohibition of arbitrariness and penalties for corruption; 3) Effective judicial protection by indipendent courts.

The *Rule of Law Report*, drawn up annually by the Commission since 2020, has identified four thematic areas – Justice, Anti-corruption, Media freedom and pluralism, Checks and balances – shared by other international monitoring instruments, within which to verify compliance with the principle of the rule of law. In turn, the four thematic areas are divided into sub-categories – freedom of thought and expression, equality before the law, transparency, a free media system, etc. – which in fact delimit the perimeter within which power can be exercised in modern liberal democracies, both by citizens and institutions. From this point of view, many points of contact emerge from the rule of law principle with the other values contained in Article 2, defining a network of relations between the various values which are difficult to separate from one another. Attempts to operationalise the general principle focus predominantly on institutions, but still say little about the degree to which citizens internalise the principles attributable to the rule of law.

The Special Eurobarometer 508, *Values and Identities of EU citizens*, [16] groups the data collected through the survey into four main top-

---

[15] European Commission, *2020 Rule of Law Report. The rule of law situation in the European Union*, p. 1.

[16] European Commission (2021), *Special Eurobarometer 508, Values and Identities of EU citizens.*

ics: 1) Freedom & Democracy, 2) Respect for Human Rights/Human Dignity/Solidarity, 3) Rule of Law/Justice, 4) Non-discrimination, Equality & Tolerance. Furthermore, the Report is divided in three sections – *Personal values of European citizens*, *Identities of EU citizens* and *EU citizens and attitudes towards European Union values*.

It is not possible here to propose an analysis of the results that would do justice to the complexity of the levels covered by the survey. In general however, as emerges from the report, European citizens show a high level of adherence to European values and in particular to those identified with the rule of law: topping the list of responses are the independence of the judiciary (82%), equality before the law and the right to a fair trial (82%), and freedom of thought, expression and religion (81%). On the contrary, there are two topics on which European citizens are most divided: the right to political asylum (66%), and the rejection of the death penalty (57%). The differences between the various countries are significant in places, and the nature of a survey aimed at analysing citizens' perceptions of phenomena rather than the nature of the phenomenon itself could provide a useful interpretation. From this point of view, the principle that 'the law should treat everyone equally and everyone should have the right to a fair trial in an independent court' reaches 94% support in Denmark and falls to 70% in Italy.

If one turns from the attitude towards the values of the European Union to the analysis of the 'Personal values of European citizens', it emerges that for European citizens two values seem to be more important than the others: 'being in charge of decisions about your life' (78%) and 'taking care of those close to you' (77%). More generally:

> At EU level, the highest level of agreement is observed for self-transcendence values (80%), followed closely by openness to change (78%) and conservation (76%). Differences are most of the time rather small when comparing across countries. This means that the value orientation in general is similar across EU Member States. Nevertheless, between the first three values at EU level, self-transcendence values score the highest in all but five countries. Indeed, in Bulgaria and Hungary, a highest score is recorded on conservation values and in Denmark and the Netherlands, a highest score is recorded for openness to change values. In Poland, conservation and self-transcendence values score the highest at the same level. [17]

Regarding the third level examined by the Special Eurobarometer, the survey looks at how people identify themselves: occupation, ethnic back-

[17] *Ivi*, pp. 12-13.

ground or race, gender, age, sexual orientation, religion, nationality, etc. In some respects, it may seem surprising that Europeans first identify with their family (81%), nationality (73%) and gender (72%). At the bottom we find 'being European' (56%), 'political orientation' (54%), and 'religion or beliefs' (53%).

The three levels on which the survey is divided refer to interesting elements for the contemporary debate: a contrast is emerging between the values of the European Union (those of Article 2) and the values of European society, which many nationalist parties in the Central-Eastern European area refer to as the authentic European values, against the Europe of Brussels, promoter of Western, cosmopolitan and liberal values. This confrontation between Europe and the European Union takes on the tones of a 'cultural backlash' [18] underlying the rise of various forms of populism, sovereignism, and nationalism. It would be opportune to further investigate this finding, which would seem to highlight a mismatch between the priorities of European citizens in terms of personal values and their adherence to the values of the European Union.

3. Conclusions

The general reflection proposed here invites further levels of investigation, starting with the verification of the hypothesis of a mismatch between the personal values of European citizens and the processes through which they construct their identity and their adherence to European values.

Moreover, on the level strictly inherent to European values, there is such a close correlation between the various values set out in Article 2 that they cannot be considered in isolation, but as part of a single heritage that defines the framework of contemporary democracies. The principle of the rule of law alone is not sufficient to guarantee the democratic nature of institutions if it is not broken down into all its elements and rooted in European society. As some scholars wrote:

A political system with regular elections, but clear limits on media freedom, on election campaigning, and on autonomous activity by civil society is not on the road to being an illiberal democracy; it is on the road to not being a democracy at all. [19]

---

[18] P. Norris, R. Inglehart, *Cultural Backlash. Trump, Brexit, and Authoritarian Populism,* Cambridge 2019.

[19] J.-W. Müller, "Should the EU Protect democracy and the rule of law inside Member States?", *European Law Journal*, 21, 2, March 2015, p. 143.

From this point of view, the principle of the rule of law needs to free itself from the widespread perception that it is a:

> domain belonging to jurists, lawyers, bureaucrats or politicians […] Yet at its most fundamental, the rule of law needs to be thought of from a citizen's perspective. For not only does the rule of law, when enforced, guarantee freedoms and liberties for citizens and enable us to live peacefully, but it is if and when it becomes a citizen-based societal principle that its many attackers are best countered.[20]

What is the real rooting of the values of Article 2 among European citizens? It remains to be seen whether the two levels – the values of European citizens and identification with the values of the European Union – are heading in the same direction or whether an internal rift, long underestimated by the European institutions, does not nurture citizens' support for the integration process, but on the contrary allows the infiltration of forms of thinking that challenge the values of democracy.

[20] A. Merdzanovic, K. Nicolaidis, "Advocacy for a citizen-centric rule of law agenda: How do we bring the rule of law to life?", *European Law Journal*, 27, 2021, p. 298. See also, A. Merdzanovic, K. Nicolaidis, *A Citizen's Guide to the Rule of Law: Why We Need to Fight for the Most Precious Human Invention of All Time*, Stuttgart 2021.

Chapter 4

EUROPEAN CONSTITUTIONAL IDENTITY IN THE LIGHT OF EU ENLARGEMENT

Federico Savastano

ABSTRACT: *This paper intends to take as its starting point the constitutional changes in EU candidate states with the aim of framing them in the debate on the relationship between constitutional identity, national identity and European integration. The subject of constitutional changes in EU Member States is not distinct, in substantive terms, from that of the changes required of the states that wish to join it. Nor is their accession process and especially not their entry neutral in terms of defining the characteristics of European integration. In fact, the integration process is in constant flux, continually evolving and involving the supranational order and the states that help determine it. It is neither static nor closed, it is not fully defined, and its intrinsic and inevitable openness also keeps the systems of the participatory states open and dynamic.*

1. The directions of the European Federalizing Process

Where is Europe going? [1] This was Beniamino Caravita's question – one of the first Italian constitutionalists to urge academics and doctrine to reflect upon this topic – in one of his research projects, in the belief that the time had come to review the European federalizing process in order to understand its prospects, its directions and, indeed, to envisage new guiding principles. [2] The reasons for that reflection were dictated by the many crises that had been facing the European Union for a long time: the financial crisis, migration, Brexit, the crisis of the rule of law in some eastern countries, and the issue of possible and/or necessary institutional reforms. This sce-

---

[1] See B. Caravita, *Quanta Europa c'è in Europa? Percorsi e prospettive del federalizing process europeo*, Torino 2020; Id., *Trasformazioni costituzionali nel federalizing process europeo*, Napoli 2012. B. Caravita, M. Condinanzi, A. Morrone, A. Poggi, "Dove va l'Europa? Percorsi e prospettive del federalizing process europeo", *federalismi.it*, 7, 2019, pp. 2-28.

[2] This paper intends to propose a vision that underlies a research path developed in a recent wider publication, see F. Savastano, *Trasformazioni costituzionali nell'allargamento dell'Unione europea*, Torino 2023.

nario was then worsened by two unforeseen but disruptive events: the pandemic and the invasion of Ukraine.[3]

To answer the starting question – Where is Europe going? – we need to take a step back and ask ourselves, especially in the light of these two new disruptive events, what is Europe? Pandemic and war, for different reasons, in different ways and at different times, have rekindled the debate on the very nature of the European Union and in particular on its ability to provide unitary answers to common problems.[4]

The enlargement of the European Union was back on the agenda in 2022: on the one hand because of the granting of candidate status to Ukraine and Moldova, and on the other hand because of the acceleration in the entry programming of Albania and North Macedonia, which started their accession negotiations with the assessment phase of the transposition of the EU acquis.

For decades, the Community chose its members according to purely political logic.[5] Over time, it progressively proceduralised the accession process, first by clarifying the need for them to be democratic states,[6] then by elaborating the Copenhagen criteria, which gave a legal form to the negotiations with the candidate states. These criteria, however, are anything but merely formal: they enable the European institutions to assess the effective application of EU law in the candidate states so as to guarantee a stable and mutually beneficial membership to the Union, its members and the candidate itself. The efforts that a state must make in order to apply and then join are therefore high, also because they do not only concern the type of interventions to be made on its own internal order, but also the quantity of subjects with respect to which it has to adapt to the corpus of the Union.[7]

---

[3] E. Morin, *Le 15 lezioni del coronavirus. Cambiamo strada*, Milano 2020, p. 23.

[4] A. Poggi, "Dove va l'Europa al tempo del Covid 19: riflessioni in tema di territorio dell'UE", *federalismi.it*, 19, 2020, pp. 439-440.

[5] An example is the problematic accession of the United Kingdom, which had to wait until de Gaulle's French veto fell before it could join the European Communities in 1973, ten years after first applying for membership.

[6] Greece, Portugal and Spain all joined in the 1980s as a result of applications submitted in the late 1970s, after the fall of the dictatorial regimes that had characterised them.

[7] See, especially B. Caravita, *Quanta Europa c'è in Europa?*, cit. The title refers precisely to the quantitative data on the impact of European law on the legal systems of the Member States (pp. 123-127) and the candidate states (pp. 128-131). In 2012, *Rivista Federalismi* devoted a series of editorials to the topic of the European dimension of certain fundamental legal fields. In this regard, see S. Staiano, "La Costituzione e il suo contesto. Dimensione nazionale e dimensione europea", *federalismi.it,* 1, 2012; L. Violini, "La dimensione europea dei diritti di libertà: politiche europee e case law nel settore della tutela dei diritti fondamentali. Sviluppi recenti", *federalismi.it,* 1, 2012; U. Triulzi,

Studying what is asked of those who want to join the Union provides a basis for answering the question, what is Europe?

2. Identity and borders

European identity is not unitary but is a plural one, and it has been built on a continuous dialectic between different factors that have influenced each other chronologically and culturally.[8] This composite identity has shaped a history made up of moments of unity and commonality of values.[9] We must therefore read the history of the European continent as an alternation of moments of unity and fragmentation, which followed one another in a continuous dialectic, each leaving a legacy that went on to enrich the plural fabric of the matrix that is the Europe we know today.[10] This matrix has created a system of values shared by all the Member States and today it is the main tool for distinguishing what Europe is from what Europe is not. In fact, the very idea of Europe was born out of the contrast with what was outside and what was different: Greeks and Persians, Romans and Barbarians, Westerners and Easterners, Christians and Muslims.[11]

Similarly, today the borders of Europe are no longer mere geographical boundaries, but the delimitation of a shared space of common constitu-

---

"La dimensione europea delle politiche di sicurezza in Italia", *federalismi.it,* 2, 2012; G.M. Roberti, "La dimensione europea della politica di concorrenza", *federalismi.it,* 3, 2012; G. Napolitano, "La politica europea per il mercato interno dell'energia e il suo impatto sull'ordinamento italiano", *federalismi.it*, 4, 2012; T.E. Frosini, "La dimensione europea della forma di stato e di governo", *federalismi.it*, 5, 2012; M. De Poli, "Riflessioni sulla dimensione europea della disciplina bancaria", *federalismi.it*, 6, 2012; A. Sciaudone, "La dimensione europea delle politiche agricole", *federalismi.it*, 7, 2012; A. Poggi, "Politiche nazionali di riforma dei sistemi universitari e processo di integrazione europea: autonomia della didattica e accentramento della ricerca", *federalismi.it*, 8, 2012; F. Cintioli, "La dimensione europea dei servizi di interesse economico generale", *federalismi.it*, 11, 2012; R. Rordorf, "La dimensione europea dei mercati finanziari", *federalismi.it*, 13, 2012; A. Celotto, "La dimensione europea delle fonti del diritto", *federalismi.it*, 14, 2012; S. Staiano, "I partiti europei fuori tempo", *federalismi.it*, 15, 2012; M. Cecchetti, "La dimensione europea delle politiche ambientali, un acquis solo apparentemente scontato", *federalismi.it*, 16, 2012.

[8] See P. Faraguna, "Constitutional Identity in the EU – A Shield or a Sword?", *German Law Journal*, 7, 2017, pp. 1617-1640.

[9] B. Caravita, "I valori europei all'epoca del Coronavirus", *federalismi.it*, 19, 2020, p. 435:

History teaches us that in our continent phases of great unity can be followed by phases of dramatic fragmentation and that crises, and their management, can give the final push in one direction or the other.

[10] On this subject, see P. Grossi, *L'Europa del diritto*, Roma-Bari 2007.

[11] F. Chabod, *Storia dell'idea d'Europa*, 8th ed., Bari 2010.

tional values and democracy. Identifying these values is equivalent to identifying the characteristics of European integration. After all, the European Union has always been capable of acting as a collector, catalyst and creator of a system of rights and uniform values inherited and re-proposed in a new guise to its Member States.

The set of norms that can be derived from all sources of European law and order that constitute the *acquis* corresponds to a European Union identity card. It contains the common values and constitutional traditions, the political principles by which it is inspired, the mechanisms of financial conditionality, the deficit values granted in relation to GDP, the competition and market rules; the four freedoms, fishing, and all the matters in which European legislation is substantially uniform.

In other words, the candidate states are being asked to become everything that Europe already is, and it is therefore from the demands being made of these countries – and thus from the analysis of their accession negotiations – that you can see what Europe is today. Looking at what the candidate states' legal systems must become provides a clear definition of the Member States' legal systems.

This paper follows this path with the aim of framing it in the debate on the relationship between constitutional identity, national identity and European integration. [12] The subject of constitutional changes in the EU Member States is not distinct, from a substantive point of view, from that of the changes required of the states that wish to join it. Nor is their accession path and especially not their entry neutral in terms of defining the features of European integration. In fact, the integration process is in constant flux, constantly involving the supranational order and the states that help determine it. It is neither static nor closed, it is not fully defined, and its intrinsic and inevitable openness also keeps the systems of the participating states open and dynamic. It is based, in other words, on an ongoing dialogue with the Member States, on a dialectic from which a new common identity continually emerges, which immediately relates again to the state systems: that "continual tension that unceasingly resolves itself in integration processes" on which the legal system is based in Smend's integration theory. [13]

A new Member State becomes part of this tension and a new player in the dialectic with the centre of the system, beginning to adhere to it and, at the same time, influencing it through its own identity. Thus accession be-

---

[12] It has taken up the distinction between constitutional and national identity defined by T. Cerruti, "Valori comuni e identità nazionali nell'Unione europea: continuità o rottura?", *federalismi.it*, 24, 2014, pp. 8-9.

[13] R. Smend, *Costituzione e diritto costituzionale*, Milano 1988, p. 33.

comes even more of a constitutionally relevant moment for the European Union and for the Member States: if new states interact with the supranational order, these new players will also determine its content, thus affecting the set of norms and values which the existing Member State has long been debating. From this point of view, the rationale of Article 49 of the Treaty on European Union (TEU), which identifies the values set forth in Article 2 TEU as a fundamental requirement for submitting an application for membership, is well understood: if a State wants to enter into the overall dialectic and contribute to the Union's own order of integration, it must demonstrate the standards of liberal-democracies. It cannot, in other words, depart from that block of shared values that are the heart and product of the Member States' common constitutional traditions.

Nor can the Member States accept a system that is too distant from their own, given that, as has been said, they would in any case be influenced by it to some extent. This risk has already reared its head with the problems that have arisen as a consequence of the 2004 eastward enlargement and the inclusion of states with democracies that are not yet entirely stable. [14]

The new accessions thus entail the enlargement of that common space in which the dialectic of integration takes place. New states entering to participate, together with the other members and on an equal footing with them, in that "long and uninterrupted constituent process that has not yet reached a final order" and is probably destined not to reach it. It was designed not to reach it. [15]

The systems of the states that take part in this process are, as mentioned above, open and dynamic, both in an ascending phase, thus capable of affecting the determination of the character of the supranational order, and

---

[14] According to A. Poggi, "Unione europea e territorio: problemi e prospettive", in T. Cerruti, A. Poggi (eds.), "Territorio e territori nell'Unione europea", *federalismi.it*, 31, 2020, vi: "It was known that the territorial enlargement of the Union was problematic, that it would be necessary as early as 2004 to make incisive changes to the EU's political dimension was also known, but now the real dimension of the problem has emerged: a possible fracture between two Europeans, or perhaps a fracture between many Europeans, in particular between the Nordic and the Mediterranean".

In-depth and original in this sense is the analysis conducted by O. Pollicino, *Allargamento dell'Europa ad est e rapporto tra corti costituzionali e corti europee. Verso una teoria generale dell'impatto interordinamentale del diritto sovranazionale?,* Milano 2010.

[15] A. Morrone, "I mutamenti costituzionali derivanti dall'integrazione europea", *federalismi.it*, 20, 2018, p. 3: "In the European Union, since there is no legal order established by a constitution, but a permanent constituent process, what might appear to be implementation activity is properly the construction of an order in the making, which therefore, in its most recent manifestations (marked by the succession of treaties), looks different from those immediately preceding it".

in a descending phase, thus willing to intervene on their own constitutional norms in the name of integration. [16]

These constitutional changes, regardless of whether they result in actual revisions or are tacitly brought about by other means, are an integral part of the integration process. They are not a price to pay but they constitute the very nature of the integration process, which otherwise could not exist in its current form.

Appreciating the a priori changes that candidate states make allows one to re-read those that have occurred in the constitutional order of a Member State throughout its membership. If the candidate state feels that it does not want to make the necessary changes, access cannot be granted; similarly, if a Member State does not conform its constitution to the constant changes in the integration process, it will end up clashing with the supranational order. In defence of its own constitution, it may clash by opposing counter-limits, the rationale of which is precisely to protect the constitutional identity of the Member States; it may decide that the compromise is so untenable that it considers it more appropriate to leave the European Union, as the United Kingdom has done; it may simply remain inert and refuse to make the necessary changes, calling itself out of the harmonious integrative tension of the Union, thus ending up in a circle that will lead it to an ever-widening detachment from European principles, with the risk of taking drifts that will also distance it from common values which are the foundation and purpose of the Union. An interesting outline in this sense emerges from a combined reading of Articles 2 and 3 of the Treaty on European Union: in Article 2 TEU, the values enter the treaties as common to the Member States; Article 3(1) TEU, on the other hand, identifies them as the prerogative of the Union, which has thus made them its own (The Union shall aim to promote [...] the values of the Union, and shall do so in the interests of the Union). In Article 3(2) TEU, the Union offers citizens an area of freedom, security and justice. From the states to the Union, then from the Union to the citizens, values become the feature that identifies the relationship between the supranational order and the citizens of the Member States, between the governed and the governed, thus becoming the distinguishing feature of a form of common state, which emanates from them.

Joining the European Union therefore means reflecting a well-defined form of state, characterised by freedom, democracy, equality, the rule of

---

[16] *Ivi*, p. 5.

Precisely as a result of the constitutional embedding between state and European systems, the *ordo ordinans* that takes place in the European dimension affects both, continuously shaping them.

law and respect for human dignity and human rights (Article 2 TEU). It also means espousing a model of society, the purpose of which is the well-being of people,[17] in which citizens live in a free, secure, and borderless space,[18] based on a market economy, but which is a social market economy, oriented towards sustainable and balanced growth, without discrimination and living off the richness of its differences.[19]

This model is not the only one from which a state can draw inspiration, and today it is not the most widespread model, even and especially among the world's great powers. It is different from authoritarian regimes such as China's, or illiberal democracies such as Russia's, but also from the highly competitive and liberalist American democracy.

3. Facing new Enlargements

EU enlargement to the Balkans and the Ukrainian application for membership differ from previous enlargements precisely because of this 'greater offer' from which to choose and precisely because of the differences and peculiarities of the EU's offer. Joining the Union cannot be as a mere choice of international policy, it means firstly ascribing to its values and implementing them in one's own legal system, then promoting them in the international context, since they also imply adherence to a particular way of being a global player.[20] These concepts are functional to the general reflection, which goes back to the initial question: what is Europe and where is it going?

For decades, the integration process has witnessed the transformation of political dynamics, appropriate to an international organization, into institutionalised legal procedures fitting to a constitutional order. It is precisely the enlargements that have been the result of a constitutional decision that brought about a revolution – especially in 2004 – in the European constitutional order: enlargement of the territory, increase in the number of citizens, increase in the number of Member States, significant modification of

---

[17] Article 3(1) TEU.

[18] Article 3(2) TEU.

[19] Article 3(3) TEU.

[20] Article 3(5) TEU:

In its relations with the wider world, the Union shall uphold and promote its values and interests and contribute to the protection of its citizens. It shall contribute to peace, security, the sustainable development of the Earth, solidarity and mutual respect among peoples, free and fair trade, eradication of poverty and the protection of human rights, in particular the rights of the child, as well as to the strict observance and the development of international law, including respect for the principles of the United Nations Charter.

the political community of reference.[21] The identification of criteria for accession is part of this pattern involving the transition from the predominantly political bilateral negotiations of pre-Copenhagen to an institutionalised procedure codified in the Treaties.

Many observers have pointed out that the Union's lack of democracy has been largely overcome, while a problem persists in the formation of a common will on the political level and, in particular, on the international level. The Ukrainian crisis and the enlargement to the Western Balkans could provide an opportunity to overcome this stumbling block, taking perhaps the biggest step in the European federalisation process. This is a precious opportunity to try to *recover the compass*[22] of the integration process, to understand the ways to overcome the *existential crisis*[23] of the Union and to envision a new path for the future of Europe, investigating ways to promote the effective action of its institutions and the responsible action of its Member States, beyond the suggestions of a confused platform.

Enlargement entails an enrichment of that *Vielfalt* which is the qualifying value of the common European identity.[24] This is a plural, composite identity, based on the relationship between two constitutional principles that emerge from the Treaties: that of national identities and that of the existence of common constitutional traditions. The very essence of the Union lies in the balance between differentiation and unity, with the former assuming a founding character even with respect to the latter. This aspect of the integration process is not the result of theoretical speculation, but comes directly from the wording of the Treaties. Article 4(2) TEU requires the Union to respect the national identities of the Member States, while Article 6(3) TEU includes rights resulting from the constitutional traditions common to the Member States within the general principles of European law. It is also grounded in the systems of the Member States, which have developed mechanisms to protect their constitutional identity (counter-limits), but at the same time recognize the existence of constitutional traditions common to all Member States. This tension is the foundation of integration, and creates a situation whereby the supranational legal system is never static, since it is in constant dialogue with the legal systems of its constituent states, which, in

---

[21] According to J.H.H. Weiler, *La Costituzione dell'Europa*, Bologna 2017, p. 617. The decision on enlargement was the single most important constitutional decision taken in the last ten years and probably even more.

[22] U. Beck, *Europa Tedesca. La Nuova geografia del potere*, Roma-Bari 2013.

[23] E. Morin, M. Cerruti, *La nostra Europa*, Milano 2013.

[24] A. Morrone, "I mutamenti costituzionali derivanti dall'integrazione europea", *federalismi.it*, 20, 2018, p. 5.

turn, remain open to the Union and the influences that arrive indirectly from other states, becoming the subject of constant constitutional changes, whether tacit or expressed in actual constitutional revisions.

How does the debate on the enlargement of the European Union fit into this framework? Enlargement is a significant constitutional moment in several respects. First of all, it entails a shift in the Union's borders due to the entry of new entities into the European legal space. A new state enters an area made up of common values of which it becomes the recipient and which it will help to strengthen but also to shape, according to its own constitutional experience. Thus, all those involved in the integration process are affected by changes resulting from enlargement.

In the first place, the European legal system is affected, since the accession procedure ends with an amendment to the founding treaties and therefore entails, to all intents and purposes, a formal revision of the acts containing the fundamentals of the European constitution.

The legal systems of the new Member States, as well as those of the candidate countries, are also affected since they face an accelerated process of reforms aimed at making them conform, first and foremost, to the common values set out in Article 2 TEU, in particular with regard to the principles of the rule of law and democracy. These are changes that affect the formal and material constitution, and are accompanied by a variable, but nonetheless very large number of legislative and quasi-legislative interventions in the material sectors of associated life, which aim to bring the order into line with the acquis. This process, which is often long and intricate and, moreover, can involve different governments and legislatures with differing political leanings, results, in the event of success, in a profoundly transformed state, completely different from what it was at the time of the application for membership. The Copenhagen criteria, now articulated in six negotiating clusters, have become the reference point for guiding political and institutional choices in these states, sometimes for decades, while waiting for them to begin to be structurally oriented on the basis of Union law. After all, what are the Copenhagen criteria if not the collection and systematisation of the constitutional values, economic rules and body of law of the European Union?

Finally, the legal systems of the existing Member States are affected. As Brexit empirically demonstrated, the number of participants in the Union is a factor which affects all Member States. The Union is in fact composed of states, but also of relations between states: the importance given by the Commission reports to neighbourhood relations of the candidate states has been highlighted in the previous chapters. The Union is also composed of relations between the centre and the periphery or, in its case, between the supranational system and each individual state system. Much has been said of the mutual influence between the two, and how it is fundamental to integration, while more has been discussed of to what extent it constitutes integration. The presence of a new actor participating in the constant dialectic between the Union and the Member States is not a neutral factor for the other states.

This brings us now to the subject of common values: the Member States do not want to and cannot share European integration with countries that do not recognise themselves in the rule of law and democracy. The Treaties stipulate that the Council must decide unanimously on the entry of a new state, precisely to ensure that each Member State can always decide whether and to whom to open the doors of its own system.

The values expressed in Article 2 TEU are the true fundamental principle governing every aspect of the decision on the entry of a new state. It has been shown how they even permeate the economic and legal parameters envisaged in Copenhagen, and it has clearly emerged, from the empirical analysis of the accession processes underway, that they constitute a fundamental principle from the Union's point of view, a political objective for the candidate states and a heritage to be safeguarded and protected for the Member States. A heritage that, moreover, derives from the Member States themselves, who have built it and secured it, raising it to a shared supranational principle.

Conformity to common values is, of course, not merely the expression of a formal conditionality to be demonstrated at the accession stage and to be managed more flexibly after entry. Article 2 TEU is the yardstick for membership before and after entry, and for the entire duration of stay within the common European home. This is demonstrated by Article 7 TEU, whereby a serious and persistent breach by a Member State of the values set out in Article 2 may lead to the suspension of the rights of the state in question. For this reason, compliance with these values is a prerequisite for the very submission of an application (Article 49 TEU) and the verification takes place prior to the candidate's entry. This verification does not (or should not) stop at a high level but, as the 1995 Madrid European Council made clear, extends to the actual implementation capacity of the State. The Union can only be joined when there is certainty around the stability of the rule of law and democracy.

Ukraine's application for membership has called this assumption into question, dividing politicians and academic scholarship on the hypothesis of reverting to an eminently political assessment of enlargement. While the political arguments are undoubtedly understandable, based on the need to come to the aid of a country in a state of war that is considered a friend and strategic partner, the legal ones appear less agreeable. Part of the doctrine, as highlighted in this paper, considers the Copenhagen criteria to be a superstructure created outside the Treaties, whereas the text of the TEU would refer to a simple political dynamic: application, unanimous response, accession agreement. According to this doctrinaire approach, the verification of compliance with the values set forth in Article 2 (respect for which, it is worth reiterating, is imposed by Article 49 TEU, as well as transpiring from the overall reading of the Treaty) may take place in a subsequent transitional phase, aimed at supporting the State in the process of reforms needed to adapt to the conditions of the system of which it has become part. This solution, with the Treaties in force, does not seem to be acceptable: while the promotion of values is posed as a commitment (which can therefore also be fulfilled at a later date), respect for them is qualified as a requirement not so much for admission as for the presentation of the application itself. Respect for the values of Article 2 thus counts as much as the characteristic of being a European state for the purposes of applying for membership. Moreover, the provision that the eligibility criteria agreed upon by the European Council must be taken into account is also codified in the text. Even from a conceptual point of view, the reasoning raises some questions: if, as has been shown, the Copenhagen criteria are an emanation of the common values, and are strongly characterised by them, it would be inconsistent to separate the issue of their observance from that of compliance with Article 2 TEU.

4. The future of EU integration

The problem posed by the reaction to Ukraine's application for membership is perhaps broader, and relates to the dialectic between politics and law in the construction of Europe. It recalls the debate between Schmitt and Kelsen and brings us back to the initial question: where is Europe going? European integration is an integration through law that has been based on the creation of a common space guided by values that are its beating heart and guiding principle. Can the European Union fail to comply with the system of rules it has created at such a decisive constitutional moment as enlargement? Can it fail to do so when it is dealing with states that it is asking to conform to those principles and that system of values? The answer can only be no. But if it is true that integration is achieved through law, and is consolidated thanks to the jurisprudence of the Court of Justice and national judges, whose constant dialogue articulates, defines and deepens its terms, it cannot be ignored that it also requires coherent actions and behaviour from the Member States' governments, which also contribute to giving it a solid political connotation, constantly reinforcing it through the factual renewal of their own will to adhere to it.[25] The Ukrainian crisis in

[25] See A. Poggi, "Dove va l'Europa al tempo del Covid 19: riflessioni in tema di territorio dell'UE", in B. Caravita, M. Condinanzi, A. Morrone, A. Poggi (eds.), "I dieci anni dal Trattato di Lisbona", *federalismi.it*, 19, 2020, p. 449:

particular will be decisive in this respect, as the future of Europe also depends on what it can produce outside its borders and on how the national governments of the Member States can deal with the crisis in a united manner. The Union must therefore continue to develop around the dialectic between politics and law, finally becoming capable of acting as a great global power but following the rules that it has imposed on itself, the principles that guide it, the values that it has chosen, and that can represent its strength also in terms of international relations.

Freedom, democracy, equality, the rule of law, respect for human dignity and human rights are the foundation of a social model that the European Union embodies and assumes as the defining element of its form of state. Derogations are conceptually not possible: illiberal democracies simply cannot enter the Union because their entry would undermine its functioning, and the Member States cannot accept illiberal democracies because a weakening of Europe would also weaken them. It is a model of society that acts inwards, towards the Member States and European citizens, but also outwards, as an alternative to the models observable in the United States, the People's Republic of China or the Russian Federation. Even from this external confrontation, indications can be drawn on the identity and perspectives of the integration process: it is Federico Chabod's idea of Europe[26] – referred to at the beginning – that emerges from the contrast with what Europe is not.

The guideline for Europe is therefore to continue towards itself, to continue its federalising process in constant and perennial evolution. This means extending itself, as far as possible, to all the states that wish to become part of that dialectical process of building a dynamic integration, the goal of which is an ever-closer union that cannot be renounced and that contains within itself, preserving and transforming it, all that *Vielfalt* that enriches it and constitutes its main strength.[27]

In conclusion, integration does not take place in the courts: the Europe of rights is certainly an important component of this, but it cannot replace the potential of political will necessary for integration.

In the same way A. Morrone, "Una costituzione per l'Europa? Per uno stato costituzionale europeo", *federalismi.it*, 23, 2014, p. 8:

The Europe foreshadowed by the Convention for a European Constitution failed fundamentally because it postulated a 'Europe of rights but without sovereignty', i.e. a Europe without European politics, without institutions to govern European citizens.

[26] F. Chabod, *op. cit.*

[27] B. Caravita, *Il dibattito sul futuro dell'Europa*, cit., p. 16: According to the author, the much-discussed and criticised formula (on the occasion of Brexit) simply "should not be touched", because in it "there is an indication of a strong and significant trend line, the implementation of which is entrusted to the political, social and economic balances that will be achieved from time to time".

Chapter 5

THE 'NEW *MOMENTUM*' OF THE ENLARGEMENT POLICY AND THE NEED TO STRIKE THE RIGHT BALANCE BETWEEN REFORM AND ENLARGEMENT

Francesco Battaglia

ABSTRACT: *This article analyzes the EU strategy for enlargement taking into consideration the need to reach a balance between widening and deepening, through the perspective of European values.*
As shown by the fast-track followed to grant the candidate status to Ukraine and Moldova, the last international events have given a new impetus to the enlargement process, and it will probably re-energize and unblock even the issue of Western Balkans. However, the future strategy has to take full account of two potentially conflicting objectives: speed and quality. Speed is needed to face geopolitical challenges and to promote stability, but quality is vital to safeguard the European values, as enshrined under art. 2 TEU. Such values must be the at the heart of the enlargement process and the key benchmark against which progress towards EU membership is assessed.

1. Introduction

As underlined by the European Commission, the enlargement agenda gained new momentum in June 2022 when the European Council endorsed the Commission's recommendation recognising the European perspective of Ukraine, Moldova and Georgia and, in particular, granting candidate status to Ukraine and Moldova.[1] This unprecedented 'fast-track' decision, which has taken just four months after Ukraine submitted its application, is emblematic of the EU's strong support for Ukraine in the face of Russia's aggression launched on 24 February 2022.[2]

---

[1] European Commission, 2023 Communication on EU Enlargement Policy, 8 November 2023, COM(2023) 690 final.

[2] See N. Scicluna, S. Auer "Pushing the EU's Boundaries: Enlargement and Foreign

The EU's strong support for the European perspective of Ukraine, Moldova and Georgia, as a consequence of the changing geopolitical environment, has had a broader impact on enlargement policy, as it has also reopened the debate on the accession of the Western Balkan countries, which had been progressing very slowly due to a long period of enlargement fatigue. In general, therefore, the war in Ukraine was a turning point because it revived the enlargement process and, in this sense, the EU's reaction to the Russia-Ukraine war has been compared to that during the wars of the breakup of Yugoslavia in the 1990s.[3]

Thus, in her last State of the Union, the President of the European Commission Ursula von der Leyen, who until then had maintained a lukewarm attitude towards further enlargements,[4] in continuity with her predecessor, Jean-Claude Juncker, who had also explicitly ruled out any new accession during his mandate, changed her approach and underlined the priority of the enlargement process, affirming that it could even anticipate political deepening. In her view, "we cannot – and we should not – wait for Treaty change to move ahead with enlargement".[5]

However, the idea of giving priority to widening over deepening does not seem feasible because it would jeopardise the effective functioning of the EU. While rapid enlargement could be useful to address geopolitical challenges and to promote stability, the quality of such a process is crucial to safeguard European values as enshrined under Article 2 TEU. These values must be at the heart of the enlargement process and the key benchmark against which progress towards EU membership is assessed.

In light of these considerations, the relaunch of the enlargement process has brought the issue of institutional reform of the EU back to the fore after a long stasis on both fronts.[6] In particular, the European Parliament re-

---

Policy Actorness after the Russian Invasion of Ukraine", *Journal of Common Market Studies*, 2023, pp. 1-12.

[3] V. Anghel, J. Džankić, "Wartime EU: consequences of the Russia-Ukraine war on the enlargement process", *Journal of European Integration,* 2023, p. 488.

[4] Indeed, until the last geopolitical developments, further enlargements were considered undesirable even by a large part of EU citizens. The reputation and attractiveness of the EU in the aspiring Member States probably suffered as well. In that regard, see L. Ognjanoska, "Reinforcing the EU Enlargement Policy Towards Western Balkans: Access to the Single Market as a Credible Goal", *European Papers*, 2022, pp. 833-855.

[5] State of the Union 2023, available online on https://ec.europa.eu/commission/presscorner/detail/en/speech_23_4426.

[6] A. Miglio, "Riforma dell'Unione e integrazione differenziata: l'eterno ritorno di un binomio classico", *I post di AISDUE*, 2023, p. 264. On the need to reform before enlarging, it was even affirmed that "a widening without reform would expose the EU to the threat of an imperial overstretch, which will lead in the long run to a process of

cently voted on a proposal for the reform of the Treaties in which it affirms that the Union's institutional framework, and in particular its decision-making process, is barely adequate for a Union of 27 Member States and future enlargements therefore make a reform of the Treaties inevitable.[7]

On this basis, this paper will analyse, through a legal perspective, the 'new momentum' of the European enlargement process, together with the need to reform the Treaties so that the accession of new Member States does not undermine the protection of European values.

2. The evolving approach to the enlargement policy

Enlargement has been described by the European Parliament as the EU's most effective foreign policy instrument and one of the Union's most successful policies which will remain a strategic, future-oriented geopolitical investment in peace, security, stability and prosperity on the European continent.[8] Even the President of the European Commission, Ursula von der Leyen, has recently stressed that the reasons for enlargement have never been stronger and more compelling, because in a world that is shaken by multiple crises, it is an investment in the stability and security of the continent.[9] The President of the European Commission made this statement after the European Council meeting on 14 and 15 December 2023, where EU leaders, recalling the Granada Declaration,[10] reaffirmed their full and une-

European disintegration" (C. Calliess, "Reform the European Union for Enlargement! Proposals to Prevent an 'Overstretch in Integration'", *Verfassungsblog*, 6 July 2023).

[7] European Parliament Resolution of 22 November 2023 on proposals of the European Parliament for the amendment of the Treaties (2022/2051(INL)).

[8] European Parliament recommendation of 23 November 2022 to the Council, the Commission and the Vice-President of the Commission / High Representative of the Union for Foreign Affairs and Security Policy concerning the new EU strategy for enlargement (2022/2064(INI)).

[9] Opening remarks by President von der Leyen at the joint press conference with President Michel and Prime Minister Sánchez following the meeting of the European Council of 15 December 2023, 15 December 2023.

[10] The Granada Declaration, adopted by the European Council on 6 October 2023, states: "Enlargement is a geo-strategic investment in peace, security, stability and prosperity. It is a driver for improving the economic and social conditions of European citizens, reducing disparities between countries, and must foster the values on which the Union is founded. Looking ahead to the prospect of a further enlarged Union, both the EU and future Member States need to be ready. Aspiring members need to step up their reform efforts, notably in the area of rule of law, in line with the merit-based nature of the accession process and with the assistance of the EU".

quivocal commitment to the EU membership perspective of the Western Balkans and called for the acceleration of their accession process. [11]

The need to extend the Union's borders has thus given a new impetus to enlargement policy, which should lead to a new 'big enlargement' by 2030. [12] This 'enlargement enthusiasm', which has been supported by citizens for the first time since 2004, [13] follows a long period of general 'enlargement fatigue', characterized by a lack of enthusiasm and confidence in the overall enlargement project. After the 2004 accessions, in fact, the EU and its Member States showed an "enlargement resistance", [14] seeing new accessions as a challenge to the functioning of the EU itself. This resistance stemmed from the fact that, unlike previous rounds, the 2004 enlargement was very complex in political, economic and legal terms and had far-reaching consequences. It was the largest single enlargement in terms of people and number of countries, involving several large states with emerging democracies and weak market-based economies. In other words, the new states' legal and economic models were very far from the European ones and for this reason their accession process was, for the first time, based on incentive mechanisms to support their transformation into Member States able to accept the *acquis*. However, once the candidate states achieved their goal of EU membership, the Union lost much of its leverage over the countries that could be expected to relapse by failing to comply with either the EU's economic rules or its political ideals of democracy and the rule of law. [15]

The problem of post-accession compliance with EU law arose immediately after the 2004 enlargement, so in 2007, with regard to the accession of Romania and Bulgaria, the Commission decided, on the basis of Articles 37 and 38 of the Accession treaties, to set up the Mechanism of Cooperation and Verification (MCV), the first ever post-accession conditionality instrument. [16] In this

---

[11] European Council meeting (14 and 15 December 2023), conclusions, EUCO 20/23.

[12] Speech by President Charles Michel at the Bled Strategic Forum, 28 August 2023.

[13] M. Bonomi, I. Rusconi, "From EU 'enlargement fatigue' to 'enlargement enthusiasm'?", *ÖGfE Policy Brief*, 2023, p. 19.

[14] S. Economides, K. Featherstone, T. Hunter, "The changing Discourses of EU Enlargement: A Longitudinal Analysis of National Parliamentary Debates", *Journal of Common Market Studies*, 2023, pp. 1-18.

[15] M.A. Pollack, "Europe united? The impact of the EU's eastern enlargement, five years on", *European View*, 2009, p. 248.

[16] A. Rosanò, "Not another EU report! Il meccanismo di cooperazione e verifica quale strumento di promozione dello Stato di diritto e i suoi effetti sul processo di allargamento", *I Post di AISDUE*, 2022, pp. 357-378.

sense, scholars underlined that, depending on one's view, Bulgaria and Romania can be seen as being either the last to benefit from the old enlargement policies, or as the first to experience the EU's new and expectedly more restrictive attitude towards the admission of new Member States. [17]

Actually, the accession treaties of Bulgaria and Romania seems replicating the same flexible model used in 2004. In fact, they introduced safeguard clauses such as those used as the legal basis for the MCV. These provisions stated that if Bulgaria or Romania failed to implement commitments undertaken in the context of the accession negotiations, causing a serious breach of the functioning of the internal market or in the area of criminal law, the Commission could adopt European regulations or decisions establishing appropriate measures within a three-year period following their accession. The safeguard clauses were introduced because, at the time of their accession to the European Union, these countries still needed to make improvements in order to meet the political and economic criteria for membership. [18]

However, the application of these clauses through the MCV has not been successful. Such instruments, although intended as transitional measures, remained in force well beyond the three-year period laid down in the Accession Treaties. [19] Moreover, they have not produced the expected results, as shown in the Commission's latest Rule of Law Report. In the

---

[17] D. Smilov, "Enlargement and EU Constitutionalism in the Balkan Periphery", in W. Sadurski, J. Ziller, K. Zurek (eds.), *Après Enlargement. Legal and Political Responses in Central and Eastern Europe*, Firenze, 2006, p. 161; F. Trauner, "Post-accession compliance with EU law in Bulgaria and Romania: a comparative perspective", *European Integration online Papers*, 2009, p. 2.

[18] In that regard, even the Commission opinion of 2005 on the accession of Bulgaria and Romania, while delivering a favourable opinion, stated: "The Commission calls on the Republic of Bulgaria and Romania to pursue vigorously the improvements that still need to be made in the context of the political and economic criteria for membership and in relation to the adoption, implementation and enforcement of the acquis. (Commission Opinion of 22 February 2005 on the applications for accession to the European Union by the Republic of Bulgaria and Romania, COM/2005/0055 final)".

[19] In that regard, Articles 37 and 38 establish a) that the safeguard clauses may be invoked even before accession on the basis of the monitoring findings and that the measures adopted are to enter into force as of the first day of accession unless they provide for a later date, and (b) that the measures may be applied beyond the period of three years as long as those shortcomings persist. Despite the possibility to maintain the measures for an undetermined period of time, both Articles 37 and 38 of the Act of Accession indicate expressly that the measures are not to be maintained any longer than is strictly necessary and, in any case, are to be lifted when the relevant commitment is implemented (Regarding the duration of the measures to apply the safeguard clauses, see Judgment of the Court (Grand Chamber), 18 May 2021).

case of Bulgaria, for example, even though the Commission concluded the MCV in 2019, the report states that the perceived level of independence of the judiciary remains low and the perception of the level of corruption in the public sector remains high.[20]

Thus, as a result of the 2004 enlargement, both the institutions and the Member States have adopted a more rigid and merit-based approach to the accession of new Member States. The new approach has been clear since the first speech to the European Parliament of the former President of the Commission, Jean-Claude Juncker, when he announced a pause on EU enlargement and confirmed that no further enlargement would take place during his term of office.[21] The key phrase since Juncker's Commission has become "credible enlargement", meaning that *a)* third countries can join the European Union once the criteria of Article 49 TEU, including the Copenhagen criteria, are fully met; *b)* there can be no ambiguity on the part of leaders about the status quo within these states and the direction in which they are heading, so as to secure and maintain the support of both their own and the EU's citizens.[22]

In apparent break with her predecessor, Ursula von der Leyen, when presenting her College of Commissioners in 2019, declared her ambition to accelerate enlargement.[23] However even her approach to further accessions has remained very cautious.[24] This resistance has probably been reinforced by the democratic and rule of law backsliding witnessed in some post-2004 Member States, such as Poland and Hungary.

The new EU methodology for accession negotiations, adopted in 2020, maintains the same spirit.[25] On the one hand, it establishes a more dynamic

---

[20] Commission staff working document, 2023 Rule of Law Report Country Chapter on the rule of law situation in Bulgaria, 5 July 2023, SWD(2023) p. 802 final.

[21] European Commission, A new start for Europe. Opening statement in the European Parliament plenary session, 15 July 2014.

[22] Communication from the Commission to the European Parliament, the Council, the European Economic and Social Committee and the Committee of the Regions, A credible enlargement perspective for and enhanced EU engagement with the Western Balkans, 6 February 2018, COM(2018) p. 65 final.

[23] Speech by President-elect von der Leyen in the European Parliament Plenary on the occasion of the presentation of her College of Commissioners and their programme, 27 November 2019.

[24] For an analysis on the approach to enlargement of the last three Presidents of the European Commission see I.B. Bosoancă, "The EU eastern enlargement from today's perspective", *CES Working Papers*, 2021, pp. 367-380.

[25] The Communication from the European Commission of 2020 on the revised methodology for accession follows the proposal that France put forward in 2019 through a non-paper presented after it vetoed the opening negotiations with Albania

process by grouping the accession chapters, with the aim of pursuing full enlargement, but on the other hand it emphasises the need to make the process strictly merit-based. In addition, the grouping of chapters also entails a strengthening of the rule of law conditionality, which means that the EU will both open and close accession negotiations with the rule of law chapter. This should ensure that this issue is continuously monitored and addressed throughout the process. However, the problem of post-accession monitoring of the rule of law remains.

Similar considerations apply for the 2023 Communication on EU's Enlargement Policy. While underlining that enlargement is a geostrategic investment, it states that EU membership is a free choice and that partners must embrace and promote EU values firmly and unequivocally. In this context, it affirms that alignment with the EU's common foreign and security policy is, more than ever, a signal of shared values and strategic orientation in the new geopolitical context.[26]

3. The balance between reforming and enlarging

Deepening and widening are not two alternative goals, and therefore not a contradiction between opposing sides. Nor are there 'deepeners' and 'wideners'. Instead, widening and deepening must coexist and develop simultaneously. This means that the process of European integration must continue towards an ever-closer union among the peoples of Europe, but at the same time the EU must remain an open organisation whose aim is to extend its borders. This implies that any further accession must take into account the European integration capacity, i.e. the capacity of the EU to absorb new members at a given time or over a given period of time without jeopardising the political and policy objectives set out in the Treaties. This is not a new criterion for candidate states, but a prerequisite for the success of enlargement and for deepening the process of European integration.

Actually, the 'big bang' enlargement of 2004 did not have a real negative impact on the functioning of the EU, as shown by the intensity of the legislative process. The accession of new Member States has not hindered the

---

and North Macedonia at the meeting held by the European Council in October 2019. The new methodology was outlined by the Council in the meeting of June 2020.

[26] Communication from the Commission to the European Parliament, the Council, the European Economic and Social Committee and the Committee of the Regions, 2023 Communication on EU Enlargement Policy, 8 November 2023, COM(2023) p. 690 final.

adoption of legislative acts, whose number per year after 2004 is perfectly in line with the period pre-2004. However, the entry of up to ten new Member States by 2030 would massively change the composition, make-up, and decision-making processes in all institutions. Any negotiation in an intergovernmental setting would become more complex and the functioning of the supranational institutions would be affected. It is therefore not certain that another wide enlargement would not have a negative impact on the functioning of the institutions.

Furthermore, it is worth noting that after the 2004 enlargement some difficulties arose in maintaining a comprehensive *alignment with core European values, not only because the Commission failed to ensure that the rule of law was truly embedded in the future Member States,*[27] *but also because the European institutions were not able to effectively address the backsliding of the rule of law in some Member States. This is because the only instrument to ensure that all Member States respect the common values of the EU is essentially based on unanimity.* Hence, the EU must create instruments to ensure that any further enlargement cannot undermine the EU acquis with relation to fundamental values and citizens' right. This requires a reform of the treaties to amend Article 7 TEU and introduce more effective control mechanisms which are not solely political and are based on a solid institutional procedure that secures results and prevents regression.[28] As stated by the Court, EU law is based on the fundamental premises that each Member State shares with all the others, and recognises that those Member States share those same values.[29]

Another important point is the common foreign and security policy alignment in the enlargement process, because it is essential that further accessions do not complicate the process into a closer European foreign and defence policy. This is an area where the EU needs to develop a stronger unity. In this context, war in Ukraine should not change the equation of costs and benefits in favour of new members, transforming the enlargement into a mere geopolitical strategy. Such an approach could un-

---

[27] L. Louwerse, E. Kassoti, "Revisiting the European Commission's Approach Towards the Rule of Law in Enlargement", *Hague Journal on the Rule of Law*, 2019, pp. 223-250.

[28] See C. Closa, "The quagmire of EU rule of law enforcement: Limits to jurisdictional enforcement, limited deterrence capacity and asymmetry", *EU Law Live*, 15 January 2024.

[29] Judgment of the Court (Full Court) of 10 December 2018, Case C-621/18, *Andy Wightman and Others* v. *Secretary of State for Exiting the European Union*, ECLI: EU:C:2018:999, para. 63.

dermine the *sui generis* nature of the EU, as stated by the Court since Van Gend en Loos, and its future development.[30]

Finally, enlargement requires financial preparation given that, according to a study prepared by the General Secretariat of the Council of the EU, the cost of the accession of all current candidate countries over seven years will amount to €37 billion a year, increasing the EU's budget by 21 per cent.[31] This means that any further enlargement requires a reform of the EU budget, also taking into account that states will have to pay more and receive less from the EU budget.[32]

4. Alternative (or complementary) policies to further enlargement

As shown above, striking the right balance between widening and deepening will probably require a comprehensive reform of the treaties, which will take a relatively long time. The EU and its Member States should therefore consider some alternative or complementary policies to full membership in order to make the enlargement policy more flexible, dynamic and gradual.

In this area, France and Germany made some proposals in a report on the reform and enlargement of the EU, presented in September 2023. The report proposed to apply the system of "differentiated integration" both internally and externally. In particular, external differentiation should not be limited to allowing non-EU states to participate in individual EU policies but should more generally relate to the EU's enlargement and neighbourhood policies. In other words, the Franco-German report suggests envisioning the future of European integration as four distinct tiers, each with a different balance of rights and obligations, with the last two falling outside the EU altogether: *a)* an inner circle, whose members could have even closer ties than those that bind the existing EU, such as in the areas of cli-

[30] T. Karjalainen, "EU enlargement in wartime Europe: three dimensions and scenarios", *Journal of the Academy of Social Sciences*, 2023, pp. 1-20.

[31] B. Moens, "Ukraine's accession would cost €186B, EU estimates", *www.Politico.eu*, 4 October 2023.

[32] On this point the Committee of Regions pointed out that, in the event of EU enlargement, the average GDP per capita may fall in the EU and, therefore, it asked the European Commission to carry out a detailed assessment before proposing new regulation for the post-2027 cohesion policy so that it is equipped to continue to support all regions and so that any unfavorable consequence caused by a 'statistical effect' on cohesion policy eligibility can be duly addressed (European Committee of Regions, 158th plenary session, 29-30 November 2023. Opinion: The future of Cohesion Policy post-2027, COTER-VII/030.

mate, energy, and taxation; *b)* the European Union itself, where the current and future EU Member States are bound by the same political objectives, required to comply with Article 2 TEU; *c)* associate members, which is a first outer tier, where members would not be bound to an 'ever closer union' and further integration, leaving the single market as a core area; and *d)* the European political community, which would be a second outer tier which would not include any form of integration with binding EU law or specific rule of law requirements, and would not allow access to the single market.[33]

At a first glance, the model proposed by Germany and France reorganizing the European structures into four concentric circles would change the nature of the integration process, which has developed around the idea of unity and cohesion. Indeed, the very first article of the Lisbon Treaty states that it marks a new stage in the process of creating an ever-closer union and reflects the unofficial motto of the EU: "united in diversity". From another perspective, however, the EU already knows several successful forms of differentiated integration, both internally and externally.[34] Thus, differentiation could be the key to trigger the reform of the treaties and to boost the enlargement process.

Differentiation could even be applied moderately, without any alteration of the existing integration model. In that sense, integrating candidate states only in the internal market, even as an intermediary goal, could be a solution to overcome the enlargement impasse.[35] However, the core Union should remain the political integration, while integration in the internal market should be the second inner circle, so to maintain the aim of creating an ever-closer Union which has always been a fundamental principle of European integration and thus has always endured over time.[36]

Instead, to bring states involved in the internal market into a deeper political integration, the EU should enhance the role of the European Political Community (EPC), which could serve as an important venue for this purpose. Indeed, the EPC is a form of political cooperation to achieve solidarity and strengthen common values, but it is neither an antechamber nor an

---

[33] Report of the Franco-German Working Group on EU Institutional Reform, Sailing on High Seas: Reforming and Enlarging the EU for the 21st Century, Paris-Berlin – 18 September 2023.

[34] B. De Witte, "An Undivided Union? Differentiated Integration in Post-Brexit Times", *Common Market Law Review*, 2018, pp. 227-249.

[35] L. Ognjanoska, "Reinforcing the EU Enlargement Policy Towards Western Balkans: Access to the Single Market as a Credible Goal", *European Papers*, 2022, pp. 833-855.

[36] For a different position, see C. Calliess, "Reform the European Union for Enlargement!", *Verfassungsblog*, 6 July 2023.

alternative to EU membership. Rather, as affirmed by scholars, it is a step on the trajectory for the EU, not because its members will eventually join the EU but because both sides aim to strengthen Europe on the world's stage, in opposition to competing views. It may thus work as a complement to EU enlargement.[37]

5. The proposed treaty reforms

The possibility of a second 'big bang enlargement' by 2030 has triggered the reform process of the EU institutional system, which had been dormant since the conclusion of the Conference on the future of Europe that ran from April 2021 to May 2022,[38] whose aim was not only to debate the future of Europe but to stimulate a treaties amendment.[39]

On 22 November 2023, the European Parliament adopted, by 291 votes to 274, with 44 abstentions, a Resolution calling on the European Council to convene a Convention as soon as possible, in accordance with Article 48 TEU, to launch the process of reforming the Treaties based on a revision project annexed to the same resolution.[40] In Parliament's view, in fact, the prospect of future enlargements makes a reform of the Treaties inevitable, since the EU's institutional framework and its decision-making process, in particular that of the Council, while barely adequate for a Union of 27 Member States, could not function in an enlarged Union.

---

[37] L. Lonardo, "The European Political Community: a Constitutional Experiment in Europe", *EU Law Live Symposium: The European Political Community*, June 2023, pp. 15-17.

[38] In 2022 the European Parliament stated that the conclusions of the Conference required Treaty changes, inter alia, concerning the simplification of the EU institutional architecture, greater transparency and accountability in the decision-making process and a new reflection on EU competences. It thus called for the convening of a Convention by activating the procedure for the revision of the Treaties provided for in Article 48 of the Treaty on European Union (European Parliament Resolution of 4 May 2022 on the follow-up to the conclusions of the Conference on the Future of Europe, 2022/2648(RSP)). The Council did not however follow the recommendation of the Parliament.

[39] See B. Nascimbene, "L'iniziativa per una conferenza sul futuro dell'Unione europea. Dalla 'paura' all''ambizione'", C. Amalfitano, M. Condinanzi (eds.), *Paura dell'Europa. Spunti di razionalizzazione*, Torino 2020, pp. 97-105; I. Ingravallo, "L'UE verso la Conferenza di riforma: tra funzionalismo e federalismo", *www.osorin.it*; F. Fabbrini, "The Conference on the Future of Europe. A new Model to Reform the EU?", *DCU Brexit Institute*, 12/20219.

[40] European Parliament Resolution of 22 November 2023 on proposals of the European Parliament for the amendment of the Treaties (2022/2051(INL)).

This resolution follows on from a previous Resolution adopted on 9 June 2022, by which the European Parliament had already called on the European Council to follow up the work of the Conference on the Future of Europe and to launch the process of revising the Treaties, but without presenting a revision project. [41]

Unlike the Parliament's proposal of June 2022, the Resolution passed in November 2023 contains detailed and significant amendments to both the TEU and the TFEU which include calls for the following: an increase in the number of areas in which measures are adopted by qualified majority and under the ordinary legislative procedure, including the sanctions mechanism referred to in Article 7 TFEU; a change in the system for appointing the President of the Commission, giving Parliament a more important role; a reduction in the number of Commissioners to a maximum of 15; a strengthening of the instruments for the participation of citizens In the EU decision-making process within the framework of representative democracy; an extension of the competences of the Union, for example by establishing an exclusive competence for the environment and biodiversity and a concurrent competence for health protection; and an extension of the competences of the Union in the field of CFSP and CSDP.

With regard to enlargement issues, the very first interesting point of the proposal concerns the values of the EU. In this respect, the Resolution suggests revising Article 49 TEU so to specify that "Member States must continue to respect the values referred to in Article 2 after their accession to the Union". This is certainly an interesting change, but it risks being fruitless if the treaties do not provide effective instruments for prevention and control. In this respect, the proposal recommends a significant revision of Article 7 TEU. Firstly, it would change the voting system during the procedure from unanimity to qualified majority. Secondly, with regard to the ascertainment of a clear risk of a serious breach by a Member State of the values referred to in Article 2, the draft sets a precise deadline of six months for the Council to take a decision once the mechanism has been triggered. [42] This means that if the procedure is activated, it will not remain suspended without a decision, as happened for a long time in the cases of

---

[41] European Parliament Resolution of 9 June 2022 on the call for a Convention for the revision of the Treaties (2022/2705(RSP)).

[42] The proposal modifies Article 7, para. 1, TEU as follows: "On a reasoned proposal by one third of the Member States, by the European Parliament or by the European Commission, the Council, acting by a *qualified majority* after obtaining the consent of the European Parliament, shall determine *within six months* of receiving a proposal whether there is a clear risk of a serious breach by a Member State of the values referred to in Article 2".

Poland and Hungary. Thirdly, regarding the second part of the conclusion of the procedure, the text proposed by Parliament introduces an important role for the Court of Justice. The proposed new version of Article 7, para. 2 reads as follows: "the Council, acting by a qualified majority, within six months of receiving a proposal by one third of the Member States, by the European Parliament, acting by a majority of its component Members, or by the Commission, may submit an application to the Court of Justice on the existence of a serious and persistent breach by a Member State of the values referred to in Article 2". Where a determination has been made by the Court, the Council, acting by a qualified majority, would have six months to decide whether to take appropriate measures. The procedure would thus cease to be purely political and would become hybrid, with a significant role for the Court of Justice, although the Council would retain a wide margin of discretion regarding the possibility of taking measures and their nature. On this point, moreover, the new article would be more complete on the measures that can be taken, affirming "such measures may include the suspension of commitments and payments from the Union's budget, or the suspension of certain of the rights deriving from the application of the Treaties to the Member State in question, including the voting rights of the representative of the government of that Member State in the Council and the right of the Member State in question to hold the Presidency of the Council".

On the other hand, the Parliament's proposal does not contain any innovation about the status of the Member States, thereby rejecting the idea of concentric circles with different forms of accession, and firmly maintaining the principle of unity. On this point, the proposal put forward by Germany and France, although it has the merit of using flexibility to involve the largest possible number of states within the EU, would revolutionize the nature of the EU and risk weakening the level of integration. In fact, although the Communities and then the EU have changed several times during the integration process, the idea of moving into an ever-closer Union has always been the guiding principle of this evolution.

Now, in accordance with the provisions under Article 48, para. 2, TEU, a Convention composed of representatives of the national parliaments, the Heads of State or Government of the Member States, the European Parliament and the Commission should be set up to discuss the proposed amendments and, if necessary, adopt a final proposal to be submitted to a Conference of the Representatives of the Governments of the Member States.

However, while in November 2023 Pascual Navarro Ríos, President-in-Office of the Council, stated during the debate prior to the vote on the

Resolution that "la Presidencia tiene la firme intención de proponer la adopción por el Consejo de una Decisión para transmitir las propuestas del Parlamento al Consejo Europeo ya en la próxima sesión del Consejo de Asuntos Generales del 12 de diciembre",[43] the European Council meeting of 14 and 15 December 2023, endorsing the Council conclusions on enlargement of 12 December 2023,[44] did not take any concrete decision on this point. It merely affirmed that "as the Union grows, successful European integration requires Union policies to be fit for the future and financed in a sustainable manner, based on the values on which the Union is founded, and that the EU institutions continue to function effectively".[45] Therefore, "the European Council will address internal reforms at its upcoming meetings with a view to adopting conclusions on a roadmap for future work by summer 2024".[46] The process of treaty reform therefore still appears long and will probably not be concluded before further enlargement.

6. Conclusions

The enlargement process previously remained dormant for a long time on the agenda of the European institutions. As mentioned above, the accession of new Member States had a very marginal place in the speeches of both Juncker and von der Leyen. However, the war in Ukraine and the most recent geopolitical scenario have given new impetus to the issue and brought the enlargement policy back to the centre of the European political debate. The European Council of 14 and 15 December 2023 therefore decided to open accession negotiations with Ukraine and the Republic of Moldova and to grant candidate status to Georgia. It also reaffirmed its full and unequivocal commitment to the EU membership perspective of the Western Balkans.

Enlargement has clearly become the next major political priority for the EU and a geostrategic investment. Nevertheless, the EU needs to be prepared for the upcoming of a new 'big bang' enlargement, as the accession of so many new Member States could jeopardize the Union's institutional framework, and in particular its decision-making process.

As mentioned above, it is necessary, *inter alia*, to revise the voting sys-

[43] European Parliament, Verbatim report of proceedings, Tuesday, 21 November 2023.

[44] Council conclusions on Enlargement, 12 December 2023, 16707/23.

[45] European Council meeting (14 and 15 December 2023), cit.

[46] *Ibidem.*

tem in several areas of EU competence so as to move from unanimity to majority, to establish a more effective control mechanism on EU values, which cannot remain merely political and subject to unanimity, and to amend Article 48 TEU to facilitate further treaty reforms. Such innovations obviously require an amendment of the TEU and the TFEU in accordance with the ordinary procedure under Article 48 TEU. Such institutional issues are complex as they affect the very architecture of the Union. They are also sensitive as they touch upon the respective powers, and the balance of powers, of the institutions. The discussions ahead will therefore be challenging and will require vision and courage to shape the Europe of the future. Given that the necessary comprehensive treaty reform will take a long time, the European institutions seem inclined to prioritise enlargement over reform. In other words, first widening and then deepening.

However, in the light of the existing legal framework, further accession would make further treaty reforms more difficult, because it would be more difficult to obtain the approval of all Member States and to reach unanimity within the European Council. It must be clear that any reform of the Treaties in the event of another major enlargement would be almost impossible within the existing legal framework. The decision to enlarge without prior reform could be a risk for the future ability of the EU to develop into an ever-closer union.

In any case, besides the official position expressed by the institutions, a more flexible approach to enlargement policy does seems unlikely. Indeed, all the institutions have always insisted that further accessions must remain strictly merit-based and must not jeopardies the values enshrined in Article 2 TEU. Finally, in a complex scenario where a balance between widening and deepening is absolutely necessary, the EU could use the model of differentiated integration to strengthen the links of the aspiring Member States with the EU.

Part 2

THE CONSTRUCTION OF THE EUROPEAN CONSTITUTIONAL IDENTITY IN THE MULTILEVEL LEGAL SYSTEM: THE ROLE OF THE COURT OF JUSTICE OF THE EUROPEAN UNION

Chapter 6

THE CONSTRUCTION OF THE EUROPEAN CONSTITUTIONAL IDENTITY: LIGHTS AND SHADOWS OF AN ONGOING PROCESS

Adriana Ciancio

ABSTRACT: *This chapter aims at defining the concept of constitutional identity in order to clarify in what sense it is applicable to the EU, overcoming the traditional vision according to which the idea of constitution (and related terms) is only referable to statehood. Under this premise, this chapter intends to briefly point out the strengths and weaknesses of this concept at the current stage of development of the European integration process, before going on to highlight the main reasons why the latter would be better served by a true formal constitution rather than a simple international agreement, albeit with a constitutional nature, as the Treaty of Lisbon is to be considered.*

1. Terminological clarifications

As a brief premise, it is necessary to clarify some preliminary aspects around terminology: first, what is 'identity' as such and second, more specifically, what is to be considered 'constitutional identity'? Only after answering these basic questions does it become possible to find out whether the concept of 'constitutional identity' is attributable to the EU and if so, to understand the specific extent of EU constitutional identity.

Generally speaking, identity might be defined as a sense of self-perception and/or self-awareness about some fundamental features of an individual, whilst the more specific concept of constitutional identity immediately recalls the main results of constitutionalism. At the same time, constitutionalism has been explained as the ideology behind both the process of constitutionalisation and the creation of constitutions as outcomes of the former.[1] From this perspective, constitutionalism provides the ideo-

---

[1] As suggested by N. Tsagourias, "Introduction-Constitutionalism: a theoretical

logical context within which constitutions emerge and constitutionalisation functions.[2] Therefore, constitutionalism is essentially the axiological-theoretical premises of political orders.

As a consequence, constitutional identity might be described as the self-perception which a political community has about its basic principles and founding values, no matter whether they are already set out in a formal constitution or the process of constitutionalisation is still ongoing. From this point of view, we can also introduce the concept of constitutional law as the whole set of rules and principles that express the ideology implied in constitutionalism, usually, but not necessarily, enshrined in a constitution as a unique formal document with binding effects. This topic will be covered in more detail at a later point so at the moment it is sufficient to underline that constitutionalism is not synonymous with constitution.[3]

2. Constitutionalism beyond the State

This first conclusion immediately takes us to another very important issue, namely the very possibility of discussing constitutionalism beyond the State. As we know, constitutionalism, constitutionalisation, constitution, and constitutional law are all expressions generally used to describe the political and legal culture within state legal orders. All these terms thus traditionally refer to statehood although they express different concepts. It is therefore important to define more fully the meaning of constitutionalism in order to ascertain whether and how it can operate in political arenas other than states, and, if it does, what its specific nature is.[4] Indeed, constitutionalism may also be described as:

> a set of ideas and principles which form the common basis of the rich variety of constitutions which we find in many countries of the world (…). Thus, constitutionalism encompasses institutional devices and procedures which determine the formations, structure and orderly functioning of government, and it embodies the basic ideas, principles and values of a polity which aspires to give its members a share in government.[5]

---

roadmap", in N. Tsagourias (ed.), *Transnational Constitutionalism: International and European Models,* Cambridge 2007, p. 1.

[2] *Ibidem.*

[3] The point is stressed by J.H.H. Weiler, M. Wind, "Introduction: European constitutionalism beyond the state", in J.H.H. Weiler, M. Wind (eds.), *European Constitutionalism Beyond the State*, Cambridge 2003, p. 3.

[4] As suggested by N. Tsagourias, *op. cit.*, p. 1.

[5] U.K. Preuss, "The Political Meaning of Constitutionalism", in R. Bellamy (ed.),

In this definition constitutionalism has a normative approach, including constitutional structures and procedures and prioritising values and principles. Focusing on the latter, in order to show compliance with constitutionalism, a legal system ought to demonstrate that it implements at least the following main principles and values: legal limitations to public powers, the rule of law, and the protection of fundamental rights, including political ones.[6]

As has been said, constitutionalism has traditionally been considered a matter strictly related to states due to the fact that states are the epitome of self-referential political entities and often have a stable and written constitution.[7] After deeper consideration, it is clear that this state of affairs corresponds to that typical form of organization implemented in Europe after the Westphalia Treaty under the label of 'nation state'.[8] But in current times, the homology of territory, community and political power that, according to the early-20th-century general theory (of law and state),[9] was the fundamental feature of the nation state of the Westphalian project, seems to have come to an end. Rather, in the so-called "post-national constellation",[10] the regular model of the state is increasingly challenged by tasks it is not able to cope with. Globalization, along with the increasing development of largescale financial markets and trade, international terrorism and organized crime, climate change and environmental pollution, huge flows of migration across borders, new media and relative unlimited forms of communicating worldwide, big data collection and consequent issues of privacy protection, are only some of the phenomena which highlight the need to establish new structures of government and/or different forms of social organizations.[11] These new organisational mechanisms are now dispersed across a wide range of authority sites at the local, regional

---

Constitutionalism, Democracy and Sovereignty: American and European Perspectives, Avebury 1996, pp. 11-12.

[6] Similarly, F. Lin, "Rule of Law under the Communist of China: A Study of Local People's Congress Elections", in G. Wang, F. Yang (eds.), *The Rule of Law: A Comparative Perspective*, Hong Kong 2013, p. 161.

[7] N. Tsagourias, *op. cit.*, p. 4.

[8] As stressed by B. Caravita, "Reconceptualizing Federalism", in B. Caravita, *Trasformazioni costituzionali nel federalizing process europeo*, Napoli 2012, p. 138 ff.

[9] According to G. Jellinek, *Allgemeine Staatslehre*, Berlin 1900.

[10] J. Habermas, "The Postnational Constellation and the Future of Democracy", in M. Pensky (ed.), *The Postanational Constellation: Political Essays*, Cambridge 2001, p. 58 ff.

[11] As already stressed by I. Pernice, "Multilevel constitutionalism in the European Union", *European Law Review*, 2002, p. 512.

and global levels, with their claim to legitimacy and regulatory capacity showing significant similarities to those of the constitutional state. [12] Both in response to and reinforcing this dislocation, we can observe the emergence of new forms of legal rules and political community in and between sub-state, trans-state, supra-state and other non-state processes. [13]

This is precisely the field in which the discourse on post-national constitutionalism, namely constitutionalism beyond the state, [14] is thriving. As a matter of fact, aggregations of states that share common perspectives may form bonds based on a common normative and organizational standards, principles and rules. They can also establish their own legislative, executive or adjudicative institutions to regulate their affairs and mitigate conflicts about fundamental principles and rules. [15] One such new order is the European Union, which is characterized by common normative patterns and endowed with legislative, executive and judicial powers. [16] This explains why European constitutionalism is the main starting point for the concept of transnational constitutionalism.

3. The 'Constitutional Treaty' of the EU

At this point another problem emerges: is it possible to discuss European constitutionalism despite the fact that the basic (and only) documents in which the EU fundamental organization is established are international treaties? To give an adequate answer, it is necessary to agree on the concept of 'constitution'. In a primary sense, the constitution is a *formal* document which represents, as we have just said, the outcome of a process of constitutionalisation that in different ways, times and countries is supported by the people. As a matter of fact, contemporary democratic constitutions need to be approved by the citizens, either directly or indirectly. At the same time, it is however possible to discuss a different concept of constitution. In a *substantive* sense, constitution might be described as *a set of basic legal rules according to which people live together in a community*. People feel a sense of community because they somehow recognise themselves as part of the same entity on the basis of shared fundamental rights and other basic values.

---

[12] As pointed out by N. Walker, "The idea of constitutional pluralism", *EUI Working Paper Law*, 2002.

[13] *Ibidem.*

[14] See N. Walker, "Taking Constitutionalism Beyond the State", *Political Studies*, 2008, p. 519 ff.

[15] See again N. Tsagourias, *op. cit.*, p. 4.

[16] *Ibidem.*

For the purposes of this analysis, it is important to point out that the distinctive dual nature of the European Union, [17] situated somewhere between international and national law, [18] as its usual definition as being a "*sui-generis*" organization [19] shows, is reflected in the two-fold nature of its basic legal document that in this regard might be defined as "federal Treaty". Indeed, it is undeniable that the EU was originally conceived as an international organization for economic purposes and its legal basis has therefore always been a typical international agreement. Yet, it is equally incontestable that the EU has gradually broadened its objectives, first becoming a community of law and then a union of rights and values. This is why, in subsequent developments, the EU Treaties have been given a "constitutional status", [20] evolving into what has been defined as a "Treaty-Constitution" [21] to better describe the fundamental legal document of the EU in its current shape as a political union with federal characteristics. [22] Thus, according to the initial definition of constitutionalism provided, [23] the EU has already been 'constitutionalised'. [24]

Consequently, it is possible to talk of a European constitution and EU constitutional law even though the EU still lacks a formal constitution. [25] Indeed, if we consider what we have taken to be a 'constitution' from a substantial point of view, identifiable as a set of rules to give identity to the members of a political community as they express "what they stand for, the values they want to affirm and that are distinctive for them", [26] we have to

---

[17] On the complexity of the constitutional architecture of the EU, depicted as a 'constitutional mosaic', see N. Walker, J. Shaw, S. Tierney (eds.), *Europe's Constitutional Mosaic*, Oxford 2011, p. 395 ff.

[18] As highlighted by R. Schütze, "On the "Federal" Ground: The European Union as an (Inter)National Phenomenon", *Common Market Law Review,* 2009, p. 1069 ff.

[19] For a summary of the different descriptions of the EU, see A. Rosas, L. Armati, *EU Constitutional Law. An Introduction*, Oxford 2018, p. 8 ff.

[20] R. Schütze, *European Constitutional Law*, Oxford 2021, p. 55.

[21] E. Stein, "Towards Supremacy of Treaty-Constitution by Judicial Fiat: On the Margin of the Costa Case", *Michigan Law Journal,* 1965, p. 491 ff.

[22] Similarly, also B. Caravita, "Secession, withdrawal and the experience of the European Union", *federalismi.it*, 2022, p. 2.

[23] *Ivi*, § 1.

[24] Even too much, according to D. Grimm, "The Democratic costs of Constitutionalization: The European Case", *EU Law J.*, 2015, p. 467 ff.

[25] This thesis is notably embraced by J.H.H. Weiler, "In defence of the status quo: Europe's constitutional Sonderweg", in J.H.H. Weiler, M. Wind, *European Constitutionalism Beyond the State*, Cambridge 2003, p. 7 ff.

[26] A. Ferrara, *Constitutional Narratives and the Future of Europe*, in D. Innerarity, J. White, C. Astier, A. Errasti (eds.), *A New Narrative for a New Europe*, London 2018, p. 44.

conclude that, though formally the EU Treaties are international Treaties, *ergo* intergovernmental agreements,[27] the EU already has norms that can be defined as "ontologically" constitutional, *id est* of a constitutional nature,[28] as the CJEU has long since held.[29]

In this light, we must first consider Article 2 of the Treaty on European Union (TEU) and the values this article defines as being shared among all member states which constitute – one might say – the 'common constitutional platform' in order to serve both as hermeneutic criteria and legitimacy parameters of all other European and national norms. Moreover, according to Article 49, para. 1, TEU, the EU common values are both a warning and an evaluation criterion for further applications for EU membership. It is also worth remembering that these values are protected with appropriate judicial and political safeguards as provided for in the procedure set out in Article 7 TEU to manage the "clear risk of a serious breach by a Member State of the values referred in Article 2". Furthermore, in recent times another important legal instrument, the so-called "rule of law conditionality",[30] has been introduced through secondary legislation despite several objections.[31] Moreover, as is well-known, a Charter of Fundamental Rights has been established which has eventually been given the same efficacy of the Treaties with the entry into force of the Lisbon Treaty (Article 6 TEU).

A democratic constitution is not however only a set of values and rights, but also expresses legal limitations on public powers to provide the former

---

[27] As stressed by D. Grimm, "The Democratic costs of Constitutionalization: The European Case", cit., p. 465.

[28] A. Ciancio, "Why we could and should discuss about European constitutional law", in A. Klos, J. Misiuna, M. Pachocka, A. Szczerba-Zawada (eds.), *European Union and its Values: Freedom, Solidarity, Democracy*, Warsaw 2020, p. 9 ff.

[29] See *Opinion 1/91* (1991) ECR I-6079, par. 1: "(T)he E(U) Treaty, albeit concluded in the form of an international agreement, none the less constitutes the constitutional charter of a (Union) based on a rule of law". Moreover, in Case 294/83, *"Les Verts" v Parliament* (1986) ECR 1339, par. 23, the Court referred to a "basic constitutional charter".

[30] See Regulation (EU, Euratom) 2020/2092 of the European Parliament and of the Council of 16 December 2020 on a general regime of conditionality for the protection of the Union budget. For some initial and also critical comments, see A. Alemanno, M. Chamon, "To Save the Rule of Law You Must Apparently Break I", *Verfassungsblog,* 11 Dec. 2020; and A. Dimitrous, H. Droste, "Conditionality Mechanism: What's in It?", *Verfassungsblog*, 30 Dec. 2020.

[31] Doubts on the effectiveness of the protection provided to the rule of law under Regulation 2020/2092 are expressed by A. Zemskova, "Rule of Law Conditionality: A Long-Desired Victory or a Modest Step Forward? Hungary v Parliament and Council (C-156/21) and Poland v Parliament and Council (C-157/21)", *EU Law Live,* 2022.

with suitable guarantees. This argument is usually brought against the 'constitutional nature' of the EU treaties since, although in many aspects they fulfil the specific functions of constitutions, at the same time they do not seem to comply with that basic rule enshrined in Article 16 of the 1789 *Declaration of Human and Civil Rights,* where it is clearly stated that "*any society in which no provision is made for guaranteeing rights or for the separation of powers, has no Constitution*". The EU's functioning is still not based on a clear separation of legislative and executive power as can be easily seen from a brief look at the Council's functions, which simultaneously exercises legislative powers and executive functions. Rather, the EU shows that it continues to be inspired by a principle of 'collaboration' between functions rather than by the traditional principle of separation of powers first elaborated in England by Locke and developed in France by Montesquieu some 60 years later.

It is not however difficult to overcome this argument. First, because, as is widely expected, talking about constitutional law does not necessarily coincide with establishing a constitution[32] as a codified formal document that includes the rules establishing a society's fundamental organization. Moreover, apart from the above-mentioned terminological and conceptual differences between constitutional law and constitution (or constitution in the formal or substantive sense, if preferred), what is most important is the fact that the actual functioning of the EU is based on a form of distinction of functions. In this way the division should be clear between decision-making powers, exercised by the European Council, the Commission, the Parliament, the Council and, in the specific case of the Eurozone, the ECB, on the one hand, and control powers such as those entrusted to the Court of Justice and to the Court of Auditors, on the other. It is also not possible to deny that this distinction of functions was firstly established to limit EU powers in order to guarantee the aforementioned EU shared values and principles at large as well as fundamental rights and freedoms with regard to the European institutions themselves, as also established by the EU Court of Justice in its case law.[33]

Therefore, even from this perspective one might say that (at least) after the entry into force of the Lisbon Treaty, the European Union, despite the persistent lack of a formal, documental, constitution, already has a true constitutional law which includes both Article 2 TEU and the Charter of

---

[32] See J.H.H. Weiler, "The European Union: Enlargement, Constitutionalism and Democracy", *FCE,* 1999, p. 3.

[33] Mentioned also by M. Gonzàlez Pascual, "Which Narrative for the CJUE? EU Powers and Fundamental Rights", in D. Innerarity, J. White, C. Astier, A. Errasti, *A New Narrative for a New Europe,* London 2018, p. 119 ff.

Fundamental Rights,[34] jointly representing what can be described as the 'EU constitutional core', protected through the EU's institutional set-up, which is largely entrusted with the task of guaranteeing these values and rights.[35]

Thus, as is generally considered,[36] the Treaty on European Union (TEU), the Treaty on the Functioning of the European Union (TFEU) and the Charter of Fundamental Rights currently represent the 'constitutional' legal basis of the EU since they fulfil the basic functions usually performed by (formal) constitutions in contemporary democracies. In particular, the common principles and shared values, provided with suitable judicial and political safeguards, address both the European and national legislators, provide a fundamental instrument of interpretation, and are justiciable before a judicial authority, in absolute analogy with the basic principles of national constitutions.

4. The pluralistic nature of EU constitutionalism

In order to deepen both the origins and the content of the European constitutional identity, it is necessary to recall the major role played by the Court of Justice, which initially enucleated these shared values from the so-called "'*common constitutional traditions of the Member States*'". As is well-known, these values and fundamental rights were only later formalised in primary law, specifically in the above-mentioned Article 2 TEU and the Nice-Strasbourg Charter. Hence, one might say that the Court of Justice has took the process of constitutionalisation of the EU to another level.

At the same time, it is important to highlight that this kind of 'common constitutional heritage' continues to evolve: from the domestic constitutional arenas, these values and rights reach the EU legal system and then return by permeating the constitutional framework of each Member State. A sort of circular movement can thus be observed, starting from national constitutions up to the EU level, where values and principles are often interpreted (or even re-interpreted) by the Court of Justice. Especially with

---

[34] Similarly, among others, see A. Ferrara, *op. cit.*, p. 45 ff.

[35] As already highlighted in A. Ciancio, "The European "Constitutional Core", Key Tool for Further Integration", *Consultaonline*, Liber Amicorum *per Pasquale Costanzo,* 2020.

[36] See, among others, O. Hamul'ák, V. Stehlík, *European Union Constitutional Law: revealing the complex constitutional system of the European Union*, Olomouc 2013, *passim*, spec. p. 12; and p. 160 ff., where both the Treaties of Lisbon and the Charter of fundamental rights are considered the 'Written Constitution of the European Union'.

regard to the preliminary reference (for interpretation) set out in Article 267 TFEU, the European Court can interact with the domestic ones, fostering a judicial dialogue that can both influence the national constitutional context on the one hand, and address the EU constitutional identity on the other.[37]

In this light, the so-called *'Taricco saga'* is usually mentioned as a striking example of the possibility of interpreting a Treaty provision (Article 325 TFEU) in a way that conforms to what is to be considered a basic value (the principle of legality, specifically in criminal matters) of both the Italian constitution, on the one hand, and EU Law, on the other hand. From this episode,[38] as well as from many others that cannot be detailed here, we can also identify the limits of this process of building a European constitutional identity through the activity of the EU Court, as currently embodied in the second paragraph of Article 4 TEU, where the so-called 'identity clause' is set out.[39] This results in the clearest evidence of the specific feature of EU constitutionalism, which must be considered pluralistic in nature[40] as the EU is a union of values stemming from a combination of different constitutional backgrounds and identities transposed in a common set of values and rules. The aforementioned European constitutional heritage thus acts as a sort of constitutional 'lower common denominator' among countries with different legal cultures and various political and institutional histories and backgrounds,[41] sometimes even in opposition, as is the case of far-right totalitarianism and communism. The 'EU integration process' is therefore clearly imbued with a kind of constitutional homogenization.

---

[37] According to M. Fichera, O. Pollicino, "The Dialectics Between Constitutional Identity and Common Constitutional Traditions: Which Language for Cooperative Constitutionalism in Europe?", *German Law Journal,* 2019, p. 1097 ff., spec. p. 1112 ff.

[38] For a more in-depth description of the case, see G. Zaccaroni, "The Good, the Bad, and the Ugly: National Constitutional Judges and the EU Constitutional Identity", *Constitutional adjudications in Europe between Unity and Pluralism*, special issue of *The Italian Journal of Public Law,* 2018, p. 438 ff. He also criticizes the CJEU's 'Taricco II' decision for missing the opportunity of further specifying the features of the EU constitutional identity.

[39] On the meaning to be given to this provision after the entry into force of the Lisbon Treaty, see B. Guastaferro, "Beyond the Exceptionalism of Constitutional Conflicts: The Ordinary Functions of the Identity Clause", *Yearbook of European Law,* 31, 1, 2012, p. 263 ff.

[40] As especially stressed by M. Poiares Maduro, "Three Claims of Constitutional Pluralism", in M. Avbelj, J. Komárek (eds.), *Constitutional Pluralism in the European Union and Beyond*, London 2012, *passim*, spec. p. 78.

[41] For a more in-depth exploration of the topic, see B. Ackerman, "Three Paths to Constitutionalism – and the Crisis of the European Union", *British Journal of Political Science,* 2015, p. 705 ff.

As we have said, this basic factor of constitutional homogeneity should be seen as dynamic rather than static. As a matter of fact, considering the European political integration process on the one hand, and the path of implementation of national constitutions on the other, it is clear that the two phenomena are inextricably linked and continuously evolving. This can easily be observed in those countries whose current constitutions have been established after the EU's birth, such as the Central and Eastern Member States that gained independence with the fall of the Soviet Union.[42] In this case, it is clear that the application of national fundamental rules has always gone in parallel with the EU's development and that one has naturally been influenced by the other,[43] especially after the accession of these countries to the EU. But the same is true even in countries such as Italy or Germany, where the Basic Laws came into force before the Treaty of Rome, considering all the relevant transformations the national institutions have gone through as a result of EU integration, sometimes even without formal revisions of their constitutions.

This state of affairs should not be surprising as it seems to be the natural consequence of the growth of EU public law, as a set of rules which originate from the national legal systems, which, after being harmonised at the supranational level, are then capable of further influencing the domestic set-ups from which they derive, bringing them closer and closer, as the consequence of a sort of circular motion. Thus, the final outcome is a deep interpenetration between European constitutional law and national law that makes it extremely difficult, verging on impossible, to conceive of the organization and functioning of national institutions independently of the European integration process.

5. Positive and negative aspects of an ongoing process

This way of building EU constitutional identity shows both positive and negative aspects at the current stage. Indeed, all Member States are expected to comply with the same fundamental values, including, as stated

---

[42] See the essays collected in the volumes of W. Sadurski, A. Czarnota, M. Krygier (eds.), *Spreading Democracy and the Rule of Law? The Impact of EU Enlargement on the Rule of Law, Democracy and Constitutionalism in Post-Communist Legal Orders*, Dordrecht 2006; and L. Morlino, W. Sadurski (eds.), *Democratization and the European Union: Comparing Central and Eastern European Post-Communist Countries*, London-New York 2010.

[43] For a more in-depth discussion of this process, which is considered bidirectional, see W. Sadurski, *Constitutionalism and the Enlargement of Europe*, Oxford 2012.

in Article 2 TEU, the protection of human rights, freedom, equality, democracy and, more generally, the rule of law in a society based on pluralism, non-discrimination, tolerance, justice, solidarity and gender equality, even though with different meanings, interpretations and applications, depending on each country's history and legal traditions. This state of affairs poses at least a problem of interpretation in order to identify a 'basic common meaning' to be attached to each of these traditional constitutional terms and categories. This issue can be framed within a broader one, related to difficulties in 'translating' constitutional words, i.e. the transposition of constitutional concepts from the national to the supranational level.[44]

By way of example, one might wonder what the exact content of the rule of law is. As is well known, this is currently a hotly contested issue in the EU integration process, considering all the disputes between some eastern countries and the EU Institutions when it comes to establishing whether judicial independence is a fundamental characteristic of this core value. The most troubling aspect of this process emerges from this example, namely the difficulty of carving unique, solid, precise, well-defined content out of each value included in the same idea of European constitutional identity, since each term expressed in Article 2 TEU can take on different meanings in different countries depending on their respective legal cultures and institutional backgrounds.

At the same time, if these values are not fully respected in any Member State, the EU institutions have the right to resort to all the remedies provided by EU law to safeguard them. Thereby, the so-called European 'constitutional identity' appears to be engaged in a fundamental task: to guarantee democracy with its corollaries of rule of law, pluralism and the protection of human rights even within each Member State's legal system against any violations led by contingent political majorities and different governments over time.

Returning to the reported example, the Court of Justice, in the famous 'twin decisions' of February 2022,[45] could dismiss the appeals lodged by both Hungary and Poland against the 'Rule of Law Conditionality Regulation' on the grounds that it did not fall within the bounds of the Article 7

[44] For a focus on the difficulties of detecting the basic concepts of constitutionalism when it comes to translating them from the national to the European level, see N. Walker, "Postnational constitutionalism and the problem of translation", in J.H.H. Weiler, *European Constitutionalism Beyond the State*, Cambridge 2003, p. 27 ff.

[45] CJEU, 16 Feb. 2022, in Cases C-156/21 and C-157/21. See K.L. Scheppele, "European Union's Top Court Rules Against Hungary and Poland in Rule of Law Showdown", *World Justice Project,* 2022.

TEU procedure as it was adopted as secondary legislation.[46] By contrast, in a very clear way, the Court deemed that the European Union is now a community of values, and these values must be protected in any way. Thus, the procedure laid down in Article 7 TEU is only one procedure, but it does not mean that the EU cannot introduce other instruments to guarantee those values that are to be considered fundamental and that, from this point of view, must be respected by all Member States under any conditions.[47] From this point of view, one cannot fail to also notice some positive steps in this process of constructing the EU constitutional identity, as is highlighted by the reported long-distance dispute between the Hungarian and Polish governments,[48] on the one hand, and the European institutions in general (not only the Court of Justice but also the Commission) on the other hand.

6. Does the EU still need a formal constitution?

To conclude there is another question to be resolved, namely *whether the European Union still needs a formal constitution.* As is well known, this issue has been debated for a long time, especially, but not only, in Germany, particularly at the time of the 'Treaty establishing a Constitution for Europe' which never entered into force. Since it is not possible to go into the details of that debate at this point,[49] and limiting the response to brief considerations, the answer to be given seems positive, for several reasons.

The first stems from a sociological and political point of view. Once it has been admitted that the EU is no longer a purely economic community, but also a political one which already has an anthem and a flag, but doesn't

[46] On the complex path that led to the adoption of Reg. 2020/2092, also P. Lindseth, C. Fasone, "Rule-of-Law Conditionality and Resource Mobilization. The Foundations of a Genuinely 'Constitutional'EU?", *Verfassungsblog* 2020.

[47] Given this premise, the Court explains that the procedure under Article 7 and the one established by Regulation 2020/2092 pursue different aims and have a distinct subject matter. Therefore, the CJEU deemed that the EU legislator is entitled to establish additional procedures regarding Article 2 TEU values as long as these procedures complement (and do not seek to recreate or supersede) primary law procedures, as underlined by L. Pech, "The Court of Justice greenlights the rule of law conditionality mechanism", *Verfassungsblog*, 2022.

[48] For a detailed examination of this issue, see T. Drinóczi, A. Bien-Kacala, "Illiberal Constitutionalism: The Case of Hungary and Poland", *German Law Journal,* 2019, p. 1140 ff.

[49] For further details, see A. Ciancio, "The European "Constitutional Core", Key Tool for Further Integration", *Consultaonline, Liber Amicorum per Pasquale Costanzo,* 2020, p. 1 ff.

yet have a constitution, it immediately seems that something important is lacking, at least as far as the symbolic value of the constitution is concerned, especially in times of growing nationalism in many Member States. Indeed, in order to cope with a widespread distrust of the 'political project', it is necessary to identify integration factors which can replace the lack of 'natural' cultural identifiers such as a common language with the aim of consolidating among European citizens a feeling of collective identity capable of rooting each national identity in the wider supranational context and strengthening the perception of belonging to the 'European common home'. In other words, it becomes urgent to create what others, *mutatis mutandis*, call a sense of "civic solidarity" among strangers.[50]

Furthermore, from a more-strictly legal perspective, there is another reason, which is namely the need to solve all the problems that the current institutional set-up and related functioning of the EU have been showing for 15 years. Among other issues, for example, in a community based on the principle of solidarity, it is necessary to strengthen the 'social content' of European citizenship. Indeed, for the very first time during the Covid-19 pandemic, the European Union showed an effort to effectively protect not only liberal freedoms, but also the right to work and other social rights.[51] Then, time has therefore come to stabilize efforts in this direction but this goal cannot be achieved unless the division of powers between the supranational level and the national one is reviewed and the political scope of the Union is enhanced. As has been stressed for a long time,[52] the eurozone should be completed as a minimum and, at the same time, the EU parliament ought to be placed at the centre of the EU's functioning. Indeed, politics should be the preferred tool for integration rather than the judicial path followed so far. This would allow us to overcome all the problems that the 'compromise' embodied in the current Treaties seems to leave the Member States with when they are faced with a crisis. As is well known, a major part in this malfunctioning is to be found in the 'odd' division between economic policy, which has been retained by the Member States, and monetary sovereignty, which has been transferred to the EU.[53]

---

[50] J. Habermas, "The Crisis of the European Union in the Light of a Constitutionalization of International Law. An Essay on the Constitution of Europe", *European Journal of International Law*, 2012, p. 345 f.

[51] A. Ciancio, "Shaping the Social Dimension of the EU: Lessons from the Pandemic Crisis", in *Comparative Law in Times of Emergencies*, Roma 2022, p. 529 ff.

[52] On the point, see A. Ciancio, "How we might recover from the economic and social crisis through European integration deepening", *Przeglad Prawa Konstytucyjnego,* 2014, p. 169.

[53] For a more detailed discussion of the issue, see A. Ciancio, "The European

Therefore, it seems that a formal constitution would help to manage this distribution of powers differently in order to protect all those rights that are to be considered fundamental, which are not only the traditional liberal freedoms, but also the social rights that must be guaranteed throughout Europe. The purpose of a new, true constitutional construction would entail vesting EU institutions with effective economic and financial powers along with redefining the reciprocal relations based on the policies adopted at the European level by the Parliament, as the only EU institution with direct democratic legitimacy.[54] In this way, European citizens would be satisfied in terms of the democratic control and legitimacy of the EU and its institutions and procedures, and furthermore the EU would emerge from the impasse in which the Treaty of Lisbon seems to leave Member States in the event of serious crisis.[55]

At this point, the question becomes: *what would be the added value of a formal constitution over further revisions of the Treaties?* As a matter of fact, the answer appears consequential and already contained in the definition of constitutionalisation provided above as a process that – in whatever way – *ought to be supported by the people,* giving birth to the constitution as its outcome. Indeed, in current times this kind of procedure seems to be the preferred way to enhance European citizens' trust in a union that already has its own constitutional identity but that still needs to gain both reliability and efficiency as a true political one.

Central Bank: Issues of Constitutional Law", *Przegląd Prawa Konstytucyjnego,* 2016, p. 13 ff.

[54] See A. Ciancio, "A true European Constitution to recover from the economic and social crisis through European integration deepening", in F. de Quadros, D. Sidjansky (eds.), *The future of Europe. The reform of the Eurozone and the deepening of political union*, Lisbon 2017, p. 29 ff.

[55] See, *ex multis*, S. Fabbrini, "The constitutional conundrum of the European Union", *Journal of European Public Policy,* 2016 p. 84 ff.

Chapter 7

THE CONSTITUTIONAL IDENTITY OF MEMBER STATES AND OF THE EUROPEAN UNION *

Elena-Simina Tănăsescu

ABSTRACT: *Constitutional identity is a vague concept that refers to the core content of the legal aspects highly considered by a community of people. Although it has evolved rather in connection with states endowed with Constitutions, as of recently it has started to be used also in the context of the European Union, a supranational organization that only enjoys a functional and not a formal Constitution. Against this background, the constitutional identity of the Member States of the European Union is nowadays contrasted with the main values and legal aspects highly considered at supranational level. The example of Romania is not different in this regard, save for the manner in which the Romanian Constitutional Court has chosen to operate with this concept.*

1. The Constitution and its identity

The concept of constitutional identity is one of those vague concepts which make law a science and an art at the same time; it is an indeterminate concept that refers to meta-legal aspects rather than strictly normative ones.

Thus, in the US, where it was born, the concept of constitutional identity refers to historical, political, cultural aspects, to everything that 'surrounds' the text of a Constitution. For instance, for Lawrence Tribe the concept of *constitutional identity* remains eminently subjective and cannot be deduced objectively.[1] According to Tribe, the only reality with which a lawyer can operate is the *identity of the Constitution*, which can be determined by means of interpretation and application of the rules it contains,

---

* This paper draws on the speech given by the author at the XXX FIDE Congress organised in Sofia in June 2023.

[1] L. Tribe, *American Constitutional Law*, 3rd ed., New York, 2000, 70 ff. See also L. Tribe, "A Constitution We are Amending: In Defense of a Restrained Judicial Role", *Harvard Law Review,* 97, 1983, p. 433.

whereas the constitutional identity of a community of people cannot be inferred from the norms and rules of behaviour that the respective community bestows upon itself because such norms and rules can either be codifications of past practices, or may seek to prescribe new patterns of human behaviour.

Quite differently, Gary Jacobsohn deems that the constitutional text is usually a critical component of constitutional identity but "not coterminous with it".[2] For him, constitutional identity seems to be relevant for understanding some of the meta-legal characteristics that encircle the constitutional phenomenon itself (constitutional norms). Blending a mix of political aspirations and commitments that are expressive of a nation's past, as well as the determination of those within the society who seek in some ways to transcend that past,[3] constitutional identity deals rather with the legal culture[4] within which a constitution operates. It is "changeable but resistant to its own destruction, and it may manifest itself differently in different settings".[5]

In any event, the concept of constitutional identity is based on the sociological and anthropological notion of identity, which refers to what one perceives as being their own individuality, a self-expressed self-conception. Therefore, a collective identity refers to traditions and values, including legal ones, considered to embody the essence of the respective group of people or rather the underlying and/or foundational elements of those traditions and values. A collective identity is not static, it may be dynamic and construed or even imagined.[6] A homogeneous group of people is not a necessary pre-condition of national or constitutional identity, but their social cohesion based on common values may be able to generate one. Thus, in legal terms, constitutional identity refers to the core content of the legal aspects highly considered by a community of people. Or, in the words of the Supreme Court of India, "the Constitution is a precious heritage; therefore, you cannot destroy its identity".[7]

---

[2] G.J. Jacobsohn, *Constitutional Identity*, Cambridge 2010, p. 78.

[3] G.J. Jacobsohn, "Constitutional Identity", *The Review of Politics,* 68, 2006(3), pp. 361-397.

[4] See L.M. Friedman, *The Legal System: a Social Science Perspective,* New York 1975, or D. Nelken (ed.), *Comparing Legal Cultures*, Aldershot 1997.

[5] G.J. Jacobsohn, *Constitutional Identity*, Cambridge 2010, p. 7.

[6] A. Schnettger, "Article 4(2) as a Vehicle for National Constitutional Identity in the Shared European Legal System", in C. Calliess, G. van der Schyff (eds.), *Constitutional Identity in a Europe of Multilevel Constitutionalism*, Cambridge 2020, p. 9.

[7] Supreme Court of India [1980] in *Minerva Mills Ltd. v. Union of India* (Writ Petition n. 356/1977).

2. The EU and constitutional identity

It is interesting to note that with this last understanding the concept of constitutional identity has reached the European continent. Indeed, in various European states the concept of constitutional identity is either juxtaposed to that of the identity of the Constitution [8] or it connects the characteristics of the fundamental law with other types of identities specific to a community of people, such as national, ethnic, linguistic, religious, ideological, institutional, etc.

In the specific case of the European Union, the Declaration on Western European Union appended to the Treaty of Maastricht mentioned "a genuine European security and defence identity", while Article F of the Treaty referred to "the national identities of its Member States" that have to be respected by the Union. However, the concept of national identity of Member States was discussed mainly by scholarship and went rather unnoticed at the level of EU institutions until 2009, when it was explicitly and extensively articulated in Article 4, para. 2 [9] of the Lisbon Treaty.

I will not go into the analysis of the differences between the concepts of national identity and constitutional identity, [10] or into the history of their codification in the EU treaties. Nor will I even mention the various uses [11] and possible misuses [12] of those concepts in the institutional practise of var-

---

[8] D. Grimm, "Comments on the German Constitutional Court's Decision on the Lisbon Treaty – Defending Sovereign Statehood against Transforming the European Union into a State", *European Constitutional Law Review*, 2009(5), pp. 353-373.

[9] This paragraph states:
2. The Union shall respect the equality of Member States before the Treaties as well as their national identities, inherent in their fundamental structures, political and constitutional, inclusive of regional and local self-government.

[10] S. Martin, "L'identité de l'Etat dans l'Union européenne: entre «identité nationale» et «identité constitutionnelle»", *Revue française de droit constitutionnel,* 91, 2012(3), pp. 13-44; A. Levade, "Identité nationale ou constitutionnelle ?", in M. Fatin-Rouge Stéfanini, A. Levade, V. Michel, R. Mehdi (dir.), *L'identité à la croisée des Etats et de l'Europe. Quels sens ? Quelles fonctions ?*, Bruxelles 2015, pp. 187-206.

[11] Among many other see C. Calliess, G. van der Schyff (eds.), *Constitutional Identity in a Europe of Multilevel Constitutionalism*, Cambridge 2020; F.-X. Millet, *L'Union européenne et l'identité constitutionnelle des Etats membres*, Paris, 2013; L. Burgorgue-Larsen (dir.), *L'identité constitutionnelle saisie par les juges en Europe*, Paris 2011).

[12] Among many other see J. Scholtes, "Abusing Constitutional Identity", *German Law Journal,* 22, 2021, pp. 534-556; T. Drinoczi, "Constitutional Identity in Europe: The Identity of the Constitution. A Regional Approach", *German Law Journal,* 21, 2020, pp. 105-130; M. Claes, J.H. Reestman, "The Protection of National Constitutional Identity and the Limits of European Integration at the Occasion of the Gauweiler Case", *German Law Journal,* 16, 2015, pp. 917-970.

ious states and in the case-law of different jurisdictions. Legal scholarship is profuse with in-depth scrutiny of these practices, and equally abundant with theoretical approaches of all related concepts.

It is sufficient to take note that, at least over the past 20 years, constitutional identity has become an essential element of constitutional reasoning, both at national and supranational level. The European Court of Justice (ECJ) famously used the concept of EU constitutional identity [13] in its Judgements of February 2022 [14] pertaining to the rule of law conditionality [15] attached to funds provided from the EU budget and set off a new debate across Europe: is there such a thing as EU constitutional identity and what can possibly be its relationship with Member State national identities?

For my part I believe that if we agree that EU treaties are constitutional in function, we also have to agree that they are able to possess a functional constitutional identity and they are capable of expressing basic core and foundational values of the European people(s), while at the same time protecting the common traditions of the Member States of the EU. Thus, the relationship between EU and national constitutional identities may be construed as inclusive and harmonious. True to the integrative function of the European Union as a supranational organisation, the EU constitutional identity prioritises the people of the EU and deals with Member States as instruments of that European people. The specifics of European integration, with all its complexity and challenges, rely on the fact that EU law takes precedence over national law, but also on the fact that EU values are not supreme or imposed on Member States from outside or above, but they are an integral part of the national/constitutional identity of those Member States – otherwise EU integration, which has those very values as a core element, could never have happened in the first place.

Against this general background I would like to elaborate a bit on the

---

[13] ECJ, C-156/21 para. 127: "The values contained in Article 2 TEU have been identified and are shared by the Member States. They define the very identity of the European Union as a common legal order. Thus, the European Union must be able to defend those values, within the limits of its powers as laid down by the Treaties".

Also, para. 232: "In that regard, it must be borne in mind that Article 2 TEU is not merely a statement of policy guidelines or intentions, but contains values which, as noted in paragraph 127 above, are an integral part of the very identity of the European Union as a common legal order, values which are given concrete expression in principles containing legally binding obligations for the Member States".

[14] See ECJ, judgments of 16 February 2022 in Cases C-156/21 *Hungary v Parliament and Council* and C-157/21 *Poland v Parliament and Council.*

[15] Regulation (EU, Euratom) 2020/2092 of the European Parliament and of the Council of 16 December 2020 on a general regime of conditionality for the protection of the Union budget.

situation in Romania. I would also like to compare the situation there to that in Italy in order to highlight what they have in common but also what sets them apart.

3. Romanian constitutional identity

Romania joined the European Union on the 1st of January 2007. A constitutional revision, accomplished back in 2003, prepared the EU accession and granted constitutional standing to the principle of primacy of EU law in Article 148.[16] The post-accession conditionality imposed through the Co-operation and Verification Mechanism established by the Decision 2006/928/EC of 13 December 2006 was meant to assess the progress made by the new Member State in the areas of judicial reform and fight against corruption based on a set of specific benchmarks.

The Romanian Constitutional Court (RCC) discovered the concept of constitutional identity[17] only upon Romania's accession to the EU and located it in the eternity clause enshrined in Article 152 of the Constitution.[18]

[16] Article 148 [*Integration into the European Union*] states: "(1) Romania's accession to the constituent treaties of the European Union, with a view to transferring certain powers to community institutions, as well as to exercising in common with the other Member States the abilities stipulated in such treaties, shall be carried out by means of a law adopted in the joint sitting of the Chamber of Deputies and the Senate, with a majority of two thirds of the number of deputies and senators. (2) As a result of the accession, the provisions of the constituent treaties of the European Union, as well as the other mandatory community regulations shall take precedence over the opposite provisions of the national laws, in compliance with the provisions of the accession act. (3) The provisions of paragraphs (1) and (2) shall also apply accordingly for the accession to the acts revising the constituent treaties of the European Union. (4) The Parliament, the President of Romania, the Government, and the judicial authority shall guarantee that the obligations resulting from the accession act and the provisions of paragraph (2) are implemented. (5) The Government shall send to the two Chambers of the Parliament the draft mandatory acts before they are submitted to the European Union institutions for approval".

[17] Legal scholarship has attempted to identify other basic elements in the Romanian Constitution, such as pluralism, which grant the fundamental law an integrative function. See E.S. Tănăsescu, "Despre identitatea constituțională și rolul integrator al Constituției" [On Constitutional Identity and the Integrative Role of the Constitution], *Curierul Judiciar*, 2017(5), pp. 243-247.

[18] Article 152 [*Limits of revision*] states: (1) The provisions of this Constitution with regard to the national, independent, unitary and indivisible character of the Romanian State, the republican form of government, territorial integrity, independence of justice, political pluralism and official language shall not be subject to revision. (2) Likewise, no revision shall be made if it results in the suppression of the citizens' fundamental rights and freedoms, or of the safeguards thereof. (3) The Constitution shall not be revised during a state of siege or emergency, or in wartime.

It may be relevant for this discussion that the eternity clause has existed in the Constitution since its adoption in 1991, and it was not altered in the 2003 revision. On that occasion, the RCC [19] noticed that sovereignty is not covered by the eternity clauses of the Romanian Constitution, unlike the independence of the state, "*although the independence is an intrinsic dimension of national sovereignty irrespective of the fact that it is self-consecrated in the text of the fundamental law*". Since EU accession was a decision taken by the Romanian state in full independence and "*not imposed on Romania by an external entity*", the constitutional revision consisting in the addition of Article 148 to the text of the fundamental law "*does not infringe the limits of the revision of the Constitution*".

Although briefly mentioned in a few decisions, the concept of constitutional identity has never been clearly articulated in the case-law of the Romanian Constitutional Court. [20] Thus, in decision 964/2012 the RCC declared that the legal status of MPs belongs to the constitutional identity. In other decisions (683/2012 and 64/2015) the Court stated that EU law takes precedence over Romanian law as long as "*it does not infringe upon the national constitutional identity*". Furthermore, in decisions 887/2015 and 104/2018, the RCC ruled that "*Romania cannot adopt a normative act contrary to the obligations it undertook as member state of the EU*", but "*all these have a constitutional limit expressed in what the Court has defined as «national constitutional identity»*".

In this context it is worth mentioning that, when in doubt with regard to the meaning and impact of the word "spouse" in the case of same-sex couples for the free circulation of persons, the RCC sent a preliminary question to the European Court of Justice (ECJ). Upon receipt of the ECJ judgement, [21] it declared constitutional the Article of the Romanian Civil Code which forbids the recognition of same-sex marriages, but interpreted it as not precluding the free circulation of persons within the EU, without mentioning the concept of constitutional identity. [22]

However, in a case dealing with the fight against corruption and involving judicial organisation, specifically a special prosecutorial section meant

---

[19] RCC, Decision 148/2003.

[20] For a critical view of the lack of active role of the RCC in defining constitutional identity see M. Guțan, "Este Curtea Constituțională a României un port-drapel al identității constituționale naționale?" [Is the Romanian Constitutional Court a Flagship of National Constitutional Identity?], *Revista română de drept European,* 2022(1), pp. 28-45.

[21] ECJ, Case C-673/16, *Relu Adrian Coman and Others*, Judgment of the Court (Grand Chamber) of 5 June 2018.

[22] RCC, Decision 534/2018.

for the investigation of crimes committed only by magistrates, the RCC seized the opportunity to elaborate on the concept of constitutional identity. In a nutshell, and leaving many other aspects aside, in Decision 390/2021 a majority of judges of the RCC stated that the primacy of EU law applies only to ordinary national legislation and not to the Romanian Constitution because it cannot be conceived as "*suppressing or ignoring the national constitutional identity, as provided by Article 11(3) corroborated with Article 152 of the fundamental law and which must not be relativized in the EU integration process*". For the first time the RCC further explained that "*by virtue of this constitutional identity the Constitutional Court is empowered to guarantee the supremacy of the fundamental law on the territory of Romania* (see mutatis mutandis the *Judgement of the German Constitutional Court of 30 June 2009, 2 BvE 2/08)*". It also proclaimed that national courts do not have the power to examine the compliance with EU law of national provisions deemed constitutional by the Court in the light of Article 148 of the Romanian Constitution. Two judges signed a separate opinion stating that the aforementioned conclusions contradict not only binding EU law and the established case law of the European Court of Justice, but also Article 148 of the Romanian Constitution, which provides for the systematic and compulsory primacy of EU law over national law.

The answer of the European Court of Justice has been clearly articulated in Judgement *RS* (C-430/21) of 22 February 2022. In short and also skipping over much of the substance of this landmark ruling, the ECJ reiterated that ordinary courts cannot be prevented from assessing the compatibility with EU law of national legislation which a constitutional court has found consistent with a national constitutional provision providing for the primacy of EU law. More importantly for the topic here discussed, the ECJ stated that, although it is true that Article 4(2) TEU does protect the national identity of Member States, "*that provision has neither the object nor the effect of authorising a constitutional court of a Member State […] to disapply a rule of EU law, on the ground that that rule undermines the national identity of the Member State concerned as defined by the national constitutional court*" (para. 70). It also invited the RCC, when in doubt, to resort to the mechanism of the preliminary ruling because a "*constitutional court of a Member State cannot, on the basis of its own interpretation of provisions of EU law, including Article 267 TFEU, validly hold that the Court has delivered a judgment exceeding its jurisdiction and, therefore, refuse to give effect to a preliminary ruling from the Court*" (para. 72[23]).

[23] Judgement RS (C-430/21) of 22 February 2022

The situation described above may not seem different from the one existing in other Member States of the EU, but it is probably better understood if compared with the Italian example.

Thus, the "Taricco saga" [24] presents an Italian Constitutional Court rather delicate in its approach with the ECJ, acknowledging the primacy of EU law and underlining the common values on which EU integration is grounded. Decision 390/2021 of the RCC, an *accident de parcours* as it may well be, displays a different approach of the RCC towards the supranational organisation and its jurisdiction. Unlike its Romanian counterpart, the Italian Constitutional Court has presented arguments in favour of European integration and it has repeatedly addressed preliminary questions to the ECJ in order to clarify an issue that had the potential to become a disruption for European integration but ended-up as a fruitful exercise in judicial dialogue. The RCC not only did not refer the matter to the ECJ, but explicitly and emphatically refused to do so. [25]

It is interesting to note that in Romania we have witnessed a sharp discrepancy between the position adopted by the RCC and the one unanimously expressed by political authorities. Just as happened in Italy during the "Taricco saga", in Romania MPs and the Government [26] made their attachment to the European project known and stressed the importance of the principle of the primacy of EU law. [27] Especially after the press release posted on the website of the Constitutional Court in December 2021 without any signature, [28] which expressed an even more EU hostile position than Decision 390/2021, [29] Romanian political authorities hastened to position themselves in favour of European integration and claim the European identity of Romania. For a moment it seemed that the constitutional identity defined by political actors was different from the constitutional identity defined by the constitutional jurisdiction. Whose version would prevail?

---

[24] G. Piccirilli, "The 'Taricco Saga': the Italian Constitutional Court continues its European journey", *European Constitutional Law Review,* 2018(14), p. 814

[25] The RCC asserted that:

"It remains at the discretion of the Constitutional Court to apply the judgments of the Court of Justice of the European Union in the context of constitutionality review or to ask itself preliminary questions in order to determine the content of the European rule". (Decision 104/2018, para. 83).

[26] https://www.g4media.ro/premierul-nicolae-ciuca-despre-disputa-ccr-cjue-privind-supermatia-dreptului-european-asupra-legislatiei-nationale-prevalenta-dreptului-uniunii-europene-e-inscrisa-in-constitutia-romaniei-ccr-a-dat.html.

[27] https://spotmedia.ro/stiri/opinii-si-analize/cum-ne-scoate-ccr-din-ue-miza-ratata.

[28] https://www.ccr.ro/comunicat-de-presa-23-decembrie-2021/.

[29] https://www.ft.com/content/8974c833-e57c-4aba-849f-9000bf31888f.

It is thought-provoking how chameleonic the concept of constitutional identity can be. If the RCC were to use the eternity clauses in the Romanian fundamental law in order to protect its constitutional identity against a constitutional amendment by political actors, it would merely perform its constitutional duty. Indeed, were those political actors to oppose or disapply such a type of ruling of a constitutional court they would be liable for disregard to the rule of law.

Yet, since the RCC interpreted the eternity clauses in the Romanian fundamental law in order to safeguard the constitutional identity against European integration, it overstepped its powers because EU accession represents a fundamental decision made by political actors not just since the country formally joined the EU (on the 1st of January 2007), but since the revision of the Constitution in 2003, as the RCC itself acknowledged in Decision 148/2003. Indeed, upon validating Article 148 into the Romanian Constitution, which "*has not been imposed on Romania by an external entity*",[30] the RCC accepted that the constitutional identity of Romania has been reunited with EU core values, i.e. with the constitutional identity of the EU. Therefore, the RCC can no longer manoeuvre with constitutional identity in order to limit the primacy of EU law or, indeed, to oppose a structural and fundamental decision already taken by political actors. Such a manipulation of constitutional identity would only emphasize the parochial distinctiveness of the collective identity and not its core foundational values.

It is therefore interesting to ponder the impact of the relationship between the constitutional identity of the EU and the constitutional identity of Member States, which becomes functional only if the concept of *constitutional identity* employed in both cases refers to the common core values that shape the legal aspects highly considered by a community of people and not the constitutional peculiarities that singularise or particularise a specific group.

---

[30] RCC, Decision 148/2003.

Chapter 8

CONSTITUTIONAL IDENTITY BY EXCESS (GERMAN FEDERAL CONSTITUTIONAL COURT) AND BY DEFAULT (SPANISH CONSTITUTIONAL COURT). PENDING DIALOGUES WITH THE COURT OF JUSTICE OF THE EUROPEAN UNION

Antonio López Castillo

ABSTRACT: *The aim of this paper is to highlight the context and details of the well-known European jurisprudence of the Federal Constitutional Court, and the failed preliminary relationship between the CJEU and the Spanish Constitutional Court in the Melloni case. In this work, we will also try to clarify aspects of this situation and examine its silent influence on the German Federal Constitutional Court Judgment Euro Order II. We will then consider a reformulation of its parametric perspective in Right to be forgotten I and II, and the way in which the Second Chamber tries to integrate it into its traditional approach of controls tools, specifically that of identity control. Finally, we will close with a critical assessment of the prospects for a correct resumption of a preliminary ruling between these constitutional courts and the CJEU.*

SUMMARY: 1. Introductory remarks. – 2. Lisbon: the shaped constitutional identity clause. – 3. Melloni: constitutional identity clause *in absentia*. – 4. Euro order II: a first appeal to the constitutional identity clause, speaking loud and clear, without asking the CJEU anything. – 5. By way of conclusion: how to get out of the quagmire? All speaking in a rigorous cooperative manner.

1. Introductory remarks

The explicit provision for a national identity clause in Article 4(2) of the current Treaty on European Union has generated wide-ranging debate about its meaning and potential scope. In particular, there has been much discussion over whether its meaning is an autonomous concept, since it is an existing European concept, or whether it is derived through its connection with the constitutional orders which it refers to by definition. As to its potential scope, the debate centres on whether it acts as to limit or safeguard the remaining liabilities of the Member States.

As a turning point in this debate, we must consider the LISBON judgment of the German Federal Constitutional Court (GFCC). Based on the doctrine laid down in Maastricht, the Court has developed a novel constitutional identity control clause, granting itself a complementary and extensive possibility of reviewing the European actions of constitutional bodies. At the bottom in the Court's mind is the effective safeguarding of national democracy (2).

In what follows, an attempt will be made to characterise a very controversial debate on constitutional identity which starts from the Lisbon Judgement (2009). This judgement, at that same time, will become the constitutional reference point for many other Constitutional and Supreme Courts of the Member States. A distinction will have to made between approaches that distort this contribution of the German Court – such as that of Poland, among others [1] – and other approaches that are implicitly or explicitly relevant to the issue or are better understood in the light of the Lisbon judgment.

Related to the Lisbon Judgement, we will use the 2014 Melloni judgment of the Spanish Constitutional Court (SpCC) as an example of implicit contribution to the debate. We are deeming this 'implicit' because the Court could have brought up the constitutional identity clause, but did not, for reasons we will critically analyse in this paper. As a case of explicit application of the Lisbon Judgement, we will consider the Euro Order II judgment (2015) of the Second Chamber of the GFCC.

In the Melloni case the SpCC sought, in the context of a preliminary ruling, to have the CJEU lay down consistent standards for the interpretation of the European Charter in a case concerning a criminal conviction in absentia. The results of this did not turn out particularly well for the SCC as we will see later (3).

In view of this failed application of the jus fundamental standards of EU Charter, the GFCC in a very similar case, decided not to involve the CJEU and proceeded directly to the first application of the identity clause drawn in the Lisbon Judgment (4).

As a result of these rulings and in the light of this shift in dialogue, the CJEU set out to further shape the standards already contained in a comprehensive reading of the EU Charter. [2] From this perspective, the constitu-

---

[1] See, for instance, K. Wetz, *Funktionen von Verfassungsidentität als gerichtliches Konzept in der Europäischen Union*, Tübingen 2021; Ch. Callies, G. Van Der Schyff (eds.), *Constitutional identity in a Europe of multilevel constitutionalism*, Cambridge 2021.

[2] See, for instance, A. López Castillo (dir.), *La Carta de Derechos fundamentales de la UE. Diez años de jurisprudencia*, Valencia 2019.

tional courts felt encouraged to reconsider their own function as interpreters of constitutional (national and Charter) standards, some (the German one) having done so more than others (the Spanish one).

Following this path, the First Chamber of the GFCC in two parallel decisions (2019) endorsed the distinction established by the CJEU of the Melloni (2013 CJEU) and Akerberg Fransson (2013 CJUE) cases. By doing so the Chamber sought to reclaim its central position as a body for the protection of fundamental rights, whether in cases fully determined by EU law (Melloni) or in cases only partly determined by EU law (Akerberg Fransson). Some more recent developments of the Second Chamber of the GFCC such as the Euro Order III Case and the still pending verdict of the SpCC, should be read in this perspective (5).

In short, if we are to think about re-establishing a frank dialogue between these and other courts and the CJEU then it would be appropriate for both the national and European Courts to consider the original meaning of their pronouncements, as set out by GA Cruz Villalón:

> I think it useful to recall that the Court of Justice has long worked with the category of 'constitutional traditions common' to the Member States when seeking guidelines on which to construct the system of values on which the Union is based. Specifically, the Court of Justice has given preference to those constitutional traditions when establishing a particular culture of rights, namely that of the Union. The Union has thus acquired the character, not just of a community governed by the rule of law, but also of a 'community imbued with a constitutional culture'. That common constitutional culture can be seen as part of the common identity of the Union, with the important consequence, to my mind, that the constitutional identity of each Member State, which of course is specific to the extent necessary, cannot be regarded, to state matters cautiously, as light years away from that common constitutional culture. Rather, a clearly understood, open, attitude to EU law should in the medium and long term give rise, as a principle, to basic convergence between the constitutional identity of the Union and that of each of the Member States. [3]

[3] See A.G. Cruz Villalón, at point 61, in OMT Opinion (see a full explanation at points 59-63). See, for instance, M. Claes, J.H. Reestman, "The protection of National Constitutional Identity and the Limits at the Occasion of the Gauweiler Case", *German Law Journal*, 16(4), 917, 2015, pp. 919-20 (https://doi.org/10.1017/5207183220001 9957).

2. Lisbon: the shaped constitutional identity clause

The GFCC's Lisbon Judgment of 30 June 2009 certainly put the focus on the invocation of a substantive aspect of the democratic principle, which had been assumed to be a basic element driving Germany's direction in the evolving integration process since the GFCC's Maastricht Judgment.[4] What was new in the Lisbon Judgment was the effective application of this constitutional parameter of principle to manage the inadequacy of some legal provisions which were not only ordered in an abstract form, but prescribed in detail, and that these provisions defined their due intervention in accordance with the reinforced democratic standard. This democratic standard as a presupposition determined and also limited the possibilities of German commitment to a Union of sovereign states like the EU.

Although the constitutional identity clause was not expressly established in the Maastricht decision, the basis for its recognition was laid. The recently unified Germany became conscious of its sovereign status both ad extra and ad intra, in aliquot partem within the EU. The GFCC took a unique procedural route to the individual safeguarding of national sovereignty to fulfil this responsibility and the Court did not hide in any way its manifest purpose of strengthening the national basis of democracy.

The Lisbon ruling also reiterated a traditional jurisprudential reference of the GFCC, relating to the constitutional reservation of jurisdiction for the purpose of verifying any possible excess political and jurisdictional action by organizations and institutions. The GFCC intended to contribute, aware that the lack of specific procedural means for this purpose could be seen as a brake, and expressly warned the legislator that, as long as a specific procedural regulation to certainty was not adopted, there was nothing to prevent the Court from constitutional control pathways to verify an ultra vires action on or outside the integration program, either as a consequence of insufficient or excessive invocation of competence conferring titles, or due to the intensity of effects that, regardless of their legal basis and the intensity of their exercise, reach elements or affect substantial and intangible aspects of the identity clause.

That said, one might ask whether such statements can be considered misleading and, in any case, what space is left for the community application of

[4] See A. López Castillo, "Alemania en la Unión Europea a la luz de la sentencia Lisboa, de 30 de junio de 2009, del Tribunal constitucional federal alemán", *Revista española de derecho constitucional*, 87, 2009, pp. 337-360; H. López Bofill, "What is not constitutional pluralism in the EU: National constitutional identity in the German Lisbon Judgment", in A. Sáiz Arnáiz, C. Alcoberro Llivina (eds.), *National Constitutional Identity and European integration*, Cambridge 2013, pp. 221-242.

EU law, if the national democratic principle acts as a limit, a condition and a presumption for Germany's approach and commitment in the EU?

An attentive reader of the Lisbon Judgement will easily notice the centrality of a national-democratic discourse that in what follows, without prejudice to what has been stated, and for purely indicative purposes, must be limited to a double reference. The first, barely mentioned, concerns equality in representation, while the second, to be considered briefly, is in response to the meticulous identification of some of the material areas indicated for the purpose of specifying a state reserve of powers.

Leaving aside here the interesting question of equality in representation, despite electoral thresholds among other things in a system characterized as decreasing proportional,[5] the Second Chamber significantly advanced the meaning of this newly adopted constitutional identity clause by identifying material areas and issues reserved to the state and maybe falling into a self-referential circularity by saying 'it has always been like this'.

According to the Lisbon Judgment these areas would be everything concerning decisions on substantive and formal criminal law, on the disposition of the monopoly on the use of force by the police within the state and by the military externally, fundamental fiscal decisions on public revenue and public expenditure, the latter being particularly motivated, inter alia, by social policy considerations, decisions shaping living conditions in a social state and decisions of particular cultural importance, for example on family law, the school and education system and with the treatment of religious communities.[6]

Some perplexity was undoubtedly caused, not only by such a statement, that it seemed to be already overstepping in certain areas, but also because of concern about the nature and function of the GFCC in the exercise of its specific (attributed) jurisdiction. It also seemed clear that its status as the supreme interpreter and ordinary safeguard of the Constitution, which is reflected in its pronouncements in the various proceedings it hears, whether as a guarantee of the division of powers, or for the purpose of protecting fundamental rights, etc., does not it place on the same level as the power of reform or constituent power. Although it is true that, as a consequence of the predetermination, *ex* Article 79.3 German Fundamental Law (GFL), it can control some intangibility clauses of integrable content through constitutional interpretation – which has perhaps led to misunderstanding arising

[5] A recent European regulation, which is still pending ratification by Spain, will bring new relevance to this issue (see GFCC Order, of 6 February 2024, 2 BvE 6/24, 2 BvR 994/23).

[6] See Lisbon Judgment, para. 252; see paras. 253-260.

from its willful activism –, in no case could it replace it. Nor could it become the executor of a constituent will to which, *ex* Article 146 (GFL), obiter dictum, the final decision regarding eventual German participation in a hypothetical supranational process of state construction was left.

However, based on this controversial attempt at positive delimitation of a state reserve, progress was made in the GFCC´s Lisbon decision in the integration of an imprecise constitutional identity clause, for whose ordinary observance the set of constitutional bodies was asked to take care of by virtue of a (constitutional) requirement of integration responsibility on which, ultimately, the GFCC would have to control and decide.[7]

But the supervisory intervention of the application of EU law on German soil does not stop at the ultimate safeguarding of inalienable standards (not because it is constitutional fixed, but because it is so upheld by the GFCC).[8] Similarly, it is focused on such cases of ultra vires of the integration program, by excessive exercise of the conferred powers, by virtue of a subsidiary exercise of its control jurisdiction that has its early reference in the Kloppenburg Judgment (1987).[9]

The relevance of this form of constitutionality control leading to the safeguarding of non-attributed powers, with similar results to a conflict of powers, which the GFCC once again assumed in Lisbon without prejudice to the lack of explicit provision for this purpose in its regulatory law, had its first episode in an interesting ruling by the 2nd Chamber of the GFCC.[10] Presupposing the subsidiary control jurisdiction, similar to what was already the case regarding the protection of fundamental rights (from Solange-I to Bananen, passing through Solange-II), it thus advanced the modulation of the application standard in the exercise of its jurisdiction from both a procedural

---

[7] The invocation of a responsibility for European integration, in order to ensure parliamentary coverage for the Government´s foreign action, already in the jurisprudence of the GFCC regarding the deployment and possible entry into action of German troops, was thus seamlessly passed in the GFCC Lisbon Judgment, to a principle with a similar name but dissimilar function (see, for instance, BVerfG 2 BvE, 1/03, 7 May 2008).

[8] For instance, when it comes to a wide conception of budgetary national reserves (see GFCC Judgment of September 7, 2011, 2 BvR 987/10, 2 BvR 1485/10, 2 BvR 1099/10).

[9] In which, for the first time, an arbitrary refusal by the Federal Financial Court to submit a preliminary ruling to the ECJ was declared unconstitutional on the grounds of infringement of the fundamental legal guarantee of access to the legal judge, prior recognition of a non-reviewable area of discretion, regarding the interpretation of the meaning and scope of community law and, specifically, the determination of the direct effect of certain provisions of a directive.

[10] Honeywell Judgment, July 6, 2010, 2 BvR 2661/06.

and substantive perspective. This was also done in a doubly complementary way. On the one hand, it interpreted the meaning and scope of EU regulatory provisions, taking into account the criteria that the CJEU has traditionally indicated to national courts as instruments through which to approach an interpretation that could be shared by other interpreters in the EU law. On the other hand, it pointed to the criteria of sufficiency and evidence of the alleged violation, indicated as control standards in the Lisbon judgement, the verification of a significant structural breakdown of the order of jurisdiction to the detriment of the Member States.

The balanced Lisbon model would support an exercise of ultra vires control by the GFCC – it is emphasized in the Dissenting Opinion (VP) of Judge Landau –, not only in extraordinary and hypothetical cases of structural questioning of the jurisdictional order in the EU, but in more concrete and real cases, in which, due to their obviousness, clarity and notoriety, an ordinary case of ultra vires could be appreciated. [11]

In relation to the modulation of the ultra vires standard of application *ad casum*, on the discrepancy between the appeasement criterion of the majority and the demand for Lisbon's forcefulness in the individual vote, a space of consensus was established in the 2nd Chamber, of which the dissident Judge himself gives an account, with regard to minor issues, because their impact on the order of jurisdiction was of little relevance or because the impact occurred only with respect to the powers inside the Union.

3. Melloni: constitutional identity clause *in absentia*

The preliminary ruling resolved by the CJEU Melloni decision (2013) emphasised the expressive cliches of the autonomy of an order characterised by its primacy of application, without fully understanding the meaning of the questions posed by the SpCC, in an equivocal manner and by means of a way of arguing that is manifestly improvable.

The SpCC raised three concatenated questions of the following tenor:

---

[11] A few years later, the 2nd Chamber focused on this type of control culminating, after some previous attempts, with the Weiss/PSPP Judgment, 5 May 2020 (see in Spanish, X. Arzoz Santisteban, *Las transformaciones judiciales. Karlsruhe y los derechos fundamentales de la Unión Europea*, Madrid, 2022; A. López Castillo, "Del tránsito presidencial en la Sala 2ª del TCFA y de su reflejo en la superación de su disparatada sentencia Weiss", 5 May 2020, *Revista Española de Derecho Constitucional,* 122, 2021, pp. 333-366.

See, for instance, N. Petersen, K. Chatzia Thanasiou, *Primacy's Twilight? On the Legal consequences of the ruling of the Federal constitutional Court of 5 May 2020 for the Primacy of EU Law*, Brussels 2022.

1. Article 4a(1) of Council Framework Decision 2002/584/JHA of 13 June 2002 on the European arrest warrant and the surrender procedures between Member States, as amended by Council Framework Decision 2009/299/JHA of 26 February 2009, must be interpreted as precluding the executing judicial authorities, in the circumstances specified in that provision, from making the execution of a European arrest warrant issued for the purposes of executing a sentence conditional upon the conviction rendered in absentia being open to review in the issuing Member State.
2. Article 4a(1) of Framework Decision 2002/584, as amended by Framework Decision 2009/299, is compatible with the requirements under Articles 47 and 48(2) of the Charter of Fundamental Rights of the European Union.
3. Article 53 of the Charter of Fundamental Rights of the European Union must be interpreted as not allowing a Member State to make the surrender of a person convicted in absentia conditional upon the conviction being open to review in the issuing Member State in order to avoid an adverse effect on the right to a fair trial and the rights of the defence guaranteed by its constitution.

The SpCC, trying to abandon its previous demand for a maximalist standard, formulated its questions for preliminary rulings, highlighting its previous interpretation of the meaning and potential scope of Article 53 EU Charter. This was a literal interpretation of the rule of the best possible standard, always starting, by default, from the lowest common denominator of the ECHR (as it had declared by way of a prior constitutional review of the failed EU constitutional treaty).[12]

It was, in any case, a perfectible approach that, without prejudice to casuistic nuances and modulations, in general terms, did not necessarily contradict the requirement of primacy (effectiveness and uniformity) of the EU Law. In fact, if the CJEU understood that the primacy of the EU Treaty was put at risk by the proposed interpretation outlined by the SpCC, it was not because of the tenor and meaning of a rule expressly articulated in the Charter, but because, in a case involving a matter fully regulated by the EU Treaty, the CJEU would not consider a hypothesis of a complementary constitutional standard to be possible. However, the CJEU's response, which was perfectly acceptable in general terms, is more controversial if, as was the case in Melloni, the European law standard that is formulated bare-

---

[12] See SpCC Declaration 1/2004, Grounds 5-6 (see A. López Castillo, A. Sáiz Arnáiz, V. Ferreres Comella, *Constitución Española y Constitución europea. Análisis de la declaración del Tribunal Constitucional*, Madrid 2024).

ly observes the common conventional minimums established by the ECtHR when interpreting the equivalent guarantees within the framework of the ECHR (Article 6).

In this case, the SpCC did not invoke the constitutional identity clause (nor did the Spanish government in the hearing[13]), even though it alluded to the connection of procedural guarantees with the dignity of the individual in the case of criminal liability in a transnational context. In realty, the SpCC was trying to combine a twofold aim. On the one hand, it was an idle question, the abandonment of a maximalist requirement in the interpretation of the constitutional guarantees of due process, leaving behind its demands for a new in-person trial for those convicted in absentia. This prior requirement was considered excessive, in any case, in relation to the regime of 'simplified extraditions' that the European arrest warrant entails. On the other hand, the intention was to enter into a logic of cooperation with the CJEU, as a 'judicial body' (Article 267 TFEU), in order to safeguard a common interpretation of EU Law, giving the CJEU the opportunity to clarify the meaning and scope of Article 53 of the EU Charter.

The question of Article 53 of the Charter, which is essentially related to the integration of fundamental legal guarantees, ex Articles 47(2) and 48(2), is awkwardly presented. First of all, because of the confused invocation of a national margin of appreciation, when the intention was to waive the requirement of absolute content, previously formulated with regard to the constitutional regime for the extradition of persons sentenced in absentia. But also, by the breakdown of an alternative hermeneutic offer, according to which the questioned meaning of Article 53 of the Charter could be understood either as a functional equivalent of the corresponding clause of the ECHR, or as a rule superimposed on the jurisdictional dividing line reiterated in its Article 51.2, or, finally, as a hybrid, fungible to some extent, depending on the casuistry to be resolved.[14]

The CJEU, in its responsibility, far from understanding the cooperative sense of the SpCC's initiative (in a relatively incongruous manner, it must be said, with its traditional corps of doctrine on its specific nature as a constitutional jurisdiction with restricted power of attribution), replied with rough answers.

The CJEU held that the SpCC had to rule out the application of its maximalist standard, without fully understanding that this decision had already been discounted by the SpCC itself (and which became real, in general terms, in its subsequent decision, by distinguishing the constitutional stand-

[13] See a reference in AG Bot, Melloni Opinion, at point 141.

[14] See in detail AG Melloni Opinion, at points 91-92, 93-94 and 95.

ard required, *ad intra* and *ad extra*), and that it was not an alternative to oppose the European *ius* standard. The CJEU also held that the controversial regulation of the Euro-warrant system, far from being questionable, had to be considered as secondary legislation that was consistent – 'in accordance", as the CJEU stated – with the fundamental legal guarantees of (Articles 47 and 48.2 of) the EU Charter of Fundamental Rights and Freedoms.

By definitively ruling this way on the adequacy of the standards contained in the EU Charter for the protection of fundamental rights, the CJEU proceeded to declare the conformity with primary law of the alternative requirement to the defence at trial of a mere notification of the commencement of proceedings voluntarily evaded by the person who is later convicted in absentia.

As such, the question under debate is not so much whether or not European Union law has seen its primacy of application recognised in contrast with a better national standard (a constitutional or conventional European one), but rather whether the European law standard has been the consequence of a judgement contrasting secondary law with primary law or whether it has been the painful result of interpreting the meaning and scope of Articles 47 and 48.2 oft he EU Charter of Fundamental Rights in the light of such a provision of secondary law.

In other words, the ECHR was given the opportunity to integrate fundamental legal guarantees of the EU Charter such as effective judicial protection and due process in a consistent manner with national standards (constitutional and conventional) where the destruction of the presumption of innocence was at stake in a charge of criminal liability. The CJEU undertook a kind of practical correspondence, by means of a presumptive judgment, in which the final objective of the defective rule in question (promotion of effective cooperation between Member States in the prosecution of crime) was not only made to take precedence over these unavoidable national (and, moreover, European) standards, but was also seemingly confused with a presupposed pattern of mutual trust which, as has become clear in subsequent case law of the CJEU itself, far from being diluted in appealing to the objective of promoting cooperation between jurisdictions, is sustained and reinforced by the effective application of the appropriate European *ius* fundamental standards in the common areas of freedom, security and justice.

The SpCC was frustrated in its attempt to cooperate dialogically with the CJEU and, apart from the manifest perfectibility of the tenor of its questions, the truth is that it was met with an inappropriate and inattentive response. Equally as surprising was the standard that was set (which could be described as 'rickety') which generated confusion, not to say alarm, within the SpCC. Despite this, the TC maintained its intention to abandon the maximalism resulting from interpreting the meaning and scope of the fundamental legal guarantees of Article 24.2 of the Spanish constitution in light of their development through the organic law on criminal prosecution, leaving their 'absolute content' ad extra inoperative and, in any case, relating to the application in Spain of thc regime of the European arrest warrant. For this very reason, its weakness in the face of such an ill-advised response on the part of the CJEU is not well understood. Nevertheless, a more decided reaction is lacking.

The SpCC would have done well to react less inconsistently by rephrasing the questions with additional argumentative support and by invoking a re-reading of the Charter standard not so much in the light of a secondary law which, integrated in accordance with the concurrent standards, should have been interpreted less unrestrictedly by the CJEU .[15] The restrictive interpretation in this case of the Charter's jus fundamental clauses, in the light of secondary law, is not a congruent way of proceeding for the purpose of integrating the standards that make up the EU Law's reference parameter.

In this case, the Plenary of the SpCC, having failed to reach a shared response, in the face of the emphatic insistence of some of its members on the inexcusable assumption of the response given by the CJEU, tried a solution, apparently in accordance with its traditional interpretation of the meaning and scope of Article 10.2 EC. This was an ingenious, relatively inconsistent and, formally, inattentive response to a preliminary ruling which, if it is not reformulated and answered, is binding. However, far from considering it a binding declaration, the SpCC, with the vote of a large majority of the members of the Plenary, held that this response from the CJEU could be useful, together with other references taken from the case law of the ECtHR, for the purpose of integrating the minimum necessary content which, as an essential and inexcusable parametric element, must be observed when integrating the constitutional standard applicable in all cases, including those of application of the rules of the European arrest warrant.

In short, what could have been a great opportunity to consolidate the common standards through the preliminary ruling dialogue, turned out to be an ill-advised and doubly unsuccessful exercise in the face of a surprising parametric decantation by the CJEU which the SpCC did not know how to deal with. It did not understand that it had an alternative way out

[15] An example of successfully overcoming a challenging hermeneutic dispute, after some questionable decisions, between CJEU and Italian CC, could certainly be the Consob case (see D. Sarmiento, *The Consob Way – or how the Corte Costituzionale taught Europe (once again) a masterclass in Constitutional Dispute Settlement*, 2021, accessible by registration: enlawlive.com).

other than the plenary opposition between the orthodox demand for full compliance with the preliminary ruling (a position upheld in two of the three separate opinions) and the heterodox decision to avoid a preliminary ruling interpretation which the plenary majority merely took into consideration, as if it were just another element of hermeneutic reference, for the purpose of integrating the operational constitutional standard ad extra.

Indeed, given the CJEU's lack of understanding of the deep constitutional significance of the (poorly posed) question, the SpCC could have opted for a third way, consequently reassuming a responsibility that it had already brought into play in its first preliminary rulings. But, far from that, the Constitutional Court failed to engage in effective dialogue with the CJEU, reformulating the meaning of questions which not only did not seek to question the common standard of the Charter, but which sought to contribute to its better configuration, in line with the necessary minimum content. Had this content not been misunderstood at the time, [16] it could have been invoked by the Constitutional Court under the constitutional identity clause.

Since then, the SpCC has continued to ignore its responsibility for immediate and direct dialogue with the CJEU and let opportune, if not obligatory, occasions go by without deciding to ask questions for preliminary rulings. [17]

4. Euro order II: a first appeal to the constitutional identity clause, speaking loud and clear, without asking the CJEU anything

Indeed, through the Euro Order II Judgment, of 15 December 2015, the GFCC put into play an identity check that should have enabled it to precisely establish constitutional limits which, in any case, could call into ques-

[16] See, for instance, P. Cruz Villalón, ("La identidad constitucional de los Estados miembros: dos relatos europeos") and F. Rubio Llorente ("Derechos fundamentales, principios estructurales y respeto a la identidad nacional de los Estados miembros de la Unión Europea"), A.J. Menéndez Menéndez ("Una concepción alternativa de la identidad constitucional en el derecho comunitario: De las excepciones idiosincráticas a la resistencia constitucional colectiva"), in A. López, C. Aguado (dirs.), *Identidad: derecho y política*, Madrid 2013.

[17] See, for instance, SpCC Judgment 1/2018, 11 January 2018 (A. López Castillo, "La confluencia entre Tribunales constitucionales, TEDH y TJUE", in A. González, S. Oubiña (dirs.), *El vértice de los sistemas judiciales*, Madrid 2018; SpCC Judgment 89/2022, 29 June 2022; P. Cruz Villalón, "De la persistencia de un viejo dictum: la STC 89/2022, en contexto", in D. Fromage (ed.), *Jacques Ziller: a European scholar*, Firenze 2022, pp. 230-241.

tion the effectiveness and primacy of European Law and hinder its application in any specific case in question (i.e., even if this was the result of a legitimate, subsidiary and not disproportionate EU action or legislative provision). This check by the Court must be considered independently of its possible intervention to delimit the scope of a given attribution to the EU by examining the 'integration programme' included in each of the authorisations of the 'integration legislator' (or 'ultra vires' control).

This approach, which strictly speaking became a practical denial of the effectiveness and primacy of the EU law, as these systemic inferences were developed and outlined in the case law of the CJEU, affected the functionality of the pragmatic equivalence clause which, as a requirement for compromise in order to reconcile standards of protection that are not necessarily identical, has indeed acted as a contingent expression of compromise in order to overcome logically irreducible requirements.

It is well known that the equivalence principle, as a point of convergence, has been able to coexist with the remnants of additional standards of protection in the various legal systems. However, this is not the aim of the 'constitutional identity' clause, which had been established and applied in this case, even if the previous use of similar terms in European jurisprudence (such as the use of 'identity' or 'inalienable essentiality' in the controversial Solange decision of 1974) might suggest otherwise.

In view of what happened in the troublesome (Spanish) Melloni case, the 2nd Chamber, by omission of a formal dialogic relationship, affirmed the guarantee of the constitutional identity clause, *ex* Articles 23.1 and 79.3 LF, which, as well as allowing control of the manifestations of national public power, also reaches cases of application of predetermined national ius European law and, if the control effect is taken into account, it also indirectly reaches cases of immediate and direct application of EU Law. This is what was expressly announced regarding the principle of guilt (culpability principle) in criminal matters by referring back to Article 1.1 German Fundamental Law involving the dignity of the person.

Thus, as if it were a strictly national matter, the 2nd Chamber spoke loudly and clearly issuing its own opinion as if it were a kind of 'doctrinal statement'. In doing so, at the end of 2015, the 2nd Chamber confirmed the GFCC's intention to consider a certain period of observance of the jurisdictional division between the CJEU and the GFCC to be over, calling for a complementary jurisdiction to protect a fundamental right to personal dignity guaranteed under Article 1 GFL, regardless of whether its possible disregard or undermining may have been directly caused by EU Law.

Overcoming, in passing, the cases of tactical withdrawal, ranging from Solange-I to Solange-II (1986) and Bananas (2000), in which, without prejudice to the occasional non-observance of core fundamental *ius* contents, a control jurisdiction was declared in abeyance, which would only be reactivated in cases of systemic shortcomings and structural failure. The Court moved to call for a complementary supervisory jurisdiction based on constitutional identity, which would include fundamental rights through its nourishing connection to the clause on personal dignity, *ex* Article 1. 1. GFL.

In the performance of this complementary (ad hoc or casuistic) jurisdictional function, this constitutional parameter would be unconditionally applicable to any actions of public authorities within the national system, not only with regard to national actions not predetermined by EU Law, but also with regard to those predetermined or, where appropriate, with regard to actions which, by action or omission, through evasion of their responsibility for integration, do not undertake the corresponding actions to the effect of preventing the application of EU Law.

Such a situation does not go so far as to call into question or undermine the effectiveness of the obligations derived from the EU Law in the constitutional sphere in which it constitutes a supreme operational interpreter, by assuming a protean responsibility. The GFCC has set itself into the task of interpreting EU Law in accordance with the GFL, by judging the constitutionality of the national legislation applicable to the case, as a prior step to the interpretation of the regulations of EU Law, of which that legislation was the cause, and it did so in accordance with the constitutional interpretation in accordance with its own law, despite the redundant wording. In this way, the GFCC used its unilateral interpretation of EU Law to maintain that the issue was clear and that it therefore did not need to raise any preliminary questions.

The CJEU would do well to understand that what the GFCC has decided to declare means as much as saying that, in the event that EU Law could admit an interpretation that is in accordance with the inexcusable constitutional requirement, as an integral part of the constitutional identity, its application on German soil is possible. In other words, if that conclusion had not been reached, the GFCC would have had to declare the non-application of EU Law in the case in question.

The expectation of the primacy of application of EU Law that the legislator of integration agrees to, has its unassailable and insurmountable limit in the 'constitutional identity clause.' Thus, in the opinion of the GFCC, it can be reconciled with the combination of non-hierarchical regulations within the framework of the Union ("Verbund").

In its responsibility the CJEU had the indirect option of assuming an interpretation previously formulated unilaterally by a court whose interpretation did not produce external effects to the legal system in question. Alternatively, if the CJEU were to establish a different interpretation, it would have to assume a risk of disobedience, in case of disagreement. In this context, the full jurisprudential sequence of the last few years of passing over into the controversial 2nd Chamber could make sense.

5. By way of conclusion: how to get out of the quagmire? All speaking in a rigorous cooperative manner

a. GFCC: Clearing the path to reactivate an interrupted dialogic with the CJEU

In clear contrast to the way of proceeding in Euro Order II, bearing in mind, on the one hand, that the aim of the 2nd Chamber was to place itself at the centre of the decision making process, where fundamental legal content would be at stake, and taking into consideration, on the other hand, the appreciable evolution of the CJEU since then (that is to say, since the Melloni judgments of the Spanish Constitutional Court and Euro-order II of the German Constitutional Court), developing more attentively the common fundamental law standards in order to ensure a congruent application of the Euro Order, in accordance with the fundamental law clauses of the Charter.

It is precisely in this context that the 1st Chamber of the GFCC is going to overcome a drift from the 2nd Chamber, which would even show signs of high-flown discordance, without prejudice to sharing its objective of ensuring its participation in the management of common standards, trying to avoid an eccentricity that does not facilitate its intended development as a relevant actor in the task of applying such fundamental standards.

The intended recovery of its centrality as the supreme Garant of fundamental rights in the national sphere is presented in the light of a renewed perspective of the traditional dividing line of the legal system. The GFCC, or rather its 1st Chamber, would now formally leave behind an explicit Maastrichtian affirmation (de facto suspended) whereby, by overruling the *Eurocontrol* doctrine, the application of the fundamental law standards of the GFL was upheld, independently of the European law regime of the matter in question, in the event of its violation being accredited by way of *amparo* appeal. In fact, the GFCC, 1st Chamber altered that perspective, but not the idea underlying the endeavour to occupy the centre of decision-making, by means of two twin judgments of 6 November 2019, known as *Right to be forgotten* I and II.

An intended relocation has just become possible, because of the explicit assumption of the distinction advanced by the CJEU, in its two judgments of

26 February 2013, between cases that are fully predetermined by the EUD (Melloni) and cases in which a certain margin of national discretion persists (Akerberg). By applying this European legal standard, if the case is decided by way of a preliminary ruling, the 1st Chamber itself assumes a responsibility for integration (all political and jurisdictional bodies prescribed above). In doing so, the GFCC may once again emerge as the final national instance in matters of fundamental rights, at any time and in any case.

The 2nd Chamber, with a renewed presidency, soon took on this novelty in the Euro Order III Judgment of 1 December 2020, in which, without prejudice to the maintenance of the constitutive dividing line of the legal system and its tool of controls, as the statement made clear, that in this specific case, in view of the common criteria applied, it would not have been necessary to invoke an effective constitutional identity control. Justly, because of that, it should not go unnoticed that the Second Chamber managed the *ius* European cases with bifocal glasses depending on whether it looked closely (to rule out, in this case, a possible identity check), or from afar (if it decided to establish a common standard, by way of comparative contrast, searching for a confluent jurisprudential configuration of the CJEU, the ECtHR and other constitutional courts).

b. SpCC: still waiting for a correct dialogic relationship with the CJEU.

The SpCC is waiting to leave behind the first (and only) dialogical frustration of the (Melloni) attempt to taking part in a common task, that of participating in the arduous process of jurisprudential configuration of EU Law fundamental standards. However, to make that purpose viable, the SpCC must deal with its own doctrinal conception of the meaning and scope of a constitutional foundation (Article 93 of the Spanish Constitution), a presumed *ius* European clause that, which, despite criticism, is still considered sufficient support for the European integration process. This sufficiency, to a large extent, rests on an auxiliary use of Article 10.2., a generic clause applicable whenever it comes to integrating constitutional standards in the light of those of EU Law (like international Law).

If the opportunity arises to enter into dialogue with the ECJ, the SpCC would do well to consider the possible invocation of a constitutional identity clause which, when taken seriously, serves not so much to sustain veiled attacks on the primacy of application of the common rule, by means of a manifest breach of common values or by virtue of an hypertrophic invocation of national singularities, as to contribute to shaping and reinforcing it, as one more actor in this vast community of interpreters. Achieving a uniform EU Law application would then be a result and a method to build a community of law based on common values.

Chapter 9

RULE OF LAW, EFFECTIVE PROTECTION OF RIGHTS AND INDEPENDENCE OF THE JUDICIAL SYSTEM

Ludovica Durst

ABSTRACT: *This chapter focuses on the interpenetration that exists between the principle of judicial independence and that of the effective protection of rights, underlined by the ongoing rulings of both the CJEU and the ECtHR. Indeed, the renewed importance attributed to the guarantee of this principle has emerged today in the light of a series of internal events in some Member States characterized by marked interventions in the reform of their judicial systems. The effects of the newly introduced disciplines are such that they are resulting in what is now being called a real 'crisis of the rule of law' as a core value of the EU. So disruptive is the scope of these reforms as a backslide of the integration process that it is even being traced back to the political features of 'illiberal democracies' or forms of 'democratic regression'.*

1. Effective protection of rights and independence of judges under the European rule of law framework

For constitutionalist doctrine, the issue of judicial independence is an inalienable prerequisite of a state system that is intended to be oriented toward fairly satisfying the demands for justice of its citizens and guaranteeing the execution of laws according to the principle of balance of powers. Such a system inherently takes on the definition of *rule of law*.[1]

[1] The concept is rooted in Dicey's 1885 *Introduction to the Law of the Constitution*. Even though the *rule of law* is considered the backbone of modern states and democratic systems, and one of the oldest principles regulating the function and exercise of public powers, it still remains a vague concept. Its definition is not clear, nor are its requirements and implications or how much it overlaps with similar ideas such as

Falling fully within the constitutionalist tradition, the principle of judicial independence has been envisaged and implemented in all contemporary constitutional charters, at the crossroads between law and politics, revealing a tension that is entirely internal to the role of the judiciary which is both *power* and *countervailing power*. In the national dimension, it generally has a twofold meaning: as a principle of independence of the individual judge, in the sense that the magistrate has no other constraint than the law to exercise their function; and the independence of the judiciary as a whole, meaning that it must not depend on any other authority and must rule autonomously.

This dual internal and external function is also ascertained by the Court of Justice of the European Union (CJEU)[2] and in the EU *Justice Scoreboard*, which provides the annual report on the measurement of the main indicators of the functioning of member states' justice systems (based on quality, efficiency, independence) and the perception of their effectiveness by citizens and businesses.

Accordingly, 'external independence' refers to:

> *when the body concerned exercises its functions autonomously, without being subject to any hierarchical constraint or subordinate to any other body and without taking orders or instructions from any source, thus being protected from interventions or pressures from outside likely to impair the autonomy of judgment of its members and influence its decisions.*

At the same time, 'internal independence' means both the maintenance of an equal distance (impartiality) from the parties involved and their respective interests with regard to the subject matter of the proceedings, and when individual judges are protected from undue pressure within the judiciary, including the Supreme Courts, whose role is essential to ensure the uniform application of EU law, although individual independence cannot

---

Rechtsstaat or *European rule of law*, as discussed by G.M. Salerno, "European Rule of Law: un principio in cerca d'autore", *federalismi.it*, 19, 2020. See also, G. Amato, B. Barbisan, C. Pinelli (eds.), *Rule of law vs majoritarian democracy*, Oxford 2021. M. Belov, "Rule of law and democracy in times of transitory constitutionalism, constitutional polycrisis and emergency constitutionalism: Towards a global algorithmic technocracy?", in M. Belov (ed.), *Rule of Law in Crisis. Constitutionalism in a State of Flux*, London-New York 2023. J. Waldron, "The Rule of Law", *The Stanford Encyclopedia of Philosophy* (Fall 2023 Edition), Edward N. Zalta & Uri Nodelman (eds.). Id., *Thoughtfulness and the Rule of Law*, Cambridge (MA) 2023.

[2] CJEU *Wilson case* (Judgment of 19 September 2006, C-506/04), but see also Judgment of 21 January 2020, *Banco di Santander*, C-274/14; Judgment of the Grand Chamber 18 May 2021, *Asociatjia Forumul Judecatorilor din Romania and others*, Joined Cases C-83/19, C-127/19, C-195/19, C-291/19, C-355/19 and C-397/19.

be affected due to hierarchical organization.[3] This configuration of guarantees of independence, beginning with subjection to the law, is common to the constitutional experiences of all modern democratic countries.

With respect to this general framework, a very peculiar question is how this principle is affirmed and implemented at the supranational level. This is not so much with regard to its implementation by the European Courts (European Court of Human Rights and EU Court of Justice) in terms of their composition and functions, but with regard to its relevance in judgments on matters concerning the Member States. In this sense, there is a line of continuity between Strasbourg and Luxembourg, and even of mutual appeal in the jurisprudence recently developed by the two courts around the problem of guaranteeing democracy and the rule of law, hinging on the question of judicial independence. It is sufficient to mention the inescapable normative reference constituted by the provisions of Articles 6 and 13 of the European Convention on Human Rights (ECHR) which guarantee the right to a fair trial and to an effective judicial remedy and which assume the value of general principles also for EU law. There is also the corresponding Article 19 (para. 1, subpara. 2) of the TEU which entrusts Member States with the task of establishing the judicial remedies necessary to ensure effective protection in areas governed by EU law, and Article 47 of the Charter of Fundamental Rights of the EU (EU CFR) which enshrines the right to an effective remedy and to an independent and impartial tribunal, pre-established by law.

It is precisely the combined provisions of Article 19 TEU and Article 47 EU CFR that give rise to the principle of independence, in its dual external and internal declination. There are in fact two aspects that particularly stand out: the interpenetration that exists between the principle of independence and that of the effective protection of rights, emphasized by the ongoing rulings of both European courts; and the renewed importance currently attributed to the guarantee of these principles in the light of a series of internal events in some Member States, characterized by marked interventions in the reform of their respective judicial systems.

The effects of these new disciplines have been such that they have resulted in what is now being called a true 'crisis of the rule of law' as a core value of the EU, with a disruptive scope, from a systemic point of view and in light of the integration process, that is even being traced back to the political features of "illiberal democracies" or forms of "democratic regression".[4]

---

[3] The 2023 EU Justice Scoreboard. Communication from the Commission to the European Parliament, the Council, the European Central Bank, the European Economic and Social Committee and the Committee of the Regions, COM(2023) 309, p. 40.

[4] T. Drinóczi, A. Bień-Kacała (eds.), *Rule of Law, Common Values, and Illiberal*

As also noted by the Court of Justice, the principle of separation of powers, as a means of ensuring respect for the principle of the rule of law, can take different forms given the variety of parliamentary models and the degree to which the principle is applied at the national level. It follows that, with reference to the operational division of powers and the resulting independent and effective judicial review, EU law does not prevent a Member State from being legislator, administrator and judge at the same time, provided that these functions are exercised in accordance with the principle of the separation of powers which is one of the characteristics of the rule of law. Likewise, the principle of judicial independence does not prohibit the appointment of judges by the executive branch, provided that once appointed they are free from influence or pressure concerning the performance of their duties.[5]

Underlying the *Scoreboard* is therefore the recognition of the fundamental role of the efficiency of judicial systems in implementing EU law and preserving the rule of law and the values on which the EU is founded. Indeed, when applying EU law, national courts act as EU courts and guarantee the rights and obligations enshrined in European law. Therefore, having efficient judicial systems is also essential for mutual trust, a pro-investment climate, the sustainability of long-term growth, and ultimately for the proper functioning of the single market.

It should thus come as no surprise that the reform paths taken by the Member States have come under the spotlight of the Luxembourg court, urged on by a dual and parallel impulse: on the one hand, by European political institutions and other Member States, concerned about the weakening of the rule of law and mutual trust among the components of the Union; on the other hand, by the domestic courts of the Member States con-

---

Constitutionalism. Poland and Hungary within the European Union, London-New York 2022; A. von Bogdandy, "Towards a Tyranny of Values? Principles of Defending Checks and Balances in EU Member States", in A. von Bogdandy *et al.* (eds), *Defending Checks and Balances in EU Member States. Taking Stock of Europe's Actions*, Berlin 2021; A. Jakab, "What Can Constitutional Law Do against the Erosion of Democracy and the Rule of Law? On the Interconnectedness of the Protection of Democracy and the Rule of Law", *Constitutional Studies*, (6) 2020; F. Zakaria, "The Rise of Illiberal Democracy", *Foreign Affairs*, 76(6) 1997. See also, A. Bakardjieva Engelbrekt, "Rule of Law and Judicial Independence in the EU: Lessons from the Union's Eastward Enlargement and Ways Forward", in J. Reichel, M. Zamboni (eds.), *Rule of law*, vol. 69, Stockholm 2023.

[5] CJEU Judgment of 19 November 2019, Joined Cases C-585/18, C-624/18 and C-625/18 – *A.K and others* (Independence of the Disciplinary Chamber of the Supreme Court) and Judgment of 2 March 2021, C-824/18 *A.B. and others* (Appointment of Supreme Court judges).

cerned, which often act themselves as a 'last resort' through the submission of preliminary questions (Article 267 TFEU), to resolve the specific dispute pending before the domestic court.

Indeed, the issue of respect for the principle of independence of judges within the framework of the European Union – especially in its external dimension – directly affects the EU's ability to be a 'Union of law', specifically with regards to the content of the fundamental right to a fair trial, as established by the Court of Justice. This principle is therefore of cardinal importance both as a guarantee of the protection of all individual rights deriving from EU law and the safeguarding of the values common to the Member States set forth in Article 2 TEU, notably the value of the rule of law.

2. The independence of the judiciary under scrutiny by the Court of Justice: between effective judicial protection and respect for the principle of rule of law

It is precisely Article 19 TEU, by virtue of a renewed interpretative focus by the Court of Justice (which has also recognized its direct effect), that has become the pivotal normative reference in the most recent case law, thus allowing for incisive intervention by the CJEU in an area, that of justice, which at first glance falls outside the competencies attributed strictly to the EU and which is nonetheless considered an integral part of the *acquis communautaire* in the context of the accession process of new Member States.

This scrutiny, initiated on national measures deemed potentially capable of affecting the independence status of domestic judges, has contributed to the birth of a new strand of European jurisprudence aimed today at characterising problems of judicial independence in terms of a violation of the rule of law (rule of law crisis), and therefore in relation to one of the common values on which the Union is founded, under the aforementioned Article 2 TEU. Indeed, it has been noted that the Court has established a bridge between Article 2 TEU, Article 19 TEU and Article 47 of the Charter by virtue of the possibility of applying Article 19 TEU whenever a body, which is considered to be a Court or a Tribunal, has jurisdiction over questions concerning the interpretation and application of EU law, and allows each court to act, in its 'institutional capacity', before a national court when its independence has been affected by a law or administrative conduct. [6]

---

[6] G. Pitruzzella, "L'integrazione tramite il valore dello 'Stato di diritto'", *federalismi.it*, 27, 2022.

The magnitude of this change is not small, so much so that it is argued that talking about independence today is not the same as 10 or 20 years ago, because of the pressure of the primacy of law over the democratic principle.[7] And this is not only because of the relevance of this type of crisis, which involves first and foremost a number of recently acceded states, but also because of the reference to a parameter, Article 2, which must be recognized as having a strongly expansive scope of intervention by European institutions – beyond the material limits defined by the Treaties – and which, moreover, involves a concept, that of the rule of law, which is not unambiguously defined.

Indeed, the manner in which Article 2 violations are responded to allows for the deployment of a much broader armamentarium of a political nature than that constituted by legal remedies alone, but not necessarily more effective. Evidence of this difficulty is the European debate on the ineffectiveness of the tools provided by EU law to prevent and respond to threats or violations of the aforementioned principle, based mainly on the procedure under Article 7 TEU (both preventive and sanctioning) and the use of infringement procedures, to which additional dialogue mechanisms and tools have recently been added. Among these, in particular, the *EU Framework for strengthening the rule of law* (starting from 2014), which precedes the activation of the infringement procedure, if the three phases into which it is divided do not give a positive outcome (evaluation, recommendation, follow-up of the recommendation). While the use of the tools provided by the Treaties, such as infringement procedures, action for non-compliance, or for violations of the rule of law, is inescapable, these in fact have not always proven to achieve effective, or at least politically uncontroversial, results.[8]

The new jurisprudential direction has thus enabled the Court of Justice to bring measures relating to the status of national judges under its jurisdiction, precisely through the integration of the requirement of independence with the obligation to guarantee effective judicial protection, under Article 19(1) TEU in conjunction with the aforementioned Article 47 EU CFR. Therefore, on the one hand, the Court affirms the inseparable link between effective remedies and independent judges, from which

[7] G. Raimondi, "L'indipendenza delle corti nel diritto costituzionale, comparato ed europeo: la prospettiva della Corte europea dei diritti dell'uomo", in G. Pitruzzella, O. Pollicino, M. Bassini (eds.), *Corti europee e democrazia. Rule of law, indipendenza e accountability*, Milano 2019.

[8] F. Battaglia, "La tutela dello Stato di diritto nell'Unione europea fra strumenti di natura politica e mezzi giurisdizionali", in F. Anghelone, F. Battaglia, F. Cherubini (eds.), *Uniti si può. I valori dell'Unione europea in tempo di crisi*, Roma 2019.

the obligation of member states to protect the independence of their judges under Article 19 TEU also derives. On the other hand, on the basis of this recent case law, it explicitly refers to the values on which the Union is founded, with reference to Article 2 TEU.[9] Specifically, with the first of these decisions, the *landmark* ruling on the *Portuguese Judges' Trade Union Association case* regarding the reduction of judges' salaries due to austerity requirements, the Court of Justice affirmed that the independence of the courts is part of the essential content of Article 47 of the Charter. Indeed, the court affirmed that it is of 'primary importance' to preserve the independence of the courts in order to ensure the principle of effective judicial protection of the rights that individuals derive from EU law (drawn from Article 19 TEU), linking these principles to the value of the rule of law enshrined in Article 2 TEU and emphasizing how the Union is founded on certain values common to the Member States, including, precisely, that of the rule of law.

Later, in the so-called 'conditionality judgments', the Court made it clear that Article 2 TEU is not merely a statement of political guidelines or intentions but contains the values that are integral to the 'identity' of the EU as a common legal order, values that are embodied in principles, including obligations binding on states. The Court also clarified that adherence to these values still remains a sovereign choice of the states, but once it has taken place it becomes a binding 'constitutional moment' of their membership in the Union, which does not allow for regressions.[10] A new interpretation of conditionality thus appears, which becomes a tool for pursuing constitutional goals within the Union.[11]

With regard to the so-called conditionality judgements, it should also be noted that these are decisions related to the application of Regulation 2020/2092. The latter, in order to remedy the often unsatisfactory outcomes obtained by resorting to other means, provides for a system of horizontal conditionality in financial matters, aimed specifically at curbing threats to the European budget caused by violations of the rule of law, on the basis of the rules on the implementation of the Union's budget referred to in Article 322 TFEU.[12] The concrete implementation of this instrument,

---

[9] L. Pech, D. Kochenov, *Respect for the Rule of Law in the Case Law of the European Court of Justice A Casebook Overview of Key Judgments since the Portuguese Judges Case*, SIEPS 2021:3.

[10] See G. Pitruzzella, *op. cit.*, with reference to the *Repubblika case* (Judgment of 20 April 2021, C-896/19).

[11] A. Baraggia, "The 'conditionality' Regulation under the ECJ's scrutiny: a constitutional analysis", *European Law Review,* 47(5), 2022, pp. 687-698.

[12] E. Maurice, "Rule of law: the uncertain gamble on conditionality", *European is-*

approved in December 2020 with only Poland and Hungary voting against, encountered various critical issues and saw, in fact, the presentation of two appeals by the aforementioned states which were rejected by the Court with two decisions of 16 February 2022.

The 'twin judgments' *Hungary v. Parliament and Council* and *Poland v. Parliament and Council* (C-156/21 and C-157/21), in which the Court affirmed the validity of the regulation making the disbursement of European funds conditional on respect for the rule of law, were an opportunity to reiterate that the Union is founded precisely on values common to the Member States, including the rule of law, which define its very identity as a common legal order. These common values, it should be reiterated, were accepted by all Member States at the time of their accession to the Union and cannot therefore be disregarded thereafter.

It follows that respect for the principles of the rule of law – given also their 'concrete substantive content' in Union law – constitutes a 'result obligation' for the Member States, arising directly from their membership in the Union, to which the very enjoyment of all other rights deriving from the application of the Treaties is subordinate. What emerges here with all clarity is the peculiar connection recognised by the Court between respect for the rule of law and the financial interests of the Union, which can be seriously jeopardized if the former is violated. This legitimates the Union's interventions to protect the budget, since it represents, again in the Court's words, one of the main means of giving concrete expression to the principle of solidarity between Member States, based on that mutual trust which is indispensable for the implementation of Union policies. Indeed, 'sound financial management' can only be guaranteed if public authorities act in accordance with the law, if violations of the law are effectively prosecuted, and if arbitrary or unlawful decisions by public authorities can be subject to effective judicial review by an independent and impartial judiciary.

There is thus a mechanism that provides a different remedy than that under Article 7 TEU, as the Court points out. Article 7 TEU allows for a reaction to any serious and persistent violation of one of the founding values of the Union or to any clear risk of such a violation, whereas the contested regulation applies only to violations of the principles of the rule of law and only if there are well-founded reasons to believe that such violations have an impact on the budget. In other words, it must be demonstrated that there is a real link between the violation of a principle of the rule of law and an injury or serious risk of injury to the sound financial management of the Union.

---

sues, 660 (14th March 2023). M. Bonelli, "Constitutional Language and Constitutional Limits: The Court of Justice Dismisses the Challenges to the Budgetary Conditionality Regulation", *European Papers vol. 7*, 2, 2022, pp. 507-525.

The use of the instrument specifically provided for in Article 7 TEU (para. 2) has indeed been more difficult, which is why the way has been opened to extra-Article 7 special instruments, characterized by the system of conditionality, such as the Cooperation and Verification Mechanism (CVM) adopted in 2007 for Romania and Bulgaria, in order to demonstrate the actual progress made by the two countries in the post-accession phase, particularly in the areas of justice and the fight against corruption. Thus, while both Poland and Hungary have been subjected to the Article 7 procedure for the first time, it should be noted that it has remained at a *de facto* preliminary level, failing to reach final completion due to the Council's hesitation to fully follow it up. It was precisely in this regard that the European Parliament passed its Resolution of 18 March 2022 condemning the Council's inability to make significant progress in the ongoing Article 7 procedures in response to the threats to common European values in Poland and Hungary, as well as to effectively implement Article 7 TEU with regard to the compression of the integrity of common European values, mutual trust, and the credibility of the Union as a whole.

As a matter of fact, among the various instruments available to the Union for the protection of the rule of law, the intervention of the Court of Justice has proved to be the most effective, both through recourse to the infringement procedure, under Articles 258-260 TFEU, and in connection with the procedure for an interpretive preliminary reference, under Article 267 TFEU.

With regard to *infringement procedures*, it should be recalled how they have been used strategically by the Commission since 2019 as part of the action program to strengthen the rule of law. This is the case, for example, with the series of proceedings concerning Poland over reforms implemented in the judiciary, culminating in a number of condemnatory rulings by the Court of Justice. These rulings established that the new disciplinary regime for judges is incompatible with EU law, as it fails to provide the necessary guarantees to protect them from political control and thus to preserve their independence (Case C-791/19) in relation to the provisions concerning the Disciplinary Chamber of the Supreme Court. Lastly, the infringement proceedings originating from the concerns raised by the 2019 Polish reform and the jurisprudence of the Constitutional Tribunal, which expressly challenged the primacy of EU law by deeming certain provisions of the Treaties incompatible with the national Constitution, led the Court of Justice to first issue a judgment condemning Poland for the implementation of the interim measures (in relation to the suspension of the powers of the Disciplinary Chamber of the Supreme Court on proceedings against judges), and ultimately to uphold the Commission's appeal by declaring Poland in breach of its obligations. In its reasoning, the Court first of all reiterated its jurisdiction to monitor compliance of Member States with values and principles such as the rule of law, effective judicial protection and the independence of judiciary, as well as the obligation for Member States to prevent any regression of their legislation on the organization of justice by refraining from adopting rules that could undermine the independence of judges and the value of the rule of law. Finally, it confirmed the damage caused to the independence and impartiality of judges by the reform of the Disciplinary Section of the Supreme Court and the incompatibility of the measures adopted by the Polish legislator with the guarantees of access to an independent, impartial and legally constituted judge. [13]

Despite the sanctions imposed, the infringement procedures also present some critical issues, even just with respect to the broader scope of application of Article 7 for the purposes of protecting the rule of law. This is why, precisely in order to fill the gap resulting from the political difficulties for resorting to the procedures of Article 7 and those of infringement, the additional dialogue and monitoring tools mentioned have been progressively implemented. Intrinsic limits have also emerged with regard to the conditionality mechanism, despite the potential shown by the use of economic-financial leverage as a tool for ensuring states remain aligned with common European values and standards.

In short, what clearly appears is the difficulty of adequately calibrating the use of these tools in the relations between the Union and member states. Ultimately, in light of what has been said, albeit in the context of a range of remedies all aimed at restoring and guaranteeing respect for the rule of law in the European Union, a leading role seems to be traced back to the submission of preliminary questions, aimed at verifying the existence of the characteristics of independence of the judiciary, as an essential aspect of the dialogue with national judges and of the good functioning of the Union's legal system. It is clear that, while respecting the competence of the Member States with regard to their respective judicial systems, the effective judicial protection of rights deriving from Union law cannot be compromised.

3. The role of the preliminary ruling procedure as the keystone of the European judicial architecture and guardian of the rule of law

In parallel with the tools for protecting the rule of law described above, the preliminary ruling has taken on an undisputed importance. This has per-

[13] CJEU Ruling 5 June 2023 case C-204/21 *Commission v. Poland* (Independence and private life of judges).

mitted the substantial jurisprudential intervention referred to previously, originating from the questions regarding the profiles inherent to the independence of the judiciary, on the basis of the existence of a 'connecting factor' between the (extensive) interpretation of Article 19, para. 1, requested by the referring judge, and the dispute pending before them. These decisions have contributed to marking the impact of this problem on the entire European system, since by involving the common principles and values represented by the rule of law, they have ended up highlighting the same relationships between the primacy of European law and national 'counter-limits' (*ultravires*), as well as between features related to the definition of a European constitutional identity compared to those of the Member States.

In this regard, not only are those justice reforms relevant which, by modifying, for example, appointment procedures, the role of judiciary councils, or salaries, can impact in concrete terms on the independence of judges, directly or indirectly; but even more so those interventions capable of influencing the very use of the preliminary ruling appeal, considered as the keystone of the Treaty system, which by taking away the power or obligation from the national judge effectively prevent the activation or nullify the outcome of the ruling made. Therefore, in the opinion of the Luxembourg Court, the evaluation regarding the non-application of such internal provisions should undoubtedly be left to the national judge. [14]

In other words, having stated the discretion of the judge to request a preliminary ruling to the Court of Justice as an aspect of the principle of judicial independence, national measures that limit this discretion violate EU law: for example, if they provide for disciplinary procedures against the judge for having initiated a preliminary ruling, or for failing to apply the ruling of the Member State's Constitutional Court by which that Court refused to give effect to a ruling of the Court of Luxembourg which had decided following a preliminary ruling. [15] Therefore, the referring judge, precisely because of the duplicity of their role, of *caesura* and bridge between the national and the Euro-unitary system, ends up in a difficult position, on which the main tensions of belonging to both systems are released whenever aspects of integration are lacking, especially where the national supreme courts are also involved. [16]

---

[14] CJEU, Great Chamber, 2 March 2021 *Poland*, Ruling C-824/18 *A.B., C.D., E.F., G.H. e I.J.vs. Krajowa Rada Sądownictwa* (National Council of the Judiciary, KRS)

[15] See CJEU, Ruling 22 February 2022, case C-430/21, *RS* (Effects of decisions of a Constitutional Court).

[16] See also, K. Lenaerts, "On Checks and Balances: The Rule of Law within the EU", *Columbia Journal of European Law*, 2023, 29(2) pp. 25-64.

A further aspect which is particularly significant in light of the principle of cooperation and collaboration between the Courts and of the problem of mutual trust and mutual recognition of guaranteed standards, is represented by some cases on the application of the European arrest warrant (EAW). In particular, in the well-known *LM case* the question, raised before an Irish judge regarding the surrender of a Polish citizen to Poland – about whose possible general shortcomings of the judicial system the Venice Commission had also expressed concern – led to a preliminary request to the Court if general violations of the principle of judicial independence in Poland, following the rulings rendered by the CJEU, meant that there no longer existed a sufficient basis for the mutual trust necessary for the execution of the EAW in question. The assessment of whether there was the risk of violation of the fundamental right to a fair trial through a systematic or generalized violation of the principle of independence (as per Article 47 of the Nice Charter) was, rather problematically, left by the Court to the judicial authority executing the warrant. From this perspective, as reported in the judgment, it is also necessary to take into account the factual context which constitutes the basis of the European arrest warrant and the information provided by the issuing Member State.

In this framework, specific attention must therefore be paid to the role of the national judge and the requirement of independence in relation to the development of the notion of judge, or rather of 'judicial body', for the purposes of identifying the legitimized national subjects to raise a preliminary ruling pursuant to Article 267 TFEU. These requirements are: the legal and non-conventional origin of the body, its permanent nature, the obligatory nature of its jurisdiction, the fact that this body applies legal rules and does not decide according to equity, the contradictory nature of the proceedings as well as respect for the guarantees of independence and impartiality by the individual members and the body as a whole.

Indeed, the preliminary ruling, as a tool for the uniform application of EU law, ends up assuming a fundamental systemic function of preserving the values of the rule of law and the overall good functioning of the legal system, revealing potential for conflict resolution which in some cases is more effective than other measures such as infringement procedures or sanctions for significant violations of the rule of law. In fact, as clearly emerges once again from European jurisprudence on the crisis of the rule of law, the system of implementation of EU law and guarantee of fundamental rights of the Union is hinged on the essential role of both the national judge and the European judge, and on the essential possibility of 'dialogue' between them, offered by the preliminary ruling. Both participate in the 'European judicial architecture', by which the primacy of EU law is ensured, through a full and correct attainment of the potential for disapplying national legislation.[17] When the independence of the judge becomes a discriminating criterion for the very possibility of qualifying the internal judicial body for the purposes of activating this dialogue, it becomes clear how the definition of a shared standard of compliance with these requirements ends up influencing the very functionality of the integrated judicial system, which finds an essential factor in the network between judges.

If the independence of judges is essential for the proper functioning of the preliminary ruling mechanism, as it can only be activated by an independent judge, the risk, in the face of (judicial) reforms that ultimately undermine the democratic functioning of the rule of law, could paradoxically be precisely that of excluding the possibility of dialogue between national and European judges, with consequent repercussions of the effects of the lack of independence of national judges on the functioning of the European constitutional and judicial system.

4. Constitutional identity and rule of law in the multilevel legal system

The events of Poland and Hungary (but also Romania and others Member States) share the problem of respecting the principle of effective judicial protection, including access to justice, by independent and impartial judicial bodies as an essential element of the rule of law. Indeed, it can be underlined that, although they became known in relation to the violation of the rule of law, and therefore with reference to Article 2 TEU, the question of the effective judicial protection of rights represents the crucial aspect of these events, as it directly affects the protection of those fundamental rights which increasingly shape the European constitutional identity.

The independence of judges is therefore valid both as an 'individual right' pursuant to Article 47 of the Charter, but also as a structural principle of the European legal system, with reference to the preliminary ruling (Article 267 TFEU), as well as to the principle of loyal collaboration (Article 4 TEU), and, finally, to those common values of the Union, including the rule of law (Article 2 TEU), which are implemented in Article 19 TEU. As stated by Pitruzzella,[18] if a national measure undermines the independence of the judicial bodies, the constitutional architecture of the EU is threatened. As can be seen from the jurisprudence of the Court, without independence there cannot be effective judicial protection of the rights

[17] G. Pitruzzella, "L'integrazione tramite il valore dello 'Stato di diritto'", cit.

[18] *Ibidem*. Likewise, see also K. Lenaerts, *On Checks and Balances*, cit.

conferred by the Union; without judicial independence, a national court cannot engage in a dialogue, based exclusively on law, with the Court of Justice; without independence, mutual trust between the Courts disappears, jeopardizing the Area of freedom, security and justice.

Finally, given the connection of the principle of independence to the value of the rule of law, it is worth recalling some considerations regarding the debate and tensions that currently revolve around the rule of law, which not surprising since 2020 constitutes a new chapter which was previously absent, in the annual *Overview of the Year reports* of the jurisprudence of the Court of Luxembourg.

These tensions undoubtedly also derive from the different meaning and interpretation with which the concept of rule of law is embedded in the national constitutions and legal traditions of the states, and from how it is interpreted by the Court of Justice in the exercise of its own jurisdiction. [19] Here the concept of rule of law merges with the community of fundamental and founding values of the EU, the protection of which is entrusted to the procedures inscribed in the Treaties and to the instruments aimed at protecting what is recognized as a 'substantial constitutional identity' of the EU. [20]

The problems opened by this perspective are significant, and obviously do not only remain in the legal sphere, but involve and question, as we have seen, the potential developments of the European integration process: from possible outcomes feared by some as 'Polexit', to the issue of majoritarian tendencies, to the issue of the 'juridification' of referrals to the Court and the consequences of the decisions taken in Luxembourg in the face of 'defending' the position of the national states, in order to avoid 'excessive pervasiveness' of the CJEU and preserving that space which shall pertain to political choices (and not juridical ones). [21] The risk of aggravating the most divisive factors and the unprecedented breadth of European law should be stemmed precisely by those references, also made by the Court (see in particular in the judgments on conditionality), aimed at underlining the char-

---

[19] T.E. Frosini (ed.), *Rule of Law come costituzionalismo*, Bologna 2023. A. Circolo, *Il valore dello Stato di diritto nell'Unione europea. Violazioni sistemiche e soluzioni di tutela*, Napoli 2023.

[20] J. De Poorter et al. (edited by), *European Yearbook of Constitutional Law 2022. A Constitutional Identity for the EU?*, Berlin-Heidelberg 2020. J. Scholtes, *The Abuse of Constitutional Identity in the European Union*, Oxford University Press, 2023.

[21] On the "judicialization of political issues" see M. Cartabia, "The Rule of Law and the Role of Courts", *Italian Journal of Public Law*, 10(1) 2018. On the relationship between politics and democratic processes with judicial decisions see also M. Nettesheim, "EU Rule of Law or Rule of Lawyers?" in this volume. G. Amato, B. Barbisan, C. Pinelli (eds.), *Rule of Law vs Majoritarian Democracy*, Oxford 2021.

acteristics of a Union of values not imposed from above, but deriving from the contribution of Member States and common constitutional traditions.

Only future developments will allow us to verify whether an approach of this type, which leaves room for the autonomy of states in the implementation of the rule of law (as a 'framework of reference'), without involving the imposition of a single constitutional model (precluded also by Article 4 Paragraph 2 TUE), will be able to guarantee the right balance between the most extensive guarantee of European values and respect for the different areas of competence (also with regard to the organization of the judicial system, which is attributed to the Member States). In this way, it would be ensured that the interpretation of European law is formed through a fruitful dialogue with the Court of Justice, which has (if anything) the last – but not only – word, and to which also national judges contribute, thanks to the preliminary ruling, in determining the primacy of European law,[22] which is not necessarily the same as supremacy.

[22] G. Amato, "Conclusioni", in B. Carotti (ed.), *Identità nazionale degli Stati membri, primato del diritto dell'Unione europea, stato di diritto e indipendenza dei giudici nazionali. Atti della Giornata di studio tra Corte costituzionale e CGUE*, Roma 2022, p. 153 ff. See, also, K. Lenaerts, "National Identity, the Equality of Member States before the Treaties and the Primacy of EU Law", *ivi*.

Chapter 10

EU RULE OF LAW OR RULE OF LAWYERS? THE COURT OF JUSTICE OF THE EU AND ARTICLE 2 TEU

Martin Nettesheim

ABSTRACT: *This paper critiques the recent case law of the Court of Justice of the European Union on Article 2 TEU. The thesis is that the legal development pursued by the CJEU leads to a highly problematic depoliticisation of fundamental questions of European integration. This damages the already underdeveloped democratic nature of the EU. It amounts to a form of eclectical "Frankenstein"-constitutionalism.*

SUMMARY: 1. Government by judges. – 2. The rule of legal experts. – 3. The development of Article 2 TEU into a federal homogeneity clause. – 4. Four characteristics of the CJEU's constitutionalism. – 4.1. Non-minimalism. – 4.2. Judicial identity politics. – 4.3. Selectivity. – 4.4. Concrete reciprocity. – 5. The political place and timelessness of CJEU constitutionalism. – 6. Judicial determination of political preferences. – 7. The decline of democraticity.

1. Government by judges

If we apply Abraham Lincoln's vision of democracy [1] to the EU, it is easy to recognize that its governance system is entirely oriented towards a "government for the people(s)". In contrast, the EU cannot be understood from the outset as a "government of the/a people", and even the standard of "government by the people", measured against the standards of a democratic governance system in the Western liberal nation state, remains unfulfilled, despite all the counter factual representations of the treaty text (e.g. Article 10 Paragraph 1 TEU) and the claims of interested actors.

For some years now, it has been observed that the Court of Justice of the EU (CJEU) has also been operating a "government for the people(s)" at the constitutional level. Fundamental questions of the quasi-federal and democratic construction of the EU are no longer decided in the political arena but answered by legal experts in an official capacity (be they public

---

[1] Abraham Lincoln, Gettysburg Address, Nov. 19th, 1863 (https://www.abrahamlincolnonline.org/lincoln/speeches/gettysburg.htm).

administrators or judges). The CJEU depoliticizes fundamental political questions and legalises highly political contentious issues. A specific but by no means uncontroversial vision of the integration process is perpetuated through legal manoeuvres of treaty 'interpretation'. Constitutional power is no longer attributed to a democratic subject, not even in its claims, but is presented as an expression of 'values' whose significance is recognized and managed by particularly enlightened legal experts. Power thereby becomes self-referential and detached from the political environment. This represents a decline in the democratisation of public authority and a problem for political culture. When the 'constitutional space' of a sovereign and democratic state is defined by lawyers without a truly clear legal basis, there is cause for closer scrutiny. The following explanations serve to substantiate the thesis that the EU Court of Justice is currently advancing a constitutional transformation that has the potential to damage the democratisation of the governance system inherent in the alliance of the EU and EU Member States.

2. The rule of legal experts

It is part of the institutional DNA of the EU to depoliticize political conflicts. The increasing prevalence of national conservative, illiberal, and autocratic thought patterns in EU Member States is not interpreted by EU institutions as a highly political moment in which various ideologies clash, creating a struggle over the future of a specific liberal world view. The same institutions also do not view the attainment of governmental power by proponents of such ideas as a politically manageable challenge. Instead, the events are seen as an annoying deviation from a historically and philosophically predefined path into the future, which is in any case politically predetermined. For the EU, there is no need for political negotiation on how to respond to deviant behaviour; instead, sanctions and coercion mechanisms are required to enforce a return to appropriate behaviour. Only those who are guided by an apolitical or depoliticized understanding of the development of the integration process can speak of 'regression' or 'back-sliding'.

From the outset, the EU has been characterized by its method of addressing political problems and challenges through expertocratic institutions, administrative 'reason', and socio-technical control ('social engineering').[2] Problems are measured and efficiently solved with expert knowledge. The

[2] S. Rehling Larsen, "The European Union as 'Militant Democracy'?", in J. Komárek (ed.), *European Constitutional Imaginaries: Between Ideology and Utopia*, Oxford 2023, 75.

EU is driven by a vision of post-conflict technical problem-solving, which for some represents the utopia of post-modern social integration,[3] but for others, is pure dystopia. It is not surprising that the EU institutions also employ these patterns when confronted with challenges at the constitutional level. It was almost a natural reflex for the European Commission to resort to technocratic-administrative control when confronted with the question of how to respond to changes in Member State government systems driven by national conservative governments. It drafted 'mechanisms', established reporting requirements, and formulated 'scoreboards', aiming for an almost mathematical determination of how far the government systems of the Member States deviated from those of an ideal state. Doubts about the success of this approach, which is based on reinterpreting a political problem as an administratively manageable task, abound on all sides (even among sympathetic observers of the European Commission).

In recent years, a new development has been observed with EU institutions striving to address situations of political conflict through case law. Instead of technocratic-administrative reasoning, the technocratic rule of legal experts is coming into play. The European Court of Justice has begun to set standards for what political justice and good governance look like and has made these standards binding for EU Member States. This also represents a depoliticization, albeit through a different path. A member of the CJEU once told me ironically that master thinkers have gathered in Luxembourg who can circumvent the political struggle over the meaning of contested concepts of good governance and determine the correct meaning based on superior insight. A constitutional concept such as the rule of law is meticulously worked out in legal terms in a similar way to the definition of a customs or agricultural law. Soon, this may also apply to democracy, solidarity, tolerance, or justice. This is constitutionally and politically relevant because the Court of Justice presents the standards it has developed to the democratically responsible legislatures of the still sovereign Member States. The legal reasoning of the Luxembourg judges trumps the political-democratic process in the Member States; it also supersedes the position of political discourses between EU bodies and Member State governments.

---

[3] See, e.g., A. von Bogdandy, P. Bogdanowicz, I. Canor, M. Taborowski, M. Schmidt, "A Potential Constitutional Moment for the European Rule of Law – The Importance of Red Lines", *Common Market Law Review*, 2018, p. 983; D. Kochenov, P. Bárd, "The Last Soldier Standing? Courts vs Politicians and the Rule of Law Crisis in the New Member States of the EU", *European Yearbook of Constitutional Law*, 2019, p. 243; A. von Bogdandy, L.D. Spieker, "Countering the Judicial Silencing of Critics: Article 2 TEU Values, Reverse Solange, and the Responsibilities of National Judges", *EU-Const*, 2019, p. 391.

3. The development of Article 2 TEU into a federal homogeneity clause

For decades now, 'constitutional transformations' have been observed worldwide, in which there is a shift of policy-making authority from democratic representative institutions to autonomous or semi-autonomous professional bodies.[4] Decision-making is shifting from politically influenced spaces to expert-oriented, isolated forums that are not directly democratically accountable. The EU is currently undergoing such a transformation, allowing us to speak of the third phase of EU constitutionalisation. In the early stages of European integration, the CJEU was primarily concerned with the development of legal doctrines and institutional requirements to make the political decisions of politically acting institutions binding.[5] In the next phase, which began with the fall of the Berlin Wall, the EU committed itself to upholding liberal-democratic patterns of fundamental rights and put the idea of the 'end of history' into practice.[6] In the latest phase of European constitutionalism, which can currently be observed, the aim is to legally 'lock in"' certain political preferences and orientations so that they can no longer be questioned through democratic means.

If the legalisation of the political dispute over what constitutes just and good governance were based on clear and sufficiently specific provisions of the EU Treaty, there would be nothing wrong with the rule of law experts and their actions would be legitimized by the Member States. However, this is not the case. Although there are numerous specific provisions in EU treaty law that limit the political leeway of the Member States, these provisions also affect the 'constitutional space' of the Member States. The Lisbon Treaty does not contain a federal homogeneity clause granting the EU institutions comprehensive oversight of constitutional development in the Member States. It was a deliberate decision by the drafters of this treaty to distinguish between values and legal obligations or legal principles. The treaty-makers made it clear that they wanted the decision on whether a Member State's government system complies with the value orientations contained in Article 2 TEU to be clarified in political processes (Article 49 TEU: political decision on admission; Arti-

---

[4] M. Loughlin, *Against Constitutionalism*, Cambridge (MA) 2022.

[5] J. Weiler, "The Transformation of Europe", *100 Yale Law Journal,* 2403, 1991.

[6] The CJEU has defended its "end of history"-claim in: CJEU, 20.4.2021, C-896/19, Repubblika, EU:C:2021:3011. See J. Scholtes, "Constitutionalising the End of History? Pitfalls of a Non-Regression Principles for Article 2 TEU", *European Constitutional Law Review*, 19, 2013, p. 59.

cle 7 TEU: political decision on sanctions; unwritten: political decision on expulsion).

The CJEU has overridden this legal situation by reinterpreting Article 2 TEU as a federal homogeneity clause – so far only for the concept of the rule of law,[7] but fundamentally for all 'values'. Article 2 TEU was conceived as a treaty provision containing the affirmation of certain political value orientations of the Member States. It has normative significance because the EU Member States have committed to the standards they want to adhere to in the three cases of accession, response to developments, and expulsion. In its decision of 22 February 2022, the CJEU claims to be able to derive a strict legal standard of the rule of law quality of the government systems of the EU Member States from Article 2 TEU, which they must not fall below ('result obligation').[8] The conclusion that a 'rule of lawyers' has replaced a European 'rule of law' is not entirely far-fetched.

Astute lawyers will always be able to provide a reason for their legal derivations and developments. However, positivist manoeuvres cannot overcome the limits of the normative authority of a governing institution. It is striking the extent to which the lawyers of the CJEU and the circle of EU federalists strive to ignore the question of democratic authority. Nothing characterizes the logic of political modernity more than the axiom that every form of public-political rule (including by legal experts) requires sufficient democratic legitimacy. Courts also do not operate outside of this logic, even if they play a politically independent role. Nothing is more important for the constitutionalized democratic constitutional state than ensuring that the political space, in which preferences and future visions, values, and interests are negotiated, is not closed off by the expertocratic dominance of administrative or legal experts.

4. Four characteristics of the CJEU's constitutionalism

Not every reader of this work will be familiar with the development of the CJEU's jurisprudence. The CJEU first dealt with interventions by Member State legislators and governments in their respective judicial systems in the

[7] C. Closa, D. Kochenov (eds.), *Reinforcing Rule of Law Oversight in the European Union*, Princeton 2016; see also D. Kochenov, A. Magen, L. Pech, "Introduction: The Great Rule of Law Debate in the EU", *Journal of Common Market Studies*, 2016, p. 1045; M. Avbelj, "Rule of Law and the Economic Crisis in a Pluralist European Union", *Hague Journal on the Rule of Law*, 2016, p. 191; D.J. Liñán Nogueras, P. Martín Rodríguez (eds.), *Estado de derecho y Unión Europea*, Madrid 2018.

[8] CJEU, 16 February 2022, C-156/21, Poland/EP and Council, EU:C:2022:44.

early 2010s. Initially, the Court attempted to combat such interventions by resorting to specific treaty provisions (e.g., the forced retirement of judges through the prohibition of age discrimination).[9] It then began to treat interventions and manipulations of the judicial system as violations of Article 19 TEU.[10] Finally, it developed a radical new approach, interpreting the general values clause of Article 2 TEU as an operative provision imposing strict legal obligations on EU Member States and thereby limiting their constitutional room for manoeuvre.[11] The limitations resulting from Article 2 TEU are binding for all EU Member States, although they were obviously developed in response to regressive developments in Hungary and Poland. The obligations developed by the CJEU lead to a significant restriction of the freedom of EU Member States to independently exercise their 'constitutional space'. To date, the CJEU has mainly focused on giving directives to EU Member States which it derives from the value of the rule of law however the European Commission has now indicated that it also considers similar derivations from the value of democracy to be necessary. The logical end of this development is a state in which the CJEU also prescribes to the Member States what they must observe with regard to human dignity, freedom, equality, and human rights. Jurisprudence is a bold act of legal development because the EU Treaty affirmatively speaks of values, not normative duties. There is no philosophical or legal rational approach by which the statement that someone values something could be inferred to imply obligations and behaviours. The CJEU also fails to rationally bridge the gap between a statement of value and a legal obligation. This is already evident semantically: the CJEU speaks in an extremely strange formulation of the fact that the treaty would have 'established' values.

Of course, neither the CJEU nor the parts of European legal science that support it have addressed the political and constitutional implications of the transformation of Article 2 TEU. They have chosen a strictly legal positivist approach, which is characterized by carrying out mental operations and constructive efforts without analysing and discussing the wider institutional and political contexts. The process can only succeed through conscious blindness and suppression because otherwise it would become too clear how precarious it is for a supranational organization with a lack of democratic accountability to turn a regulation listing values into a lever for removing essential parts of the national constitutional space. There is a

[9] CJEU, 6 November 2012, C-286/12, Commission/Hungary, EU:C:2012:687.

[10] Leading case: CJEU, 27 February 2018, C-64/16, Associação Sindical dos Juízes Portugueses, EU:C:2018:117.

[11] CJEU, 16 February 2022, C-156/21, Poland/EP and Council, EU:C:2022:44.

deep tragedy in the fact that the CJEU protects values with precarious distortions of the wording of the treaty, potentially harming the European rule of law. When socio-politically and socio-culturally important decision-making areas are depoliticized by being seized by irresponsible (legal) experts, the question arises whether this degrades the democratic quality of a governance system and signals the emergence of a liberal autocracy on the horizon.

For the criticism of the CJEU jurisprudence, it is necessary to distinguish between the four essential features of the approach developed by the CJEU, which we will now look at in Section 4.

4.1. Non-minimalism

If you have read Article 2 TEU, you might wonder where the problem lies if the CJEU advocates for values such as the rule of law, democracy, and human rights. Are not all rational-thinking people committed to these values? What is wrong with reminding the Member States, who have spoken of values in Article 2 TEU, of their statements as treaty makers? Apart from the previously mentioned fact that there is a categorical difference between the affirmative statements of values made in Article 2 TEU and legal obligations, the following is particularly relevant: the terms mentioned, as well as others in Article 2 TEU such as "justice," "solidarity," "tolerance," etc., are not only semantically highly indeterminate but also understood in very different ways. All these terms represent 'essentially contested concepts'. The concept of the rule of law can encompass very different notions. Those who choose a minimalist understanding will speak of the rule of law as soon as formal legality is ensured and minimum requirements for the stability and predictability of state action are maintained. Those who apply a maximalist understanding will also include material justice, human rights guarantees and rationality. The same applies to democracy. There is a vast difference between an approach that defines democracy by the existence of a freely and fairly elected parliament with sufficient legislative, regulatory, and oversight powers, and an approach that also requires constitutional court control, separation of powers, and diverse human rights.

The jurisprudence of the CJEU is characterized by the fact that it not only interprets the concept of the rule of law in Article 2 TEU in a minimalist way but makes a quasi-maximalist interpretation binding for the Member States.[12] For the CJEU, Article 2 TEU results in an unspecific

---

[12] For a precise analysis of minimalist, intermediate and maximalist approaches, see

"prohibition of arbitrary exercise of governmental authority".[13] It also reads a series of human rights requirements into it which moves beyond the field of uncontroversial matters and constitutes judicial policy making.[14] To justify its jurisprudence, the CJEU cannot rely on the will of the contracting Member States or on the results of a political-public discourse. It rather refers to the opinion of experts who are beyond democratic control and responsibility (The Venice Commission[15]). Juristocracy and expertocracy mutually support each other through mutual references and establish loops that can no longer be democratically penetrated. The depoliticization of discourse is taken a step further when statements by the European Commission or the opinions of politically active EU NGOs and scientists are also used as evidence.

Of course, neither the CJEU nor the voices from the academic field that support it have admitted that they have moved jurisprudence far beyond the realm of the uncontroversial and self-evident. The terms 'rule of law,' 'democracy,' and 'human rights' are treated as monolithic blocks that stand alone with a clear form. They carry the semantics of the Holy Trinity (Rule of Law, Democracy, Human Rights) like monstrances and suggest that a reasonable debate about the concrete content is not possible. There is then only affirmation and rejection, and any reminder that there can be legitimate differences of interpretation and that the boundaries where reasonable interpretation turns into unreasonable interpretation is already a sacrilege.

The jurisprudence of the CJEU on Article 2 TEU can be classified as a case of 'positive integration'. The CJEU is no longer just concerned with taking certain political options away from the Member States while respecting their fundamental political decision-making powers. The CJEU operates with a positive ideal of what the constitutional manifestations of national governance systems should look like (independent courts, etc.), and

---

Lord Bingham, "The Rule of Law", 66 *Cambridge L.J.* 67, 2007. See also J. Raz, "The Rule of Law and its Virtue", in J. Raz (eds.), *The Autority of Law: Essays on Law and Morality (1979)*, Oxford 2012, p. 214; see also J. Waldron, "The Rule of Law", *Stanford Encyclopedia of Philosophy*, 22. June 2016 (https://plato.stanford.edu/entries/rule-of-law/); C. Mollers,"Reflexion uber den Rechtsstaat", *ZRP*, 2020, p. 27.

[13] CJEU, 16 February 2022, C-156/21, Poland/EP and Council, EU:C:2022:44, Rec. 321.

[14] CJEU, 16 February 2022, C-156/21, Poland/EP and Council, EU:C:2022:44, Rec. 327.

[15] See, e.g. Venice-Commission, Report on the Rule of Law, CDL-AD(2011)003rev-e (adopted in 86th Plenary Session, Venice, 25–26 March 2011); Venice-Commission, Rule of Law Checklist, Document CDL-AD(2016)007-e (adopted in 106th Plenary Session, Venice, 11–12 March 2016).

uses this ideal to identify supposed and actual deficits in national governance structures. The ideals of constitutional governance structures are then used by the European Commission in its usual technocratic style as the basis for reports addressing compliance or deviation.

4.2. Judicial identity politics

The CJEU does not merely present its jurisprudence on Article 2 TEU as the result of a legal analysis of an important treaty provision. Instead, it elevates its jurisprudence politically: the EU's commitment to the values of Article 2 TEU constitutes the core of its identity. The English version of the decision of 16 February 2022 states that:

> The values contained in Article 2 TEU have been identified and are shared by the Member States. They define the very identity of the European Union as a common legal order. [16]

The 'cult of the self,' which is cultivated in so many social contexts, has now also reached the European judiciary.

It is unclear whether to laugh or cry when considering that the CJEU is following the identity policy pathway initiated by the Member States as treaty makers (Article 4(2) TEU). The process of juridification thus extends not only to specific political conflicts or areas of action but also to the definition of self-understanding itself (raison d'être). The EU and EU Member States can now oppose each other's 'identity' in legal or political conflicts: future disputes will no longer be treated as conflicts over interests and goals but as a struggle for each state's own identity. Thus, the nature of a dispute becomes existential. Anyone who already had doubts about the legal rationality of the approach in the search for the identity of state constitutional courts will only see a further decline in legal acumen and legal argumentation in the new battle order. The invention of an EU 'common identity' in legal literature has been widely welcomed. It gives lawyers the opportunity to muse and write about the nature of the EU under the guise of scientific work. There is a significant danger of crossing the boundary between an approach that is still supported by the self-understanding of legal science as a social science discipline and a freely associative and unscientific talk. The juridification of the search for the 'essence of the EU' does not automatically mean that lawyers have special expertise in this area.

[16] CJEU, 16 February 2022, C-156/21, Poland/EP and Council, EU:C:2022:44, Rec. 127.

Perhaps the identity-political exaltation of the EU needs to be classified into a category of public discourse described by Harry G. Frankfurt.

The efforts of the CJEU to interpret the EU's essence in terms of identity politics are particularly surprising because they are both overly simple and politically problematic. An organization with the institutional, socio-cultural, and political complexity of the EU can only be reduced to the simple denominator found in the quoted sentence at the cost of brutal losses. This is evidenced by the following consideration: would a person who has never heard of the EU be able to draw any meaningful conclusions about its real existence if presented with Article 2 TEU and the values stated therein? Politically, it is downright misleading to reduce an organization in which nearly 30 European states have joined forces, each with its own history, culture, economy, and socio-political structures, to a few universalistic values. How can one claim to want to speak about the essence of the EU without addressing the common future ('common destiny'), freedom, and solidarity? I have wondered whether the moralization of the EU by the CJEU is a reaction to the (actual or perceived) signs of crisis, deficits, and ugliness that currently characterize the integration process. Even if the EU is currently making sluggish rather than confident progress, at least its core, the legal community, should be shining brightly.

4.3. Selectivity

The CJEU only drives the development of obligations towards the Member States derived from Article 2 TEU. Its jurisprudence has only a federal-vertical dimension. The CJEU aims to introduce constitutional control over the EU Member States with the aim of pushing the European Union towards becoming a European federal state. In contrast, the CJEU does not apply Article 2 TEU to the EU institutions, even though the first and most important task of the CJEU is to monitor the legality of the actions of the EU institutions. The CJEU does not indicate that it wants to attribute an internal meaning to Article 2 TEU, even though Article 2, para. 1, TEU mainly refers to the Union being founded on the aforementioned values. The CJEU would have had the opportunity to overcome the selectivity of its understanding of Article 2 TEU. It recently had to rule on the decision of its President to withdraw the status of a member of the CJEU from an Advocate General nominated by the UK following Brexit. In this decision, which has been sharply criticized in legal literature, the CJEU completely retreats to a positivist interpretation of specific treaty provisions, without mentioning the principle of the rule of law and the principle of independence developed towards the Member States.

It is not far-fetched to accuse the CJEU of evidently applying double standards and pursuing an agenda towards the member states that it is unwilling (or unable) to enforce against itself and the EU institutions. Many observers accuse the CJEU of hypocrisy and hypercriticism with regard to its fight for the values of the rule of law. It is already paradoxical that the CJEU declares the values of Article 2 TEU to be genuinely identity-shaping characteristics but then refrains from applying them to the Union itself. The accusation of hypocrisy would gain even more weight if an institution like the EU, which is generally considered under-democratized, were to become the guardian of democracy in the EU Member States and interfere in democratically made decisions.

4.4. Concrete reciprocity

The jurisprudence of the CJEU on Article 2 TEU has another striking feature. The system of EU treaty law provides for the CJEU to react to treaty violations by declaring the observed behaviour to be contrary to EU law. The Treaty provides for further obligations in the event that an EU Member State fails to return to compliance. In contrast, the Treaty does not provide for the EU institutions to respond to a treaty violation by withdrawing rights or even excluding a Member State. This is based on the idea that there is a distinction between action and status in a political organisation: it must be seen as a constitutional achievement that poor behaviour does not affect the fundamental membership status. Reciprocity may serve as the guiding principle of a theory of justice, but that does not mean that reciprocity can find its place in every social context (think of a parent-child relationship).

In its jurisprudence on Article 2 TEU, the CJEU falls short of this level of constitutional thinking in a political association. In its decision of February 16, 2022, the CJEU established a concrete reciprocity between behaviour in conformity with values and (membership) rights:

> It follows that respect for the values referred to in Article 2 TEU by a Member State is a condition for enjoying all the rights resulting from the application of the Treaties to that Member State.[17]

The CJEU's reconstruction of the relationship between the EU and the EU Member States is thus based on a way of thinking that reconstructs

---

[17] CJEU, 16 February 2022, C-156/21, Poland/EP and Council, EU:C:2022:44, Rec. 126.

membership as an exchange: respect for values in exchange for the granting of rights. The CJEU does not explicitly specify which rights these should be. As a consequence of this legal thinking, it may be possible to withdraw all rights (de facto exclusion).

The (almost archaic) return to the concept of reciprocity ('an eye for an eye') is remarkable because this concept, which refers to concrete behavioural expectations, has already been overcome in the horizontal relationship between the EU Member States. The treaty violation of a Member State does not give others the right to question the rights of the offending state. Retaliatory measures are excluded. Traces of a concrete concept of reciprocity are found solely in Article 7 TEU, but this is limited to the relationship between the EU member states as a 'club' of equal states and confined to a narrowly defined institutional area. Article 7 TEU does not provide for any way of responding to violations by withdrawing rights granted by the treaty.

Against this background, it is particularly remarkable that the CJEU relies on these concepts when reconstructing the vertical-federal relationship of the EU Member State. It falls short of a federal understanding that does not establish a direct causal relationship between the status as a Member State and compliant or non-compliant behaviour. It is clear and needs no explanation that an EU institution does not have the legal right to adjudicate on the membership rights established in the treaty.

5. The political place and timelessness of CJEU constitutionalism

Constitutions do not exist in isolation, nor are they located somewhere in the middle of nowhere. Constitutions are products of human action. They must be reconnected to the political decision-making space, but in order to extend their counter-political guidance and binding effect, they cannot simply rely on the will of the current majority. There are two ways of developing interpretive patterns that reconnect the text and institution of the constitution to the political space. Political reconnection can be past-oriented. In this case, the central reference point is the text created by the historical constitutional legislator and their 'will'. Past-oriented interpretation techniques include historical hermeneutics, originalism, and traditionalism. Political reconnection can also be future-oriented by developing a vision of a good life for the members of a political community. This vision must include elements of political justice but regularly also extends to socio-cultural elements.

The CJEU claims – in line with wide circles of European legal scholarship – to interpret the founding treaties of the EU as a 'constitution.' However, this 'constitution' hovers strangely in space, without place or time. The CJEU cannot and will not rely on the will of the Member States (in their capacity as treaty makers) because it would then not be able to overcome the attachment to categories and patterns of international treaty-making. An alternative construction, which relies on the will of a European people, some imagined group of European peoples, or even on individuals, is politically, constructively theoretical, and empirically so implausible that it can only be discussed by voices that move in an empirically distant academic ideal world, where attention is mainly gained through daring theses and constructions. The legitimacy patterns used by state constitutions cannot be meaningfully applied to the EU and its treaties, at least as far as backward-looking approaches are concerned. However, similar difficulties arise when it comes to developing and legally anchoring future-oriented narratives. The politically powerful interpretation of the EU as a peace order is fading and it is hardly possible to implement it in the everyday interpretation of the treaties. The promise of prosperity associated with the single market project, which was to be renewed in the now politically superseded Lisbon Agenda, appears increasingly utopian. Factors beyond the control of the EU (demographic change, societal aging, technological and industrial change, new geopolitical competition, etc.) contribute to this, as does the fact that the EU institutions today see themselves more as regulatory institutions than as promoters of prosperity. The pride of the EU institutions in being 'regulatory champions' may come as a surprise given the competitive problems of European economies. Whether and how the recent narrative – the EU as protector of particularly vulnerable EU citizens – will leave socio-psychological traces is not yet clear.

How can the CJEU's claim to anchor the identity and essence of the EU in a universalistic conception of good governance be placed in this context? The EU is apparently to be described as a "shining city upon the hill" [18] that holds the flag high at a time when the number of democratic government systems is decreasing and national conservatism, illiberalism, and authoritarian orientations are spreading. The EU describes a political vision of positive co-existence, which is based entirely on universalistic concepts and values. The CJEU does not enter the field of socio-cultural values and patterns of meaning, probably not least because it would have to take a stand in contentious conflict areas. The 'glossy vision' developed by the CJEU is in any case unquestioned, uncontested, and unchallenged among

---

[18] Ronald Reagan used the metaphor in his Farewell Adress in 1989 (see https://ourlostfounding.com/ronald-reagan-and-the-shining-city-upon-a-hill/).

the players shaping the discourse. Unfortunately, it must be said that it is anything but clear whether the description of the EU developed by the CJEU can reach and resonate with significant parts of the population outside the bubble-like discourse spaces in which political and scientific elites engage with CJEU decisions. One cannot help but feel that the CJEU is preaching to the already converted.

The term "Frankenstein constitutionalism" stands for constitutional theory and constitutional law thinking that eclectically assembles elements of governance and legal institutions of different origins and functions and assembles them into a disparate creature. It describes an approach that inserts implants into a constitutional order that "function" superficially, but at the same time destroy the integrity of the whole and create an entity that breaks with political culture and societal integrity. The idea has also recently been used in the context of describing the evolution of liberal EU Member States with dominating counter-majoritarian elements into "illiberal states" [19] The CJEU's case law on Art. 2 TEU is such a form of constitutionalism.

6. Judicial determination of political preferences

It is a trivial observation that constitutions, basic laws, and other hierarchically superior statutes determine certain policy preferences and remove them from the normal political process. It is equally trivial to note that the politically democratic process shrinks to the extent that the field of constitutionally determined 'policy decisions' expands. In extreme cases, the constitutionalisation of political preferences can go so far that democracy can only be spoken of in name, and a transition to a juristocracy occurs.

The Court of Justice claims to determine subjective policy preferences to such an extent and in such a manner that it departs from the decision-making space legitimized by the wording of the EU Treaty. Its non-minimalist interpretation of the 'values' of Article 2 of the EU Treaty also fails to show an adequate sense for preserving democratic decision-making spaces. Against the backdrop of the fact that a political correction of the CJEU's decisions in the treaty amendment procedure is theoretically possible but practically impossible due to procedural hurdles (veto positions of each member state), specific political preferences are anchored in constitutional law in such a way that they are set in stone for the time horizon of constitutional thinking.

---

[19] K. Lane Scheppele, "The Rule of law and the Frankenstate", 26 *Goverance*, 559, 2013.

How is it that this development does not trigger political resistance? Why do the vast majority of Member States not resist losing their autonomy and being put into a golden cage by the CJEU? Viewing the development through the prism of vertical relationships between the EU and its Member States, it is difficult to understand the indifference of the overwhelming number of EU Member States. After all, we are talking about the loss of their freedoms in a core area of their democratic self-determination. It is not far-fetched to speak of an impairment of sovereignty or subjugation of Member States. If we look further into the future, we will see a situation on the horizon in which EU Member States have been made parts of a commonwealth whose essential structures are formulated by a court in Luxembourg.

If the development is not interpreted as a conflict between the EU and its Member States but as a political struggle over the future of a particular form of liberalism, the course of the conflict lines looks different. The self-empowerment of the CJEU is taking place at a time when a political struggle has emerged in almost all EU Member States over the meaning and sustainability of the specific form of liberalism developed by large sections of a globally oriented elite in recent decades. Choosing this perspective to analytically classify and normatively criticize the recent case law of the CJEU explains quite naturally why the introduction of constitutional supervision by the CJEU and the loss of essential parts of the 'constitutional space' is accepted so passively, even positively, by the governing actors in most EU Member States. In most EU Member States, the previously dominant political groups are under pressure – new political forces are challenging the interpretive power and creative capacity of those 'grand coalitions' that have dominated the representative democratic institutions for decades. The self-empowerment of the CJEU means that political preferences that are no longer undisputed in the domestic sphere (and are losing their majority in some Member States) are stabilized and 'entrenched' through primary EU law. Instead of engaging in the struggle for the political viability of a position, value patterns, political horizons, and interests are interpreted into the EU Treaty and thus depoliticised. Specific political value patterns, ideas, and socio-cultural orientations are thus stabilized in a time when societal struggles over their meaning and significance have erupted.

This form of stabilization significantly benefits from the fact that the belief in the neutrality, impartiality, and truthfulness of the decisions of a high court is deeply rooted in the populations of the EU Member States. The idea that the CJEU does not act as a politically interested actor but as a distant guardian of the law remains unchanged. In this way, a liberal-egalitarian political system of meaning and values is legally protected from the emergence of illiberal and national-conservative tendencies. The CJEU's case law aims to 'lock in' policy preferences that should be subject to open political discussion. It enables CJEU judges to control and steer the political economy of the EU and its Member States in a way that creates the image of a juristocracy.

In this context, there is nothing to suggest that there is a simple causal link between the challenge from politically dominant actors and the development of depoliticizing case law by the CJEU. The development cannot simply be interpreted as a "hegemony-preserving strategy" of a EU elite (Hirschl[20]). It is by no means the case that the judiciary is empowered by a political majority at precisely the moment when it comes under social pressure and can foresee that it will lose its political hegemony. Rather, the development takes place on the basis of existing treaty provisions that have an ideological surplus typical of certain types of constitutionalisation – a surplus to which judges can attach themselves in the pursuit of their vision. These provisions were drafted at a time when the belief in a liberal-libertarian end state of world affairs was still intact.

It would also be incorrect to accuse the CJEU judges of unethical behaviour. Most, if not all, CJEU judges are likely to share a political vision according to which the political finality of the European integration movement leads to a libertarian-egalitarian, market-oriented, and globalist end state. Judges with a specific socialisation, are thus committed to a specific political vision of positive co-existence, which is challenged by the rise of national conservatism and illiberalism. It would therefore be wrong to assume that the judges behind the case law see themselves only as instruments of political majorities. The same applies to those assistants who support the CJEU from positions in science and policy advice. There are manifold interactions between the judicial decision-making behaviour of the actors in Luxembourg and the political developments in the socio-political and socio-cultural spheres that cannot simply be resolved in one direction. Such questions of causality are not relevant for constitutional theory analyses. Members of the CJEU are required to differentiate between their political self-understanding as citizens of the states and the Union and their position as judges. The function of legal analysis and criticism of judicial decisions is missed if observers content themselves with repeating the CJEU's praise of liberal values and commenting favourably on its statements on identity politics.

The EU Member States therefore also bear significant responsibility for this development. It is the EU Member States that prepare the ground for

---

[20] R. Hirschl, *Towards Juristocracy. The Orgins and Consequences of the New Constitutionalism*, Cambridge (MA) 2004.

judicial decisions: they make hesitant compromises, anchor vague formulations in EU treaty law, and, where they cannot resolve tough conflicts, rejoice in the constitutionalisation of visionary idealistic ideas and programmatic promises. In addition, political forces are often too divided, too weak, and too timid to make political decisions on the future of the EU in the appropriate procedures (Article 48 TEU). At the same time, the judges of the CJEU are expected by the Member States to react to actual or perceived undesirable developments. Judicial restraint in this situation requires a high degree of self-discipline and an official ethos that prioritizes the protection of democratic processes over the possibility of inscribing one's own vision of the future in case law.

7. The decline of democraticity

Constitutional ideas and concepts are like medicine: when applied wisely and appropriately, they can properly direct the political process and prevent undesirable developments. However, if they are applied wrongly or to an inappropriate extent, they destroy what they claim to protect. Constitutional concepts and structures are supposed to frame decision-making processes in such a way that the negotiation and decision of political issues fulfil the expectations of the rule of law, democracy, and the common good. The idea of constitutionalism is misunderstood when the institutions responsible for monitoring the political process redefine their role and decide on political issues themselves. The emergence of a juristocracy characterized by over-constitutionalisation can then be observed. Even a politically liberal system can adopt autocratic structures if judges exercise unconstitutional and uncontrolled authority without being legitimized to do so.

In a under democratized political system like that of the EU, any further shift of decision-making power to (administrative or judicial) experts should be cause for concern. The problematic image that the EU presents from the perspective of democratic standards of public autonomy of political subjects is further reinforced. It is irrelevant in this context whether one agrees with the protection of specific political preferences pursued by the CJEU in content or not. The task of constitutional jurisprudence is to advocate for the preservation of open political spaces, even when developments occur there that one personally rejects. This is what distinguishes the ethos of a real scientist from political activism dressed up as academic search for truth.

Is it compatible of the European *rule of law* that the actors of an under-democratized system now curtail democratic processes in the Member States because they observe the emergence of political patterns of an understanding of good governance that break with a former consensus?

Part III

FUNDAMENTAL RIGHTS, DEMOCRACY AND JUDICIAL DIALOGUE: A CRITICAL ANALYSIS

Chapter 11

JUDICIAL REVIEW OF ELECTORAL RIGHTS BETWEEN LUXEMBOURG AND STRASBOURG *

Cristina Fasone

ABSTRACT: *This chapter explores and compares the role played by the Court of Justice of the EU (CJEU) and the European Court of Human Rights (ECtHR) when adjudicating electoral rights. These courts are in a rather awkward position, being very distant and detached from the national constituencies where electoral rights are exercised, while also facing the difficulties which all courts encounter when dealing with such sensitive political issues. Both supranational courts tend to show a deferential approach to national authorities on the matter of electoral rights, although this is much more evident for the CJEU than for the ECtHR due to the differences in their respective jurisdictions. This chapter focuses on the following specific aspects of the two Courts' jurisprudence on elections: the relationship between voting rights, citizenship and problems of discrimination; disenfranchisement, in particular of prisoners; verification of credentials; and parliamentary immunity, especially inviolability when used as an impairment to exercise the right to stand for elections and fulfil the parliamentary mandate. Finally, this chapter draws some conclusions from the comparative analysis of the two courts and highlights prospective trajectories in the supranational adjudication of electoral rights.*

1. The uncomfortable position of supranational courts when adjudicating on elections

The protection of political rights through elections is a very sensitive mat-

---

* This chapter draws on R. Bray and C. Fasone, "The Court of Justice and the European Court of Human Rights on Electoral Matters: Towards a Procedural Conception of Representative Democracy?", in C. Fasone, E. Mostacci, G. Romeo (eds.), *Judicial Review and Electoral Law in a Global Perspective*, Oxford 2024, pp. 149-172.

ter, going to the core of any representative democracy. Indeed, elections are what gives shape to the representative bond between voters and elected politicians, an issue that tends to be very country-specific and context-dependent.

At the same time, the guarantee of fair electoral procedures and access to justice to redress alleged violations of electoral rules are essential to any constitutional democracy. The timeframe for the adjudication of electoral disputes is also crucial. The (judicial) reversal of an electoral result too late during the parliamentary term – for example a seat illegitimately assigned to an MP due to errors in the counting of votes –creates problems of legal certainty and undermines the legitimacy of parliamentary decisions.

At the domestic level, there are several options to design mechanisms for resolutions of electoral disputes: they can be centralised in the hands of the Constitutional Court, like in France for parliamentary elections; they can be deferred to ordinary judges or administrative judges and subsequently 'on appeal' to the Constitutional Tribunal, like in Germany; they can involve independent electoral commissions, like in many Eastern European countries; they can be assigned to the legislature itself, like in Italy for parliamentary elections; finally, they can be conferred to specialised electoral tribunals at the various levels of government, like in Brazil and Mexico.[1]

In any event, adjudicating electoral disputes is an extremely important and delicate task as it interferes with the representative capacity of political institutions and, ultimately, with their ability to validly fulfil their mandates. Moreover, the contestation of electoral results is becoming more and more widespread even in well-established democracies, either before Courts or by means of seditious acts attacking the institutions themselves, as happened with the assault on the U.S. Capitol Building in 2020.[2]

Especially over the last two decades, in the unique European context, the Court of Justice of the European Union (CJEU) and the European Court of Human Rights (ECtHR) have become more and more involved in electoral disputes, sometimes triggering domestic backlash.[3] By their very

---

[1] On the European models adopted to solve electoral disputes, see G. Milani, *Sistemi comparati di giustizia elettorale in Europa*, Padova 2023, Ch. 1.

[2] See, for example, looking solely at the US presidential elections, *Bush v. Gore*, 531 U.S. 98 (2000), *Trump v. Anderson*, 601 U.S. _ (2024) and J Politi, "Ballot bans show how Capitol Hill riots weigh on Donald Trump's 2024 campaign", *Financial Times*, 29 December 2023.

[3] See R Bellamy, "The Democratic Legitimacy of International Human Rights Conventions: Political Constitutionalism and the European Convention on Human Rights", *European Journal of International Law*, 25, 2014, p. 1019.

nature these supranational courts are more distant and detached from the national constituencies where electoral rights are exercised and, thus, they find themselves in an uncomfortable position. Their decisions are liable to alter national political dynamics and standards of democratic competition without always being fully aware of their domestic impact. They have been accused of being irresponsible and unaccountable for their judgments despite the far-reaching consequences on democratic politics.[4] Yet, except for a few controversial cases, both the CJEU and the ECtHR have remained largely deferential to national courts and democratic bodies. For example, it would be unusual for these courts to question electoral formulas and the design of the electoral system.

It should be clarified from the outset, however, that the mandate and the standards of review for the CJEU and the ECtHR are quite different. The CJEU adjudicates almost exclusively on European Parliament's elections but in principle, it could be also involved in cases dealing with local elections where the rights of European citizens residing and voting in other Member States have been impaired. Moreover, due to the division of competences between the domestic and the supranational level, the CJEU can only rule on the common electoral principles set in the European Electoral Act of 1976 as amended.[5] Indeed, the main standards for the CJEU's review in electoral matters are represented by this Act, which defers the greatest part of the legislation on European elections to the Member States,[6] and by the Protocol on Immunities of 1965. In prospect and depending on how the problem of the rule of law backsliding evolves, the CJEU may be called to adjudicate on democratic problems surrounding national elections, but this possibility appears quite remote right now and would require a significant exercise in extensive, if not creative, interpretation of the Treaty bases (especially Articles 2 and 10 of the Treaty on European Union (TEU)). After all, protection of representative democracy was not one of the core tasks with which the European Community was entrusted.[7]

---

[4] *Ibidem.*

[5] The latest amendment to the Act is contained in Council Decision (EU, Euratom) 2018/994 of 13 July 2018, still pending approval in Spain, under Article 223 TFEU. For instance, the common electoral principles include the choice for a proportional electoral formula and the prohibition of a double parliamentary mandate, at both the national and European level.

[6] Lacking a uniform electoral procedure under Article 223 TFEU.

[7] G.F. Mancini, D.T. Keeling, "Democracy and the European Court of Justice", *Modern Law Review*, 57, 1994, p. 175; G. de Burca, "The Road Not Taken: The European Union as a Global Human Rights Actor", *American Journal of International Law*, 105, 2011, p. 649.

The standpoint of the ECtHR is instead different. It is true that, due to the opposition of some delegations, notably the UK, when the ECHR was drafted in 1950, electoral rights were not included in the text of the Convention. However, two years later a clear reference to elections was inserted in Article 3, Protocol n. 1 to the ECHR. Many have emphasised the wording of this Article, which does not recognize an individual right to vote and to be elected, but is framed as an obligation for the Contracting Parties.[8] Also taking stock of the position of the European Commission on Human Rights, starting from the seminal judgment in *Mathieu-Mohin and Clerfayt v Belgium*, in 1987,[9] the ECtHR derived from this Article both the right to vote and the right to stand for elections, at local, national and European level.[10] This unexpected move of judicial interpretation by the ECtHR has been criticised for not being thoroughly justified or explained in the judgment at stake and in further decisions,[11] but has certainly paved the way to a much more significant role for the Court in the electoral domain.[12] Such a development does not automatically imply a very intrusive approach of the ECtHR on elections, but it is clear that the protection of representative democracy is somewhat in the DNA of this Court's mandate, also drawing and often citing the work of the Venice Commission, which put together a Code of good practice on electoral matters in 2002. It is evident that the ECtHR is in general quite cautious when reviewing domestic electoral legislation. However, on the one hand, the Court tends to be more lenient toward Western democracies, with very few exceptions, than with Eastern European countries, especially where processes of democratic backsliding are ongoing.[13] On the other hand, also in other remits, for example on law-

---

[8] According to this Article:

The High Contracting Parties undertake to hold free elections at reasonable intervals by secret ballot, under conditions which will ensure the free expression of the opinion of the electorate in the choice of the legislature.

[9] ECtHR, *Mathieu-Mohin and Clerfayt v Belgium*, Application n. 9267/81, 2 March 1987.

[10] On the European elections, see ECtHR, *Matthews v. UK*, Application n. 40302/98, 18 February 1999.

[11] A. Ruiz Robledo, "The Construction of the Right to Free Elections by the European Court of Human Right", *Cambridge International Law Journal*, 7, 2018, p. 227 ff. and J. García Roca, I. García Vitoria, "Del compromiso internacional de los Estados de organizar elecctioner libres al derecho de sufragio de los ciudadanos", in J. García Roca, P. Santolaya Marchetti, M. Pérez-Moneo (eds.), *La Europa de los Derechos. El Convenio Europeo de Derechos Humanos*, Madrid 2023, pp. 1113-1153.

[12] D. Kurnosov, "Pragmatic Adjudication of Election Cases in the European Court of Human Rights", *European Journal of International Law*, 32, 2021, p. 256.

[13] P Popelier, "L.B. v. Hungary and the Quality of the Parliamentary Debate", *Quaderni costituzionali*, 3, 2023, p. 676.

making, the ECtHR has become quite keen to adjudicate on the quality of democratic procedures in order to ensure "'tolerance, pluralism and broadmindedness' of the deliberation,[14]" a standard fit to apply to electoral procedures too.

This chapter will proceed as follows: it will first provide some basic elements to compare the case law of the ECtHR and the CJEU on electoral matters. Then, it will focus on the following specific aspects of the two Courts' jurisprudence on elections: the relationship between voting rights, citizenship and problems of discrimination; disenfranchisement, in particular of prisoners; verification of credentials; and parliamentary immunity, especially inviolability when used as an impairment to exercise the right to stand for elections and fulfil the parliamentary mandate. Finally, it will draw some conclusions from the comparative analysis of the two courts and highlight prospective trajectories in the supranational adjudication of electoral rights.

2. A comparison between the ECtHR and the CJEU on the matter of electoral rights

To begin, the focus of the jurisdiction of the two supranational Courts is quite diverse. While the ECtHR was conceived as a human rights court, the CJEU was established as a court of a project of regional integration, in particular economic integration following the failure of the European Political Community in 1954.[15] Indeed, the CJEU became the engine of such integration, devising structural principles from direct effect to primacy, to forge a strong legal community where EU law could be applied as evenly as possible. Over the years, however, since the 1970s and even more so after the turning points of the Maastricht and the Lisbon Treaties, with the entry into force of the Charter, the CJEU started developing and consolidating a body of case law focused on fundamental rights' protection. It drew on the constitutional traditions common to the Member States and, not by chance, on the ECHR and on the Strasbourg jurisprudence, taking stock of the EU countries' membership of the Council of Europe and of the wording of Article 6 TEU which recalls the Convention.

Notwithstanding the different origin, still a very limited portion of these two Courts' case law deals with electoral matters, with the CJEU covering a lower proportion given the constraints of its legal bases and the eminent

[14] Since ECtHR, *Handyside v United Kingdom*, Application n. 5493/72, 7 December 1976, para. 50. See A. Zysset, "Calibrating the response to populism at the European Court of Human Rights", *ICON*, 20, 2022, p. 994.

[15] G. de Burca, *op. cit.*, p. 664.

focus on the European elections. Moreover, while the ECtHR reviews the compliance of domestic measures with the ECHR, the CJEU cannot directly target domestic law, at least in principle.[16]

The number of electoral cases in both Courts has however increased significantly over the last few years. It is possible that domestic constitutional crises, ranging from secession, Brexit, and the rule of law backsliding in Eastern Europe, have accelerated this trend toward more electoral disputes reaching supranational Courts.

Overall, the attitude of the Courts when adjudicating electoral matters has been quite cautious and both of them concede significant leeway in the way the electoral system is designed domestically. For the CJEU this is somewhat implicit in the circumstance that the Court has never been given the possibility to decide on the correct implementation of the common electoral principles enshrined in the European Electoral Act, despite the many cases brought before national Constitutional Courts on the electoral thresholds for the European Parliament's elections.[17] Nor, in principle, could the CJEU enter into the realm of the national legislation regulating the European elections, for example on the electoral campaign.

In *Mathieu-Mohin and Clerfayt v Belgium* the ECtHR patently stated that any electoral system can be legitimate. It "must be assessed in the light of the political evolution of the country concerned; features that would be unacceptable in the context of one system may accordingly be justified in the context of another, at least so long as the chosen system provides for conditions which will ensure the 'free expression of the opinion of the people in the choice of the legislature'".[18] From this reasoning of the Court and despite the difficulty for minorities to enter Parliament, it followed that even the nationwide electoral threshold as high as 10% in the election of the Turkish unicameral legislature was considered in line with Article 3, Protocol n. 1.[19] Moreover, the ECtHR does not impose any specific eligibility criteria to stand for elections.[20]

---

[16] On the way the CJEU try to circumvent this limit, see F. Nicola, C. Fasone, D. Gallo, "Comparing the Procedures and Practice of Judicial Dialogue in the US and the EU: Effects on US Unconstitutionality and EU's Preliminary Interpretive Rulings", 3 *EJLS* (2023). Special Issue. p. 156 ff.

[17] See German Constitutional Tribunal, Judgment of 9 November 2011, Second Senate, 2 BvC 4/10; Judgment of 26 February 2014, Second Senate, 2 BvE 2/13, 2 BvR 2238/13, 2 BvR 2221/13, 2 be 12/13, 2 BvE 10/13, 2 BvE 9/13, 2 BvE 8/13, 2 BvE 7/13, 2 BvE 6/13, 2 BvE 5/13, 2 BvR 2220/13; Italian Constitutional Court, Judgment 10/2025; Czech Constitutional Court, Pl. ÚS 14/14 of 19 May 2015.

[18] ECtHR, *Mathieu-Mohin and Clerfayt v Belgium*, para. 54.

[19] ECtHR, *Yumak and Sadak v Turkey,* Application n. 10226/03, 8 July 2008.

[20] ECtHR, *Berlusconi v Italy*, Application n. 58428/13, 27 November 2018. Howev-

While the CJEU (at present, at least) does not rule on systemic aspects of the electoral system, such as the existence of effective legal remedies and access to justice against violation of electoral rules or the stability of electoral legislation, these issues have been addressed by the ECtHR in some cases, using Article 6 ECHR, the right to fair trial, as the standard for review, alone or together with Article 3, Protocol n. 1. In *Ekoglasnost, for example,* the Strasbourg Court condemned Bulgaria for amending the electoral law two months before the national elections, thereby affecting the predictability and certainty of electoral rules.[21] The Court confirmed the link between conventional legality and the stability of the Bulgarian cardinal rules on the voting system during the pre-electoral year, as changes therein could lead to the perception of a link with contingent interests, which, in extreme cases, could "benefit the political parties in power" and therefore constitute a "practice incompatible with democratic order".

In the next sections the comparison between the two Courts will be grounded on cases dealing with the same or similar aspects of electoral legislation.

2.1. Voting rights, citizenship and discrimination

One interesting body of case law that both Courts have developed – though, for the reasons already explained, the jurisprudence of the ECtHR is more extended – relates to alleged problems of discrimination in the exercise of voting rights, often connected to the enjoyment of the status of national or European citizen.

In *Spain v UK*, the CJEU ruled on the UK extension of voting rights in the European elections to third country nationals resident in Gibraltar.[22] As neither the Treaty nor the Act of 1976 define precisely who is entitled to vote and stand in the elections, this competence falls within the Member States' remit, in compliance with EU law principles, such as the principle of non-discrimination. The Court held that the people who are granted such electoral rights – despite not being European citizens – must have a close link with the Member State in question and that in any case the Member

er, as we will see, the Court can consider (discriminatory) national criteria to exercise voting rights in breach of the ECHR.

[21] ECtHR, *Ekoglasnost v Bulgaria*, Application n. 30386/05, 6 November 2012.

[22] CJEU, Judgment of 12 September 2006, *Spain v UK*, C-145/04, ECLI:EU:C:2006:543; see S. Adam, "Electoral Rights under the Review of the European Court of Justice: Judicial Trends and Constitutional Weakness", *Croatian Yearbook of European Law and Policy*, 3, 2008, p. 415, p. 426 ff.

States must observe Community law and the classical principles of equality and proportionality.

The same reasoning on equal treatment applied to the opposite situation, which arose in *Eman and Selvinger.*[23] In that case, what was contested was the Dutch legislation excluding certain categories of their own nationals residing in one of the overseas territories associated with the Community (OCTs), Aruba, from voting in European elections. The CJEU held that Member States can define the criteria for exercising voting rights in these elections, provided that the principle of equal treatment is respected: the requirement of residence is not inappropriate per se, but the Dutch authorities had failed to justify the difference in treatment between Dutch nationals residing in one of the OCTs and Dutch citizens residing in other countries outside the EU, who, instead, were entitled to vote. This led, according to the Court, to patent and unreasonable discrimination.

In both cases, whose rulings were delivered before the Treaty of Lisbon was in force and therefore also before the acknowledgment that the European Parliament represents European citizens (Article 14 TEU), the Court was clear that the acknowledgment of electoral rights should be grounded on clear and strong bonds between the prospective voters and the territory, the historical roots and the tradition of the Member States. Moreover, the Court has also been attentive to cases of unreasonable and unjustified discrimination stemming from an exclusion from the community of EU voters. Equal treatment is a key principle in that respect and, in the view of the CJEU, limitations of voting rights should be based on objective reasons.

On this ground and in the post-Brexit context, the CJEU has reasserted the fundamental relationship between EU citizenship and voting rights in *EP v Préfet du Gers.*[24] The Court considered a request for a preliminary ruling arising out of the refusal by a local mayor to register a UK national on the special electoral roll for non-French citizens of the EU. Following the entry into force of the Withdrawal Agreement on 1 February 2020, the person concerned had had their name removed from the French electoral roll despite having resided in France for 38 years and being married to a French citizen. The mayor made reference to the UK rule by which UK nationals having resided abroad for more than 15 years are no longer entitled to take part in elections in that state. The entry into force of the Withdrawal Agreement

[23] CJEU, Judgment of 12 September 2006, *Eman and Selvinger*, C-300/04, ECLI:EU:C:2006:545. See P. De Groot, N. Luk, "Twenty Years of CJEU Jurisprudence on Citizenship", *German Law Journal*, 15, 2014, p. 825 ff.

[24] Judgment of 9 June 2022, *EP v Préfet du Gers and Institut national de la statistique et des études économiques*, C-673/20, ECLI:EU:C:2022:449.

triggered the loss of the fundamental status of EU citizen for UK nationals and, with that, of the right to vote and to stand as a candidate in the European and municipal elections. For the CJEU, it was irrelevant that UK nationals had previously exercised their right to reside in a Member State. As regards the fact that the applicant was also deprived of the vote in the UK, that was an automatic consequence of the UK's decision to withdraw from the EU and the 15-year rule was a choice of UK electoral law.

Likewise, at the ECtHR, most of the alleged electoral rights' limitations that come under its scrutiny essentially refer to equality of treatment of voters and candidates.[25] *Matthews v UK* (see *supra*), where UK citizens residing in Gibraltar were denied the possibility to vote in the European elections, was only indirectly related to the later infringement proceeding at the centre of *Spain v. UK* where the CJEU cited extensively the decision of the Strasbourg Court. Indeed, in 1999 the ECtHR considered that, even though Member States enjoy a broad margin of appreciation in imposing conditions on the right to vote, they cannot curtail the right to vote to such an extent as to impair its very essence and deprive it of effectiveness and, thus, condemned the UK for violation of Article 3, Protocol n. 1. As a consequence, the UK allowed nationals residing in Gibraltar to vote in the European elections from 2004 onward.

By contrast, in *Sitaropoulos and Giakoumopoulos v Greece*, where Greek citizens residing abroad alleged that their inability to vote for the Parliament from their place of residence amounted to disproportionate interference with the exercise of their right to vote, the Court considered that no infringement of Article 3, Protocol n. 1, had been committed. It did so on the basis of a comprehensive comparative law analysis of Member States' legislation which showed that most countries subject the exercise of the right to vote to residence requirements. Instead, a legislative ban on candidates holding multiple citizenship standing in parliamentary elections has been deemed an unjustified and disproportionate measure which conflicts with Article 3, Protocol n. 1.[26]

On limited occasions, where the protection of electoral rights was found to be impaired in its essence vis-à-vis the democratic process, the Court has issued pilot judgments and found against the Member State. In *Sejdić and Finci v Bosnia and Herzegovina* the ECtHR had to review the exclusion of the right of the two complainants, national citizens, to stand for election to the second chamber of the Federal Parliament and the federal collective

[25] For discrimination between candidates wishing to stand for election, see *Aziz v Cyprus*, Application n. 69949/01, 22 June 2004.

[26] ECtHR, *Tănase v Moldova*, Application n. 7/08, 27 April 2010.

Presidency owing to their Roma and Jewish origins.[27] Indeed, the state Constitution acknowledged (and still recognises) the right to stand in those elections as being vested only in the 'constituent peoples' of Bosnia and Herzegovina, notably Bosniaks, Croats and Serbs, with a view to the restoration of peace in a post-conflict and ethnically divided context. For the Court, such a total ban could by no means withstand the proportionality assessment as it lacked an objective and reasonable justification. Consequently, the Court found a violation of Article 14 ECHR – which, on the basis of the consolidated case-law of the ECtHR, is never used as a stand-alone clause of review – in conjunction with Article 3, Protocol n. 1, as well as of Article 1, Protocol n. 12, for the exclusion from the presidential elections. The landmark ruling, which has yet to be implemented after 15 years, left unaddressed the problematic domestic accommodation between ethnic divisions and political representation.

The issue was taken up recently in a major ECtHR's judgment, *Kovačević v Bosnia and Herzegovina*, where the Court acknowledged the violation of the applicant's right under Article 1, Protocol n. 12 with regard to the composition of the lower chamber of the federal Parliament and the election of the Presidency considering that the emphasis on ethnic representation in the institutional design impaired the effective political participation of all citizens.[28] For the ECtHR, "the current arrangements render ethnic considerations and/or representation more relevant than political, economic, social, philosophical and other considerations and/or representation and thus amplify ethnic divisions in the country and undermine the democratic character of elections" (para. 56).

2.2. Disenfranchisement

The ECtHR has also ruled on several cases involving the disenfranchisement of the claimants for reasons other than nationality and residence. In general, on the prisoners' voting ban, the Court has assured the Member States a wide margin of appreciation,[29] but has clarified in *Hirst n. 2*,[30] the

---

[27] ECtHR, *Sejdić and Finci v Bosnia and Herzegovina*, Application n. 27996/06 and n. 34836/06, 22 December 2009.

[28] ECtHR, *Kovačević v Bosnia and Herzegovina*, Application n. 43651/22, 29 August 2023. See J. Woelk, "Opening Pandora's Box?: On the Kovačević Case and the European Court of Human Rights' fundamental criticism of the electoral system in Bosnia and Herzegovina", *VerfBlog*, 1 September 2023, https://verfassungsblog.de/opening-pandoras-box/

[29] A. Zysset, *op. cit.*, p. 999.

pilot judgment in the field, that no violation of Article 3, Protocol n. 1, is to be detected unless, as in that case, disenfranchisement is to be considered "general, automatic and indiscriminate", and, hence, disproportionate. Consequently, in *Frodl v Austria*, Austria was condemned for violating Article 3, Protocol n. 1, because the disenfranchisement of the prisoner, Mr Frodl, had not been declared by a judge and there was no connection between the criminal offence and the sanction on elections.[31] In the subsequent case-law, the ECtHR adopted a very cautious approach with regard to prisoners' disenfranchisement in long-standing democracies. For instance in *Scoppola v Italy (n. 3)*, the Grand Chamber referred to the "historical development, cultural diversity and political thought within Europe" to justify its deference to national legislation.[32]

The reasoning of the Court developed in *Hirst n. 2* applies as well to cases of a "permanent and irreversible ban" against people affected by mental disability: if a blanket prohibition is considered in breach of the ECHR,[33] the enforcement of disenfranchisement conditions only to those persons who are effectively unable to make a free and self-determined electoral choice has been justified by the Court.[34]

It appears that the ECtHR has adopted a very different attitude in recent years when dealing with limitations of electoral rights in authoritarian regimes compared to consolidated democracies.[35] A strict approach to disenfranchisement was for example followed in *Söyler v Turkey*[36] where Turkey imposed a general voting ban on all those who committed intentional crimes, and in relation to Russia and its Constitutional Court: the Russian constitutional provisions on prisoners' disenfranchisement have been at the centre of a fierce 'battle' with the Strasbourg Court. This – disputably – led the Russian Constitutional Court, in 2016, to consider the ECtHR judgment in *Anchugov and Gadkov v Russia*, where the country was found to have violated the ECHR, as unenforceable.[37]

---

[30] ECtHR, *Hirst n. 2 v the United Kingdom*, Application n. 74025/01, 6 October 2005, not yet fully implemented, on which see, critically, R. Bellamy, *op. cit.*, p. 1019 ff. and D. Kurnosov, *op. cit.*, p. 276 ff.

[31] ECtHR, *Frodl v Austria*, Application n. 20201/04, 8 April 2010.

[32] ECtHR, *Scoppola v Italy (No. 3)*, Application n. 126/05, 22 May 2012.

[33] See ECtHR, *Alajos Kiss v Hungary*. Application n. 38832/06, 20 May 2010.

[34] See ECtHR, *Caamaño Valle v Spain*, Application n. 43564/17, 11 May 2021.

[35] Again, on this double standard, see in detail Ø. Stiansen, E. Voeten, "Backlash and Judicial Restraint: Evidence from the European Court of Human Rights", *International Studies Quarterly*, 64, 2020, p. 770.

[36] ECtHR, *Söyler v Turkey*, Application n. 29411/07, 17 September 2013.

[37] See ECtHR, *Anchugov and Gladkov*, Application n. 11157/04, 4 July 2013 and the

To date, the CJEU has had the opportunity to rule in just one case of disenfranchisement from the European elections, *Delvigne.*[38] In 2015, the Grand Chamber held that French law depriving some individuals convicted by means of a final judgment of their right to vote was not incompatible with a number of principles of the EU Charter of Fundamental Rights. After noting that Article 8 of the 1976 Act provides that subject to its provisions, the electoral procedure is governed in each Member State by its national law and that Articles 1(3) and 9 of the 1976 Act do not define, expressly and precisely, who can vote and stand as a candidate in elections to the European Parliament, this being a competence which remains with the Member States,[39] it observed that, in exercising that competence, Member States must fulfil the obligation under Article 1(3) of the Act read together with Article 14(3) TEU.[40] The Court took the view that in adopting legislation to that effect, even where it deprives an EU citizen of the right to vote in the European elections, it is fulfilling that obligation and hence implementing Union law for the purposes of the Charter.

The Court then held that the limitation on the exercise of the right to vote as enshrined in Article 39(2) of the Charter complied with Article 52(1)[41] of the Charter, asserting that the deprivation of the right to vote is "provided for by law" and "respects the essence" of this right because it "does not call into question that right as such, since it has the effect of excluding certain persons, under specific conditions and on account of their conduct, from those entitled to vote in elections to the Parliament". It held that it pursued a legitimate objective and did not conflict with the principle of proportionality since it "takes into account the nature and gravity of the criminal offence committed and the duration of the penalty".[42] In reaching this conclusion and unlike the Advocate General,[43] the Court made no reference to the rich case law of the ECtHR on the matter.

---

judgment of the Constitutional Court of the Russia Federation, Judgment n. 12-П, 19 April 2016.

[38] Judgment of 6 October 2015, *Delvigne v Commune de Lesparre Médoc and Préfet de la Gironde,* C-650/13, ECLI:EU:C:2015:648.

[39] See section 2.1. above.

[40] "The members of the European Parliament shall be elected for a term of five years by direct universal suffrage in a free and secret ballot".

[41] Any limitation on the exercise of the rights and freedoms recognised by this Charter must be provided for by law and respect the essence of those rights and freedoms. Subject to the principle of proportionality, limitations may be made only if they are necessary and genuinely meet objectives of general interest recognised by the Union or the need to protect the rights and freedoms of others.

[42] CJEU, *Delvigne* (n. 43) paras. 47-49.

[43] Opinion of Advocate General Cruz Villalón, delivered on 4 June 2015,

2.3. Verification of credentials

At the EU level, the leading case on the verification of the credentials is *Italy and Donnici* v *Parliament.*[44] In this case, the European Parliament had claimed that, in verifying the credentials of MEPs, it could leave unapplied the appointment of a candidate effected by the national authorities in the event of an infringement of the free exercise of the parliamentary mandate or the principles of universal and proportional suffrage. The Court held, categorically, that the Parliament had a 'complete lack of discretion in the matter' since Article 12 of the 1976 Act provided that, for the purposes of verifying the credentials of its members, Parliament was to "take note" of the results declared officially by the Member States and rule on any dispute which may arise out of the provisions of that Act other than those arising out of the national provisions to which the Act refers.[45]

Although the Member States had to comply with the 1976 Act in so far as it prescribed certain electoral procedures, they had the task of organising the elections in accordance with their national law, counting the votes and making the official declaration of the results. Under Article 13(2) each Member State is required to lay down appropriate procedures for filling seats which become vacant. Moreover, in the absence of EU rules, the domestic legal system of each Member State must designate the competent courts and lay down procedural rules governing actions for safeguarding rights derived by individuals from EU law.[46] The only requirements are that those rules must not be less favourable than those governing rights which originate in domestic law and that they do not render virtually impossible or excessively difficult the exercise of rights conferred by EU law (principles of equivalence and effectiveness).

If the CJEU has adopted clear self-restraint on the verification of MEPs' credentials given the division of competences between EU and national law, the ECtHR has ruled in very few cases on the matter – in domestic elections only – but with far-reaching consequences on the national legal systems at stake. Typically, the ECtHR has linked the guarantees offered by the verification procedure for MEPs' credentials both to the right to fulfil the electoral mandate derived from the right to stand as an electoral candi-

ECLI:EU:C:2015:363, paras. 117–19, citing *Hirst v United Kingdom* (n. 2) [GC] n. 74026/01, 2005-IX, *Frodl v Austria*, n. 20201/04 and *Scoppola* v *Italy* (n. 3) [GC], n. 126/05.

[44] CJEU, Judgment of 30 April 2009, *Italy and Donnici v Parliament,* C-393/07 and C-9/08, ECLI:EU:C:2009:275, paras. 50-73.

[45] *Ivi*, paras. 50 ff.

[46] *Ivi*, paras. 60-63.

date (Article 3, Protocol n. 1) and to the right to an effective remedy (Article 13 ECHR).

In *Grosaru v Romania* the applicant claimed that Article 13 ECHR had been violated in conjunction with Article 3, Protocol n. 1, as he had no effective and impartial remedies against Parliament's refusal to him allocate a seat as a representative of the Italian minority in Romania.[47] According to Court majority, the Romanian electoral legislation violated the standards invoked as no court could intervene in the proceedings, so there was no effective system of appeal.

By the same token, in *Mugemangango v Belgium*,[48] where the complaint requested the recount of ballot papers in a situation where the candidate was 14 votes short of taking a seat, the Court found a violation of Article 3, Protocol n. 1, both alone and in conjunction with Article 13, as the parliamentary body examining the request lacked impartiality insofar as it included members of Parliament whose election could have been called into question. The procedure was deficient in terms of safeguards for the parties and the body involved enjoyed too broad a discretion, without a mandate sufficiently clarified by the law. As a consequence of these two judgments the respective legal systems had to be (and were) reformed to be put in line with the ECtHR case law.

2.4. Inviolability of parliamentarians and the right to stand for elections

The CJEU has had the opportunity to decide on parliamentary immunity and, especially on inviolability, of MEPs on quite a few cases. With this regard, the Court has always stressed that the objectives of immunities are to ensure that the EU institutions have full and effective protection against hindrances or risks to their proper functioning and independence.[49]

Tacking stock of the very narrow leeway at disposal on the verification of the MEPs' credentials, the CJEU decided to frame the famous *Junqueras Vies* case as related to parliamentary immunities, a field where it enjoys a broader margin of manoeuvre.[50] The ruling forms part of the judicial 'saga'

[47] ECtHR, *Grosaru v Romania*, Application n. 78039/01, 2 June 2010.

[48] ECtHR, *Mugemangango v Belgium*, Application n. 310/15, 10 July 2020.

[49] Judgment of 10 July 1986, *Wybot*, 149/85, EU:C:1986:310, paras. 12 and 22; order of 13 July 1990, *Zwartveld and Others*, C-2/88 IMM, EU:C:1990:315, para. 19, and Judgment of 22 March 2007, *Commission v Belgium*, C-437/04, EU:C:2007:178, para. 56.

[50] Although, in principle, the framing of case C-502/19 under the remit of the verification of credentials was certainly possible: see S. Hardt, "Select Fault Lines of the Eu-

concerning the election of Catalan secessionist leaders as MEPs who have been charged under Spanish criminal law with rebellion, sedition and misuse of public funds.

For the Court, given that the functioning of the Union is founded on the principle of representative democracy (Article 10 TEU), the status of MEP arises from being elected by direct universal suffrage in a free and secret ballot, while the term of office of the Members of that institution constitutes the main attribute of that status. Consequently, the acquisition of the status of MEP, for the purposes of Article 9 of the Protocol on privileges and immunities, occurs because of and at the time of the official declaration of the election results carried out by the Member States. The 1976 Act makes it clear that the term of office of MEPs begins and ends at the same time as that five-year legislative period. On that basis, the immunities granted to MEPs are intended to ensure the independence of the European Parliament in the performance of its tasks. To this end, the CJEU has cited the ECtHR's rich case law on the different forms of parliamentary immunity established in democratic political systems.[51]

The MEPs' immunity also serves to ensure the effectiveness of the right to stand as a candidate in elections guaranteed by Article 39(2) of the Charter, which constitutes the expression in the Charter of the principle of direct universal suffrage in a free and secret ballot enshrined in Article 14(3) TEU and Article 1(3) of the 1976 Act, by allowing persons who have been elected Members of the European Parliament to complete the necessary steps to take their seats. Accordingly, a person who was officially declared elected to the European Parliament while the subject of a measure of provisional detention in the context of proceedings in respect of serious criminal offences, but who was not authorised to comply with certain requirements under national law following such a declaration – namely to swear allegiance to the Spanish Constitution – and to travel to the European Parliament, in order to take part in its first sitting, must be regarded as enjoying immunity under the second paragraph of Article 9 of the Protocol. The Court further held that the immunity laid down in the second paragraph of Article 9 of the Protocol precludes, *inter alia*, that a measure of provisional

ropean Parliamentary Mandate: The Immunity of Oriol Junqueras Vies: ECJ 19 December 2019, Case C-502/19, Junqueras", 16 *European Constitutional Law Review* (2020), p. 170 and C. Fasone, N. Lupo, "The Court of Justice on the Junqueras saga: Interpreting the European parliamentary immunities in light of the democratic principle", 57 *Common Market Law Review* (2020), p. 1527.

[51] ECtHR, *Karácsony and Others v Hungary*, Application n. 42461/13, 17 May 2016, para. 138, and ECtHR, *Uspaskich v Lithuania*, Application n. 14737/08, 20 December 2016, para. 98.

detention may impede the freedom of MEPs to travel to the place where the first sitting of the new parliamentary term is to take place, in order to complete the formalities required by the 1976 Act.

However, in the latest decision in the saga of the Catalan MEPs,[52] the General Court provided a narrower reading of the parliamentary immunities and of the formal acquisition of the parliamentary status compared to the *Junqueras* case, where the CJEU appeared to envisage an automatism between the declaration of the official results of the elections and the start of the MEPs' mandate and to consider void any further national requirement to this end. On 6 July 2022, more than three years after the European elections, the General Court ruled in a case concerning candidates whose names appeared on the original list of candidates elected to the European Parliament, but had had both their request for withdrawal of the arrest warrants concerning them and their request to sign the declaration of allegiance to the Spanish Constitution remotely refused.[53] The Court held that the President of Parliament could not prevent the Kingdom of Spain from setting the requirement to swear an oath to respect the Constitution, and the General Court had no jurisdiction to assess the legality of that requirement under national or EU law. Those questions fell within the jurisdiction of the national courts or the Court of Justice in the case of an action for failure to fulfil obligations under Article 258 TFEU or a request for a preliminary ruling on interpretation under Article 267 TFEU, but the latter was precisely the circumstance of the *Junqueras* case.

When looking at the ECtHR, instead, the case law on parliamentary immunity and inviolability has led it to make very significant and clear-cut statements of principle on the close connection between electoral rights, right to fulfil the MP mandate and immunity. For the ECtHR, Article 3, Protocol n. 1 "would be merely illusory if elected representatives or their voters could be arbitrarily deprived of them [*i.e. the immunities*] at any moment".[54]

Until a few years ago, cases where an MP was deprived of their liberty were predominantly adjudicated on the grounds of Article 6 ECHR, the right to fair trial.[55] Regarding Article 3, Protocol n. 1, the central issue to

---

[52] See C. Fasone, N. Lupo, *op. cit.*, p. 1527 ff.

[53] Judgment of 6 July 2022, *Puigdemont i Casamajó and Comín i Oliveres v European Parliament,* T-388/19, ECLI:EU:T:2022:421 (under appeal as Case C-600/22 P).

[54] ECtHR, *Lykourezos v Greece*, Application n. 33554/03, 15 June 2006, para. 56.

[55] See, for example, ECtHR, *Tsalkitzis v Greece*, Application n. 11801/04,16 November 2006; *Kart v Turkey*, Application n. 8917/05, 8 July 2008, *Syngelidis v Greece*, Application n. 24895/07, 11 February 2011,

be ascertained by the ECtHR is whether the effects of the pre-trial detention of a candidate in parliamentary elections or of an elected member of Parliament essentially impair the ability of the member to perform their parliamentary duties. The article does not prevent the imposition of measures depriving elected representatives of their liberty as such, but domestic courts in particular have to weigh up the public interest pursued through the restrictive measures against the right of the person subject to custody and explore whether less restrictive means could have been used. Moreover, the ECtHR attaches considerable importance in this balancing exercise to whether the criminal charges against the MPs have a political basis.[56]

In *Selahattin Demirtaş*, the Grand Chamber found multiple violations of the Convention, namely of Article 5, paras. 1 and 3 (right to liberty and security), Article 10, on the freedom of expression, and, notably of Article 18 in combination with Article 5 ECHR.[57] Interestingly it also considered Article 3, Protocol n. 1 violated where, by virtue of a constitutional amendment passed in 2016 in Turkey with retroactive effects, Selahattin Demirtaş was stripped of his parliamentary immunity. A member of the Turkish National Assembly from 2007 to 2018, he was a prominent political figure in the country, the leader of a left-wing pro-Kurdish political party, the main opposition party in Parliament at that time, and a former candidate in the presidential elections. Charged with being a member of an armed terrorist organisation and of public incitement to commit an offence, he had been placed in pre-trial detention since 2016. The Court held that the prolonged pre-trial detention was unreasonable, disproportionate and a consequence of political charges. Although the claimant was formally able to keep the status of MP, "it was effectively impossible for him to take part in the activities of the National Assembly on account of his pre-trial detention", which thereby "constitutes an unjustified interference with the free expression of the opinion of the people and with his own right to be elected and to sit in Parliament".[58]

3. Conclusion

While both supranational courts have managed to keep a rather deferential approach vis-à-vis national law when dealing with electoral rights, it is clear

[56] ECtHR, *Uspaskich v Lithuania*, note 51, para. 94.

[57] ECtHR, *Selahattin Demirtaş v Turkey* (n. 2), Application n. 14305/17, 22 December 2020.

[58] *Ivi*, para. 397.

that the jurisdiction of the CJEU and the limits of the EU competences constrain this Court much more than its Strasbourg counterpart. Since the 1987 landmark decision in *Mathieu-Mohin,* the ECtHR has offered a creative interpretation of Article 3, Protocol n. 1, shifting the focus from the duty of the Contracting Parties to provide for free and competitive elections to the individual rights to vote and to stand for elections. This has led the ECtHR to enrich its case law on electoral matters also protecting the stability of electoral legislation, access to justice and effective legal remedies against unfair or fraudulent electoral procedures, in addition to rulings addressing alleged discriminations in the exercise of electoral rights, the problem of disenfranchisement, the way the verification of MPs' credentials is carried out and the link between parliamentary immunity and the right to stand for elections. At the same time, the ECtHR has remained reticent to engage with the design of the electoral system and the choice of the electoral formula, which are highly context-dependent.[59]

It is true, however, that the ECtHR has not gone as far as it could in redressing potential violations of electoral rights at the domestic level when verifying MPs' credentials because it has failed to use Article 6 ECHR, the right to fair trial, as the standard of review[60] or when assessing the quality of the electoral process.[61] On this latter point, in the future,, on the one hand, the ECtHR could apply the same benchmark for the procedural rationality review devised when assessing the quality of the decision-making process;[62] on the other, to ascertain whether the national electoral system and its safeguards really assure "free expression of the opinion of the people in the choice of the legislature"[63] the Court could resort to the standards already set for other conventional rights, such as freedom of expression (Article 10 ECHR), notably "tolerance, pluralism and broadmindedness"[64] of the deliberation to assess the credentials of democratic procedures.

At the same time, in the future the CJEU could refer more frequently and extensively to the ECtHR advanced case law also in the matter of electoral rights (as it does already in other fields of law), given the use of the

---

[59] D. Kurnosov, *op. cit.*

[60] G Piccirilli, "Il disallineamento del sistema italiano di verifica dei poteri rispetto al «patrimonio elettorale europeo»", *Il Filangieri 2019*, 2020, p. 193.

[61] A. Zysset, *op. cit.*, p. 994.

[62] P. Popelier, "Procedural Rationality Review after Animal Defenders International: A Constructively Critical Approach", *EU Const,* 15, 2019, p. 272.

[63] ECtHR, *Mathieu-Mohin and Clerfayt v Belgium*, para. 54.

[64] See ECtHR, *Handyside v United Kingdom*, cit., para 50.

ECHR both in Article 6 TEU and in the EU Charter and notwithstanding the fact that the EU accession to the ECHR is still pending. To date, when adjudicating on electoral rights, the citations of the ECtHR jurisprudence by the CJEU have remained confined to a couple of cases (see sections 2.1 and 2.4.).

Finally, especially if the ongoing illiberal drift worsens in the EU, the CJEU could further exploit the potential of the EU Charter, in particular Article 39, combined with Article 2 TEU – the fundamental value of democracy – and Articles 10 and 14 TEU on the principle of representative democracy and the representative function of the European Parliament, respectively. The joint interpretation of these provisions – similarly to what has been done by the CJEU to protect the rule of law – could allow fraudulent conduct before and during the European elections to be redressed. Moreover, as already threatened by the European Commission in the infringement proceeding launched against Poland on 8 June 2023, similar legal bases (except for Article 14 TEU) could ground the EU response against the undemocratic conducts of national authorities meant to impair the electoral competition at domestic level with reverberations on the supranational decision-making. [65]

[65] See, on the so-called "*Lex Tusk*", European Commission, *Rule of Law: Commission launches infringement procedure against POLAND for violating EU law with the new law establishing a special committee*, Press Release, 8 June 2023: https://ec.europa.eu/commission/presscorner/detail/en/ip_23_3134. In that case – where the EU's prompt reaction safeguarded the quality of the electoral competition and, because of that, indirectly, supported a change in the political landscape in the aftermath of the2023 Polish elections – the Charter's provisions invoked were Articles 49 (principle of legality), 47 (right to effective judicial protection), 7 (*ne bis in idem*), and 8 (right to data protection).

Chapter 12

CONSTITUTIONAL ISSUES OF THE USE OF FACIAL RECOGNITION TECHNOLOGY

Raphaël Déchaux

ABSTRACT: *Facial recognition has been one of the most emblematic AI applications since the early 2010s. Although it has obvious security benefits, it is also a technology that raises concerns if it spreads without limits into the public (and private) space of our societies. Its efficiency is often taken for granted by decision-makers and the media alike. However, facial recognition has been under development for over a decade, and no system has yet achieved a satisfactory outcome. The risks here include both the way democracy works and the protection of fundamental rights.*

SUMMARY: 1. From digital government to generalized surveillance. – 2. From enhancing public security to infringing fundamental rights?

Among all artificial intelligence (AI) innovations, one attracts more attention than any other: facial recognition technology (FRT).[1] In the past few years, it has strongly benefited from increased data availability, computing power and the development of sophisticated machine learning algorithms.[2] While FRT is mainly used for law enforcement purposes,[3] the considerable increase in accuracy achieved has prompted many public authorities and private businesses to start using, testing or planning additional uses of FRT around the world. The French government, for example, has authorized mass use of FRT[4] for Paris, the 2024 Olympic Games host city.

Before going further, let us consider a brief definition of FRTs. These

---

[1] We assume that the reader is aware of the major issues at stake in AI law, see. R. Déchaux, "The issues of legal regulation of artificial intelligence", in C. Stamelos (eds.), *Universal Solutions to Global Problems: Holistic Analysis of Law Connecting Theory and Practice*, Cambridge Scholars Publishing, Newcastle-upon-Tyne 2023.

[2] M. Mann, M. Smith, "Automated facial recognition technology: Recent developments and approaches to oversight", *The University of New South Wales Law Journal*, 40, 1, 2017, pp. 121-145.

[3] C. Martin, "Facial Recognition in Law Enforcement", *Seattle Journal for Social Justice*, 19, 1, 2020, pp. 309-346.

[4] A. Guillard, V. Louis, "La loi 'jeux olympiques': l'arbre de l'expérimentation algorithmique cache la forêt de l'extension sécuritaire", *La Revue des droits de l'homme* [Online], 2023.

are AI systems that perform different tasks for different purposes and, in particular, enable three kinds of individual identification: personal, emotional or behavioral. The most common, so far, is the first.[5] A biometric template (*i.e.*, people's facial images captured by CCTV or from a database),[6] can be used "live" or "*ex post*"[7] for verification,[8] identification[9] or categorization.[10] More and more often, additional biometric parameters such as facial micro-expressions, posture, voice, heart rate or temperature are being 'sold' as a way to read human emotions. This is the second type of FRT. The third type is often referred to as "physiognomonic"[11] and has two purposes: detection and assessment. These AIs are designed to first identify a behavior in order to categorize it, which will then permit the implementation of actions or the guidance of operators in the field.[12] Unlike facial recognition, these systems do not necessarily seek to identify a person, but rather unusual events, crowd movements, abandoned objects or situations suggesting offences are being committed.

Facial recognition technology is not a neutral technology. When it becomes commonly used, it will be very difficult to stop its development.[13] However, at present, it is not a safe and secure technology. In this article, we shall focus on two constitutional issues that the use of FRT presents: the

---

[5] European Union Agency for Fundamental Rights, *Facial recognition technology: fundamental rights considerations in the context of law enforcement*, 2019.

[6] Like fingerprints or DNA, facial images are unique.

[7] The AI Act uses the expression "post-remote" FRT.

[8] AI compares two biometric templates, assuming they belong to the same person, to provide identity authentication. It is specifically used for Automated Border Control gates at airports. The biometrics do not necessarily have to be deposited in a central database separated from the software performing comparison: they may be stored in an identity document.

[9] AI compares a person's image with those stored in a central database. Recognition is determined by a score assigned by the software on the basis of this comparison.

[10] AI compares individual characteristics, for example, sex, age, or race, with broad biometric data in order to categorize people into specific groups (profiling).

[11] C. Lequesne Roth, J. Keller, "Surveiller les foules. Pour un encadrement des IA 'Physiognomoniques'", *Observatoire de l'éthique publique* [Online], 2023.

[12] These AIs are intended to enhance the intelligence and efficiency of classic video surveillance.

[13] Italy adopted a regulation to ban FRT from 1 December 2021 to 31 December 2023: https://edri.org/our-work/italy-introduces-a-moratorium-on-video-surveillance-systems-that-use-facial-recognition/. It was inspired by the moratorium proposed by the European Parliament: Resolution of 6 October 2021 *on artificial intelligence in criminal law and its use by the police and judicial authorities in criminal matters* (2020/2016(INI)).

risk of a transformation of our democratic rule of law (par. 1) and the need to protect fundamental rights (par. 2).

1. From digital government to generalized surveillance

FRT is used in both public and private sectors, although constitutional issues concern mainly the former. As already mentioned, recognition AIs are mainly used for law-enforcement and border management. Almost all Western countries have conducted tests using FRT over the last ten years (*i.e.* EU Member States, UK, USA), although the information available is limited, [14] while local police have also been developing this technology, as can be seen in Nice (France). [15] Facial recognition is seen as a crucial technology in the fight against crime and terrorism, akin to phone tracking. More disturbingly perhaps, there have been several attempts to use this technology in schools, for attendance monitoring in Sweden, access control in France, [16] and taking payment in canteens in the UK. Of course, these are just a few examples, and since identification is a very common process in relations between public and administrative bodies, the use of FRT could be expanded infinitely. But, (*A*), is such technology safe? and (*B*) does it comply with liberal and democratic values?

A) A safe form of technology?

Many economic and research stakeholders are wondering: why AI should be regulated and why should we restrict a technology that can facilitate our daily lives and improve our wealth? [17] One key reason is that one of the general issues of deep learning AIs, which we obviously encounter in FRTs, [18] lies in their systemic biases. [19] As they are characterized by a black box effect, *i.e.*, we

[14] European Union Agency for Fundamental Rights, *op. cit.*, p. 11; C. Lequesne Roth (eds.), *La Reconnaissance Faciale dans l'espace public – Une cartographie européenne* [Online], Côte d'Azur University 2020.

[15] After the tragic terrorist attack of 14 July 2016, the city of Nice used FRTs during its famous Carnival.

[16] On 5 December 2023, the French Education Minister, Gabriel Attal, announced the deployment of tutoring services for struggling students via "MIA seconde", an artificial intelligence start-up.

[17] See European Digital SME Alliance, *AI Act Open Letter. Supporting AI Innovators*, 2022, https://digitalsme.eu.

[18] Xiaojun Lai, Pei-Luen Patrick Rau, "Has facial recognition technology been misused? A public perception model of facial recognition scenarios", *Computers in Human Behavior*, 124, 2021.

[19] This has been a shared concern for some time now, see T. Wiehl, "Human and

do not know how the software reaches its decisions,[20] the results should be taken with great caution. For example, there is much 'hype' around the use of emotional recognition[21] but there is no solid scientific evidence to support the idea that it is possible to 'read' a person's emotions or state of mind from their face or other biometric data. It is science fiction for humans, and even more so for AI. Yet this kind of AI was chosen for the external border controls of Greece, Hungary and Latvia in the framework of the Integrated Portable Control System (iBorderCtrl) project,[22] which integrates facial recognition and other technologies to detect if a person is telling the truth. It proved to be a disaster.[23] Accordingly, human rights risks seem unacceptable here,[24] even if the AI Act only categorizes them as "high risk".[25] It appears obvious that emotional recognition could facilitate discrimination against the LGBTQ community[26] or people with mental disabilities.

Computerized Facial Recognition: Comparison and Constitutional Analysis", *Northwestern Interdisciplinary Law Review*, 2013, 6, pp. 95-124; H. Surden, "Machine Learning and Law", *Washington Law Review*, 89, 1, 2014; F. Zuiderveen Borgesius, *Discrimination, artificial intelligence, and algorithmic decision-making. Study for the Council of Europe*, 2018 [Online]; S. Wachter, B. Mittelstadt, C. Russel, "Bias Preservation in Machine Learning: The Legality of Fairness Metrics Under EU Non-Discrimination Law", *West Virginia Law Review*, 123, 3, 2021.

[20] For a technical (and classical) example: M. Tulio Ribeiro, S. Singh, C. Guestrin, "'Why Should I Trust You?' Explaining the Predictions of Any Classifier", *Proceedings of the 22nd ACM SIGKDD international conference on knowledge discovery and data mining*, 2016.

[21] M.R. Islam *et al.*, "Emotion Recognition From EEG Signal Focusing on Deep Learning and Shallow Learning Techniques", *IEEE Access*, 2021, 9.

[22] https://cordis.europa.eu/project/id/700626/eng.

[23] R. Gallagher, L. Jona, "We tested Europe's new lie detector for travelers and immediately triggered a false positive", *The Intercept*, 26 July 2019; S. Stolton, "MEP: Public has a 'right to know' about Commission's lie detector tech", *Euractiv*, 1 April 2020; D. Van Den Meerssche, "Virtual Borders: International Law and the Elusive Inequalities of Algorithmic Association", *European Journal of International Law*, 33, 1, 2022, pp. 171-204; A. Romano, "Fundamental Rights and Emotional Artificial Intelligence in iBorderCtrl: Challenges of Automation in the Migration Field", *Revista Catalana de Dret Public*, 66, 2023, pp. 237-252

[24] L.F. Ortiz-Clavijo, C.J. Gallego-Duque, J.C. David-Diaz, A.F. Ortiz-Zamora, "Implications of Emotion Recognition Technologies: Balancing Privacy and Public Safety", *IEEE Technology and Society Magazine*, 42, 3, 2023, pp. 69-75; P. Sirinelli, S. Prévost, "Reconnaissance émotionnelle, connaissance irrationnelle", *Dalloz IPIT*, 2021, p. 237; A. Hern, "Information commissioner warns firms over "emotional analysis" technologies", *The Guardian*, 25 October 2022.

[25] I. Cockerell, "Europe's borders are a surveillance testing ground. The AI Act could change that", *Coda*, 7 March 2023.

[26] P.H.C. Wilkinson, "The Legal Implications of Sexual Orientation-Detecting Facial Recognition Technology", *Dukeminier Awards: Best Sexual Orientation and Gender Identity Law Review*, 2021, 20, p. 301.

Facial recognition AIs can generate false positives and false negatives. A false positive refers to a wrong identification, such as in the situation where an image is falsely matched to another image on the watchlist. In the law enforcement context, the consequences on this person's fundamental rights are critical. A false negative refers to the opposite situation, *i.e.*, where no match is found by the AI, although the individual's biometric data is included in the watchlist, which naturally also has serious consequences in terms of law enforcement. Such errors are still very frequent today and, above all, the user must remember, as with any AI, that the matching result is only a probability. Yet, "with 80% likelihood, the person shown on one image is the person on another image on the watchlist".[27] Moreover, there is always a trade-off between false positives and false negatives and racial biases are very common in these algorithms[28] (we will develop this point later).

Finally, the issue of secure FRT functioning is connected to data quality and to the accuracy of data processing.[29] What datasets were used to program the FRT software? As the ChatGPT controversy has shown,[30] large databases of facial images must comply with data protection law and property rights. Also, major IT companies such as GAFAM have developed FRT software which has been specifically designed for unlocking smartphones. Could such biometric databases be requisitioned by US authorities for alleged reasons of national security, even if they concern European residents? This question is, sadly, rhetorical. But the origin of the photo sourced is not the only issue. When the photo taken for identification has not been taken head-on or has been taken while the subject is moving, the identification reliability drops dramatically.[31] Moreover, unlike DNA and fingerprints, the facial image of an individual changes over time. Ultimately, all these considerations lead us to conclude that this technology is not really reliable in operational terms.

---

[27] European Union Agency for Fundamental Rights, *op. cit.*, p. 9.

[28] See the first UK case: Court of Appeal, C1/2019/2670, 11 August 2020, *R. v The Chief Constable of South Wales Police*, where the Court noted that "the force had not taken reasonable steps to investigate whether the technology had a racial or gender bias, as required by the public sector equality duty".

[29] "Several factors influence the quality of facial images. These include background and object occlusion, illumination and light reflection, ergonomics, age, aging, gender, skin color and skin conditions…", European Union Agency for Fundamental Rights, *op. cit.*, p. 10.

[30] M.M. Grynbaum, R. Mac, "The Times Sues OpenAI and Microsoft Over A.I. Use of Copyrighted Work", *The New York Times*, 27 December 2023.

[31] The light conditions on the day the photo was taken are also an important factor.

B) A liberal and democratic form of technology?

Even if FRT was a safe form of technology, it should not threaten the democratic functioning of the community. Considering the public safety issues at stake, it is very likely that facial recognition, like CCTV, will not only be permitted (AI Act) but its use will grow over the next few years, provided the technology improves and that the databases reach a sufficient quantity and quality of images. The risk here is the development of a general surveillance society.[32] The Court of Justice of the European Union (CJEU) has already condemned devices allowing the generalized surveillance of citizens. In the famous *Tele2* case of 21 December 2016,[33] the Court ruled that the generalized storage and administrative access to connection data of all users of telecommunications services did not comply with Articles 7 and 8 of the Charter of Fundamental Rights and should remain the exception. More recently, a very interesting European Court of Human Rights (ECtHR) case reinforced this concern: *Glukhin v. Russia* (4 July 2023),[34] whose events were highly revealing of how facial recognition can be used by an authoritarian government. In short, Mr. Glukhin, a Russian citizen who demonstrated alone in the Moscow metro,[35] was identified and located using facial recognition technology. Firstly, the Court unanimously recognised there had been a violation of Article 10 of the ECtHR, as Mr. Glukhin had merely tried to express his opinion on a matter of public interest.[36] The Court also found a violation of Article 8, due to the use of facial recognition technology to identify, locate and arrest him.[37] Although the Court did not explicitly rule on this issue, the points it raised in its decision

---

[32] S. Zuboff, *The Age of Surveillance Capitalism: The Fight for a Human Future at the New Frontier of Power*, New York 2019; G. David, "Bertillonage in an Age of Surveillance: Fourth Amendment Regulation of Facial Recognition Technologies", *SMU Science and Technology Law Review*, 24, 1, 2021, pp. 3-64.

[33] CJEU, Grand Chamber, C-203/15, C-698/15. See I. Cameron, "Balancing Data Protection and Law Enforcement Needs: Tele2 Sverige and Watson", *Common Market Law Review*, 54, 5, 2017, pp. 1467-1496.

[34] ECtHR, *case of Glukhin v. Russia*, 4 July 2023, n. 11519/20. A.A. Gikay, "Regulating use by law enforcement authorities of live facial recognition technology in public spaces: an incremental approach", *Cambridge Law Journal*, 2023, 82, 3, pp. 414-449; M. Zalnieriute, "Facial recognition surveillance and public space: protecting protest movements", *International Review of Law, Computers and Technology*, 117, 4, 2023, pp. 695-701; F. Palmiotto, N. Menéndez González, "Facial recognition technology, democracy and human rights", *Computer Law & Security Review*, 2023, 50, p. 105857.

[35] He held up a banner bearing the words: "I'm facing up to five years [in prison] for peaceful protests".

[36] ECtHR, *case of Glukhin v. Russia*, cit., §51-56.

[37] ECtHR, *case of Glukhin v. Russia*, cit., §68.

demonstrate the dangers of generalizing the use of this technology.[38] First of all, there was uncertainty: the applicant was not certain that he had been subjected to this algorithmic identification as the Russian government did not acknowledge it. The risk of generalized surveillance through AI leads therefore to the risk of global paranoia. Moreover, Russian legislation does not require the police to record their use of this technology or to notify the person concerned of its use.[39] The lack of any detailed rules in domestic law regulating the scope and modalities of the implementation of measures involving the use of facial recognition technology, as well as the failure to provide strong safeguards against the risk of abuse and arbitrariness, are therefore both in violation of the ECtHR.[40] The Court considered that "highly intrusive" FRT not only has chilling effects on other human rights[41] but is also incompatible with the "ideals" and "values" of a "democratic society" governed by the "rule of law".[42] Therefore, live FRT requires the "highest" level of justification,[43] because "it is impossible to delimit the bull's eye of a technology that, by its nature, indiscriminately targets everyone".[44] Finally, while the Court considered that resolving crimes does indeed constitute a legitimate reason for using FRT, the repression of a peaceful demonstration clearly does not: it is an instrumentalization of the technology to enable the repression of even the slightest form of opposition.

Accordingly, in order to minimize the risks, FRT has to be framed within a number of fundamental rights and principles. First, consideration should be given to the application of the proportionality principle in the use of such AI. The use should be strictly limited to prevention or resolution of the most serious crimes. For the private sector, it should only be authorized in high security industries (defense industry, chemical industry, etc.) and under the control of an independent authority. Then, a transparent and clear provision of information is of utmost importance in the context of 'live' facial recognition technologies, since people's facial images are usually captured by cameras in public places without their knowledge and

---

[38] The Court did not wish to rule on the general conformity of FRTs with the ECHR, thus maintaining an *in concreto* assessment, §85. About the *in concreto* case law, see *S. and Marper v. UK*, 4 December 2008, n. 30562/04 and 30566/04, §81.

[39] However, there was no other reason for the police to identify him so quickly after the demonstration.

[40] Conseil d'État [France], 26 avril 2022, n. 442364.

[41] ECtHR, *case of Glukhin v. Russia*, cit., §86.

[42] ECtHR, *case of Glukhin v. Russia*, cit., §90.

[43] ECtHR, *case of Glukhin v. Russia*, cit., §86.

[44] F. Palmiotto, N. Menéndez González, *op. cit.*, p. 5.

consent. People have to be informed each time they have been recognized by an AI, thus guaranteeing their right to a remedy. Finally, FRT should never be used to restrict the freedom of speech, assembly or association because those rights should be exercised strictly anonymously.

2. From enhancing public security to infringing fundamental rights?

The legal framework for the use of biometric technologies is mainly based on data protection legislation and therefore on the right to privacy (*B*). However, the threats facing constitutional rights extend beyond this initial issue.[45] The use of FRT also raises a concern with regard to the principle of non-discrimination (*A*).

A) The non-discrimination principle

Facial recognition is not only an invasive privacy application. As with any AI, it is subject to significant biases that can lead to discrimination in the form of infringements of the principle of equality. The risks are increased by the fact that this technology is still not fully developed, as we have already seen. For example, Western AIs encounter difficulties in recognizing Asian or African faces while, in contrast, Chinese AIs have less difficulty recognizing Western faces.[46] The reason for this is probably because the datasets used for training contain more images of Western people. It is a major concern, for example, in Google's technologies,[47] which it is trying to improve[48] and similar results have been found in studies on AIs developed by Microsoft and Amazon.[49] But biases are not only about race,

---

[45] M. Simonitis, "Facial recognition technology and the constitution", *NotreDame Journal on Emerging Technologies*, 2, 2, 2021, pp. 357-380; A. Ferguson, "Facial Recognition and the Fourth Amendment", *Minnesota Law Review*, 105, 3, 2021, pp. 1105-1210; M. O'Flaherty, "Facial Recognition Technology and Fundamental Rights", *European Data Protection Law Review*, 6, 2, 2020, pp. 170-173.

[46] C. Garvie, J. Frankel, "Facial-Recognition Software Might Have a Racial Bias Problem", *The Atlantic*, 7 April 2016.

[47] J. Vincent, "Google 'fixed' its racist algorithm by removing gorillas from its image-labeling tech", *The Verge*, 12 October 2018 [Online].

[48] T. Doshi, "Improving skin tone representation across Google", 11 May 2022, *www.blog.google.com*.

[49] J. Buolamwini, T. Gebru, "Gender Shades: Intersectional Accuracy Disparities in Commercial Gender Classification", *Proceedings of Machine Learning Research, Proceedings of the 1st Conference on Fairness, Accountability and Transparency*, 81, 2018, pp. 77-

they are also about gender, as was confirmed by a 2019 study by the National Institute of Standards and Technology, an agency of the United States Department of Commerce.[50] In this study, one hundred and eighty-nine facial recognition algorithms were tested. All AI had higher rates of false positives for female faces than male faces and for Asian and African American faces than Caucasian faces. Overall, the highest bias concerned the faces of African American women. When one considers the accusations of discrimination made against American police forces, it seems obvious that the use of FRT should be subject to very strict requirements. Given that the most effective AIs do not yet work, the use of this technology, especially in police surveillance or law enforcement, could lead to awful discrimination.

Moreover, the use of facial analysis for the purpose of categorization, for example, is highly questionable. Some AIs are currently exploited to classify people according to their ethnic origin, sexual orientation or political tendencies.[51] It is very difficult to conceive of any situation where this sort of FRT would not lead to discriminatory treatment and should therefore be strictly prohibited. Furthermore, using personality detection devices for analyzing automated job interviews may be particularly discriminatory for people with disabilities: if their facial characteristics or the way they hold and/or express themselves differ from the standard and thus from the overwhelming majority of data used to develop the algorithms, these people may not be recognized as suitable for a job.

B) The right to privacy

In the *Gluckhin v. Russia* case, the Court highlighted the numerous issues relating to the right to privacy brought by FRTs. Especially for 'live' applications,[52] the risk increased when combined with political data.[53] Yet the use of facial recognition to authorize or prohibit a participant's access to a demonstration is currently becoming more and more widespread in European countries. It is probably the second most common use of AI by public authorities, after its use for law enforcement. In such situations, the Stras-

---

91. See also J. Snow, "Amazon's Face Recognition Falsely Matched 28 Members of Congress With Mugshots", *ACLU*, 26 July 2018 [Online].

[50] P. Grother, M. Ngan, K. Hanaoka, *Face Recognition Vendor Test Part 3: Demographic Effects, NIST Interagency/Internal Report*, Gaithersburg 2019 [Online].

[51] M. Kosinski, "Facial recognition technology can expose political orientation from naturalistic facial images", *Scientific Reports*, 2021, 11, 100 [Online].

[52] ECtHR, *Glukhin v. Russia*, cit., §86.

[53] *Ivi*, §72.

bourg Court naturally requires a "heightened level of protection".[54] In order to comply with the Convention and the famous *Olsson v. Sweden* case of 24 March 1988,[55] any authorization requirements must be clear, precise and strictly limited. Individuals and situations that may be covered by such identification need to be strictly limited, and "sensitive data" also needs to be specially protected. One may regret that the ECtHR did not go further in its review,[56] and we shall be closely following upcoming rulings. A link can be established here with European Union law since facial images fall into the "special categories of personal data" (Article 9)[57] in the GDPR, due to their sensitive nature. As such, EU data protection law provides for enhanced protection, and additional safeguards, compared to other personal data. In this context, one of the first issues regarding privacy protection is where the dataset used for recognition comes from. Will governments compile it on their own? Could they ask the smartphone manufacturers who use FRT to unlock their phones to send these pictures? Under which legal oversight? Some argue that FRT could never be efficient because neither the governments nor the private sector will ever be able to acquire an adequate dataset.

This is not so certain, as the Clearview AI scandal has shown.[58] The company's algorithm matches faces to a database of more than 32 billion images (over 75 million new faces added every day) indexed from the Internet. This company uses exclusively public data, such as that found on social media platforms (Meta, TikTok, etc.).[59] In January 2020, the *New York Times* published an article that revealed the activity of this compa-

---

[54] *Ivi*, §75-86.

[55] ECtHR, *Olsson v. Sweden,* 24 March 1988, n. 10465/83. It stated that "the notion of necessity implies that the interference corresponds to a pressing social need and, in particular, that it is proportionate to the legitimate aim pursued", §67.

[56] In particular, the Court has not specified which categories of crime may legitimately involve facial recognition.

[57] M. Ienca, G. Malgieri, "Mental Data Protection and the GDPR", *Journal of Law and the Biosciences*, 9, 1, 2022, pp. 1-19; Z. Guo, L. Kennedy, "Policing based on automatic facial recognition", *Artificial Intelligence and Law,* 31, 2023, pp. 397-443.

[58] G. Pathak, "Manifestly Made Public: Clearview and GDPR", *European Data Protection Law Review*, 8, 3, 2022, pp. 419-422; M. Kohn, 'Clearview AI, TikTok, and the Collection of Facial Images in International Law', *Chicago Journal of International Law*, 23, 1, 2022, pp. 195-234; B. Devany, "Clearview AI's First Amendment: A Dangerous Reality?", *Texas Law Review*, 101, 2, 2022, pp. 473-507; C. Dul, "Facial Recognition Technology vs Privacy: The Case of Clearview AI", *Queen Mary Law Journal*, 2022, pp. 1-24.

[59] "We collect only public data from the open internet", Hoan Ton-That (Clearview AI's CEO), M. Heikkilä, "The walls are closing in on Clearview AI", *MIT Technology Review*, 24 May 2022.

ny,[60] and led to a global scandal. Shortly afterwards, Twitter sent a cease-and-desist letter and requested the deletion of all collected data. This was followed by similar actions by YouTube (via Google) and Facebook in February 2020. The main reason was that Clearview AI was selling access to its database to 3,100 active users including some police departments around the world, the Federal Bureau of Investigation and the Department of Homeland Security. However, contrary to Clearview's claims that its service was being sold only to law enforcement agencies,[61] a data breach in early 2020 revealed that numerous commercial organizations, private companies and even individuals were on Clearview's customer list. This was quite worrying as multiple reports have identified the CEO's connections with far-right figures since 2016.[62] In March 2022, Clearview AI was fined $21M by the Italian Privacy Regulator in violation of the GDPR and was required to delete all Italian records from its database.[63] Similar fines and deletion orders followed in Canada,[64] Australia,[65] France,[66] and the United Kingdom[67] (but not the EU).[68] Despite these sentences, at the time of writing, Clearview AI is continuing to operate (and trying to avoid paying its fines).

From a general point of view, it is difficult for FRTs to comply with the

---

[60] K. Hill, "The Secretive Company That Might End Privacy as We Know It", *The New York Times*, 18 January 2020.

[61] From 2020 to 2022, the company repeatedly stated that its tools were exclusively designed to support law enforcement agencies.

[62] L. O'Brien, "The Far-Right Helped Create the World's Most Powerful Facial Recognition Technology", *Huffington Post*, 7 April 2020; K. Hill, "What We Learned About Clearview AI and Its Secret "Co-Founder"", *New York Times*, 18 March 2021, updated 28 October 2021.

[63] M. Heikkilä, *op. cit.*, p. 1.

[64] Z. Whittaker, "Clearview AI ruled "illegal" by Canadian privacy authorities", *Techcrunch*, 3 February 2021.

[65] N. Lomas, "Clearview AI told it broke Australia's privacy law, ordered to delete data", *Techcrunch*, 3 November 2021; J. Goldenfein, "Australian police are using the Clearview AI facial recognition system with no accountability", *The Conversation*, 4 March 2020.

[66] CNIL, Decision of 20 October 2022. Clearview will have to pay more than 5 million penalty payments (Decision of 13 April 2023).

[67] $10 million, M. Heikkilä, *op. cit.*, p. 1.

[68] For the EDPB, "In its response to MEPs regarding Clearview AI, [...] Without prejudice to further analysis on the basis of additional elements provided, the EDPB is therefore of the opinion that the use of a service such as Clearview AI by law enforcement authorities in the European Union would, as it stands, likely not be consistent with the EU data protection regime", *Thirty-first Plenary session*, 10 June 2020.

necessity, legitimacy and proportionality of the infringements of the right to privacy as required by the ECtHR. It is worth mentioning that the European Parliament expressly refers to Clearview AI in its resolution about the FRT.[69] Given that the very image of a person has become a profit-making commodity, it is clear that there is a need to regulate this business. Finally, the position of the CJEU should also be taken into account, particularly its rulings on the "Schrems saga".[70] Let us briefly recall here that the Court of Luxembourg has twice invalidated the decision of the European Commission to authorize the transfer of data from Europe to the United States by Facebook, first in 2015,[71] then in 2020.[72] After President Biden signed Executive Order 14086 on 7 October 2022,[73] the European Commission adopted an adequacy decision on 10 July 2023,[74] despite the negative opinion of the EDBP[75] and the European Parliament.[76] Given the weaknesses of the American law,[77] a "Schrems III" case will probably be ruled in the coming years. It is therefore not only the effectiveness or the use of FRT that is at stake here, but also the entire environment related to the protection of personal data.

---

[69] European Parliament Resolution of 6 October 2021, cit., §28.

[70] M. Zalnieriute, "Data Transfers after Schrems II: The EU-US Disagreements over Data Privacy and National Security", *Vanderbilt Journal of Transnational Law*, 55, 1, 2022, pp. 1-48.

[71] CJEU, Grand Chamber, 6 October 2015, *Maximillian Schrems v Data Protection Commissioner*, Case C-362/14. The Court invalidated the "Safe Harbour Privacy Principles".

[72] CJEU, Grand Chamber, 16 July 2020, *Data Protection Commissioner v. Facebook* C-311/18. This time the Court invalidated the "EU-US Privacy Shield".

[73] Executive Order 14086, *Enhancing Safeguards for United States Signals Intelligence Activities*.

[74] European Commission, 10 July 2023, *Adequacy decision for the EU-US Data Privacy Framework*, C (2023) 4745 final.

[75] EDPB, 28 February 2023, *Opinion 5/2023 on the European Commission Draft Implementing Decision on the adequate protection of personal data under the EU-US Data Privacy Framework*.

[76] European Parliament Resolution of 11 May 2023 *on the adequacy of the protection afforded by the EU-US Data Privacy Framework* (2023/2501(RSP)).

[77] The main criticism that can be leveled, among others, at Executive Order 14086 is that it still does not establish federal legislation on data protection and privacy in the United States.

Chapter 13

EUROPEAN COURT OF HUMAN RIGHTS JURISPRUDENCE AND NATIONAL MIGRATION POLICIES: EXPLORING THE HERMENEUTIC TOOLS OF 'PROCEDURALISATION' AND MARGIN OF APPRECIATION *

Giulia Santomauro

ABSTRACT: *In the context of the European Convention on Human Rights (ECHR), the act of balancing migration policies with other national interests raises significant questions regarding the applicability of universal human rights in light of states' wide discretion. This chapter aims to explore the impact of the Strasbourg Court's jurisprudence on national systematic failures in migration management and the implications for individual protection standards. Specifically, the analysis delves into the strengths and limitations of the hermeneutic tool of 'proceduralisation' of the assessment of alleged violations of the Convention and its interaction with the doctrine of the margin of appreciation. Finally, this chapter illustrates that procedural-type reviews, if aimed at complementing rather than supplanting substantive scrutiny, have the potential to strengthen a shared European responsibility to effectively guarantee migrants' human rights.*

---

* This chapter presents part of the research findings from sub-project A.2 *Systemic Deficiencies in the System of Protecting the Human Rights of Migrants: a Comparison between the Inter-American and European Courts of Human Rights*, supported by funding from the Deutsche Forschungsgemeinschaft (DFG, German Research Foundation), project number 458456362, under the title 'Human Rights Discourse in Migration Societies (MeDiMi)'.

1. Introduction

Migration can currently be considered one of the most contentious fields in Europe, making it arduous to find both common political ground at the European Union (EU) level and a consensus within the member states of the Council of Europe. Whilst international law, particularly the 1951 Geneva Convention, establishes crucial boundaries for states regarding the treatment of refugees [1], migration management intersects with various national political interests such as economic needs, counter-terrorism measures and public security.

Set against this context, states' migration policies have often been questioned from a human rights perspective in legal literature and in some instances have been brought before the European Court of Human Rights (ECtHR). Although the European Convention on Human Rights (ECHR) does not explicitly enshrine a right to asylum or express provisions protecting aliens from repatriation to countries where they might face persecution or severe human rights violations, the jurisprudence of the Strasbourg Court has gained increasing prominence in recent decades. Despite the fact that a wide margin of appreciation [2] is normally granted to the contracting states in migration-related cases, since the power to authorize who is admitted to the national territory, and under what circumstances, belongs to states "*as a matter of well-established international law and subject to their treaty obligations*", [3] the ECtHR has developed a significant body of case-law on this matter. Initially, its jurisprudence was primarily based on Articles 2 and 3 ECHR, from which an absolute prohibition of *refoulement* was derived, [4] but subsequently it extended to almost all the rights of the Con-

---

[1] See, in particular, Article 33 of the Convention relating to the Status of Refugees, also known as the Geneva Convention, which enshrines the principle of *non-refoulement*, approved at a special United Nations conference on 28 July 1951 in Geneva (UNTS vol. 189, p. 137 ff.).

[2] The margin of appreciation is an hermeneutic technique used by the ECtHR to determine the intensity of its scrutiny, which S. Greer, *The Margin of Appreciation: Interpretation and discretion under the European Convention on Human Rights* (Human Rights files No. 17) (Council of Europe 2000), p. 5, describes as: "*the room for manoeuvre the Strasbourg institutions are prepared to accord national authorities in fulfilling their obligations under the European Convention on Human Rights (ECHR)*".

[3] This standard formula was used for the first time in the *Moustaquim v. Belgium* case, n. 12313/86, 18 February 1991, § 43. Then, it was maintained, for example, in the *Boujlifa v. France* case, n. 25404/94, 21 October 1997, § 42 and in the *Nunez v. Norway* case, n. 55597/09, 28 June 2011, § 66.

[4] The Strasbourg Court derived for the first time from Article 3 ECHR the duty of contracting states not to expose migrants to the risk of ill-treatment as a result of an ex-

vention.[5] In particular, by regarding the ECHR as a living instrument, the Strasbourg Court has been able to assess the compliance of national measures with refence to rights that are not expressly provided for in the text, and safeguard individual guarantees against violations by states which are not even parties to it. Hence, through the hermeneutic technique commonly known as protection *par ricochet* (i.e., indirect protection), the ECtHR has effectively filled certain gaps in the protection of migrants and enabled a functional interpretation of the Convention, intended to uphold 'practical and effective' human rights, rather than 'theoretical or illusory' ones.[6]

Building on these premises, among various interpretative practices developed by the Strasbourg Court such as the proportionality and fair balance tests or the fourth-instance doctrine, this chapter is dedicated to the analysis of procedural-type reviews in migration-related cases. While most previous studies put emphasis on the possible adverse effects of the so-called 'procedural turn' of the ECtHR in terms of human rights scrutiny,[7] some questions remain unanswered. In particular, does the Strasbourg Court's 'proceduralisation' have the ability to advance migrants' human rights beyond individual cases, eventually strengthening a shared European

---

pulsion in the case *Soering v. the United Kingdom*, n. 14038/88, 7 July 1989. The principle of *non-refoulement* under the ECHR is an absolute guarantee, given that its scope also extends to those excluded from refugee status under Articles 1.D, E, F of the Geneva Convention. On the non-derogable nature of the principle of *non-refoulement* under the ECHR, see, for example, F. De Weck, *Non-refoulement under the European convention on human rights and the UN convention against torture: the assessment of individual complaints by the European court of human rights under article 3 ECHR and the United Nations committee against torture under article 3 CAT*, Leiden 2017.

[5] For a comprehensive analysis of immigrants and refugees' rights under the ECHR and the Strasbourg Court case-law on migration, see D. Moya, G. Milios, *Aliens before the European Court of Human Rights. Ensuring Minimum Standards of Human Rights Protection*, Leiden 2021.

[6] On the meaning and implications of the protection *par ricochet* for individual rights, see F. Julien-Laferriere, "L'application par ricochet de l'article 3 CEDH: L'exemple des mesures d'éloignement des étrangers", in C.A. Chasin (eds.), *La portée de l'article 3 de la Convention européenne des droits de l'homme*, Bruylant 2006, p. 141 ff.

[7] On the risks that 'proceduralisation' may entail a retreat from substantive human rights obligations, see, for instance, O.M. Arnardóttir, "Organised Retreat? The Move from "Substantive" to "Procedural" Review in the ECtHR's Case Law on the Margin of Appreciation", *ESIL Conference Paper Series*, 5 (4), 2015, p. 4 ff.; E. Brems, "The "Logics" of Procedural-Type Review by the European Court of Human Right", in J. Gerards, E. Brems (eds.), *Procedural Review in European Fundamental Rights Cases,* Cambridge 2017, p. 17 ff.; P. Popelier, C. Van De Heyning, "Subsidiarity Post-Brighton: Procedural Rationality as Answer?", *Leiden Journal of International Law*, 30 (1), 2017, p. 5 ff.

responsibility to secure standards of protection? This chapter aims to bridge this gap by paying special attention to states' shortcomings in allowing access to asylum which are characterized by the repeated occurrence of the same type of violations within a specific territory and timeframe, often with the tacit approval of the relevant government.[8] We also aspire to grasp whether 'proceduralisation' can contribute to creating shared responsibility among states to ensure the application and effective implementation of the Convention concerning migrants' human rights.[9] To answer these questions, Section 2 delves into a theoretical investigation of the meaning of 'proceduralisation' with regard to addressing the systemic shortcomings of states. In this analysis, attention will also be paid to the interrelated scope of different procedural approaches previously distinguished in legal scholarship and how they are connected to the doctrine of the margin of appreciation. Section 3 analyses the procedural arguments most often invoked by the ECtHR in the context of asylum cases, focusing on forced removal of migrants and summary returns at the border (Section 3.1), access to the international protection system and guarantees in the context of the asylum assessment process (Section 3.2). Finally, Section 4 offers concluding reflections on the ambivalent nature of the ECtHR's 'proceduralisation', which can be positioned on the borderline between the classic opposing notions of judicial activism and judicial restraint.

2. The Court of Strasbourg's 'proceduralisation': theoretical grounds and interrelation with the doctrine of the margin of appreciation

The ECHR encompasses explicit procedural guarantees, which can also be extended to protect irregular migrants and asylum seekers, in the form of Article 5 on the right to liberty and security and Article 13 on the right to an effective remedy.[10] However, what is particularly interesting from the

---

[8] On the concept of 'systematic' human rights violations, see P. Sardaro, "Jus Non Dicere for Allegations of Serious Violations of Human Rights: Questionable Trends in the Recent Case Law of the Strasbourg Court", *European Human Rights Law Review*, (2003) 6, p. 602. On the structural challenges experienced by migrants to access asylum in Europe, see J. Bast, F. von Harbou, J. Wessels, *Human Rights Challenges to European Migration Policy: The REMAP Study*, Baden-Baden-Oxford 2020, p. 14 ff.

[9] On the key objective of building a shared responsibility for the implementation of the ECHR, see, in particular, the *High-Level Conference on the Implementation of the European Convention on Human Rights, Our Shared Responsibility* (27 March 2015) and the resulting *Brussels Declaration*.

[10] It is relevant to note that Article 6 ECHR guarantees the right to a fair trial, but it

perspective of the advancement of human rights is the increasing use of 'procedural arguments' by the Strasbourg Court in judgments related to potential interference of state measures with substantive rights [11].

Specifically, scholars have identified a twofold procedural approach employed by the ECtHR to assess alleged Convention violations. [12] Firstly, the Court employs a practice that could be termed a 'procedural-obligations review', which involves a dynamic interpretation of the Convention aimed at deriving autonomous positive obligations for the contracting states from its substantive provisions, even if these are not explicitly outlined therein. Secondly, Strasbourg judges adopt a process that could be labelled a 'procedural quality review' involving an assessment that places importance, at times more explicitly and in other instances more indirectly, on the robustness of the national legislative process, as well as the judicial and administrative procedures carried out at the domestic level. This means that, if certain procedural requirements are satisfied, the Court is more inclined to refrain from reviewing the substantive issue at stake. [13]

Therefore, at first glance, while the procedural-obligations review appears to extend the safeguarding of individuals' substantive rights, the procedural quality review introduces a certain degree of deference in the human rights' assessment. Indeed, in the former rationale, procedural criteria are perceived as an integral part of the scope of the right in question and are translated into derived positive procedural obligations for states. This would effectively extend the protection granted to involved individuals, while restricting the room for manoeuvre for contracting states. Conversely, in the latter rationale, procedural features in the strict sense could poten-

---

applies only to civil and criminal proceedings, meaning that immigration and asylum cases are not covered by its scope.

[11] In this vein, see R. Spano, "The Future of the European Court of Human Rights—Subsidiarity, Process-Based Review and the Rule of Law", in *Human Rights Law Review*, 18 (3), 2018, p. 474 ff., who observed a shift of the Strasbourg Court from a "substantial embedding phase" to a "procedural embedding phase".

[12] On the distinction between two modes of 'proceduralisation', see, among others, J. Gerards, "Procedural Review by the ECtHR: A typology", in J. Gerards, E. Brems (eds.), *Procedural Review in European Fundamental Rights Cases*, Cambridge 2017, p. 127 ff.; O.M. Arnardóttir, "The 'procedural turn' under the European Convention on Human Rights and presumptions of Convention compliance", *International Journal of Constitutional Law*, 15 (1), 2017 p. 14 ff.; T. Kleinlein, "The procedural approach of the European Court of Human Rights: Between Subsidiarity and Dynamic Evolution", *International and Comparative Law Quarterly*, 68, 2019, p. 94 ff.

[13] ECtHR's Organising Committee for the opening of the judicial year 2015, *Seminar to Mark the Opening of the Judicial Year 2015–Subsidiarity: A Two-Sided Coin?*, 2015, p. 9.

tially overshadow the case's merits and the tests of proportionality and reasonableness when considering the balance of factors in the substantive assessment.[14] Moreover, according to this perspective, the quality of national processes corresponds to a broader margin of appreciation and *vice versa.*[15] In other words, the more the Court believes that national authorities are capable of conducting a high-quality human rights assessment, the more margin is likely to be granted.

However, both procedural approaches appear to be linked by the objective of effectiveness in upholding Convention rights.[16] In the case of the procedural-obligations review, this principle is applied in such a way that extracting positive procedural obligations from substantive rights can effectively improve the implementation of Convention standards at the national level. Regarding the procedural quality review, effectiveness is manifested in accordance with the theory that a 'good process' is more likely to lead to 'good outcomes'.[17] Based on this premise, the Court's deference may vary from completely refraining from examining the merits of the case to evaluating the quality of the domestic process, ultimately viewed as an assessment of the human rights scrutiny already conducted by domestic authorities. The underlying connection remains the effectiveness of Convention compliance, which is not only consistent with its structure but also aligns with the proactive reading that the Strasbourg Court openly professes to pursue.[18]

---

[14] According to V. Stoyanova, "Populism, Exceptionality, and the right to family of migrants under the European Convention on Human Rights", *European Journal of Legal Studies*, 10 (2), 2018, p. 120, if procedural guarantees are considered robust at the national level, the stringency with which the Court conducts its proportionality analysis at the international law level will be lower. However, the author also highlights anomalies in the proportionality test applied by the Court when using the procedural approach in migration-related cases. This is because the Court does not always follow a strict structure in its argumentation, and it is unclear and thus unpredictable how it balances competing interests.

[15] O.M. Arnardóttir, "The 'procedural turn' under the European Convention on Human Rights and presumptions of Convention compliance", cit., p. 17 ff.

[16] E. Brems, "The "Logics" of Procedural-Type Review by the European Court of Human Right", cit., p. 18 ff.; V. Stoyanova, *Positive Obligations under the European Convention on Human Rights. Within and Beyond Boundaries*, Oxford 2023, p. 150 ff.

[17] J. Christoffersen, *Fair Balance: Proportionality and Primarity in the European Convention on Human Rights*, Leiden 2009, p. 462.

[18] ECtHR, *The European Convention on Human Rights. A living instrument*, September 2022, p. 7.

3. The use of procedural-type reviews in asylum-related case-law of the ECtHR

The tendency of the ECtHR to 'proceduralise' the monitoring of the Convention's substantive provisions has been mostly observed with reference to the right to life (Article 2), to not be subjected to torture, inhumane or degrading treatment (Article 3) and to respect for private and family life (Article 8).[19] Remarkably, these rights are all crucial for ensuring compliance with the principle of *non-refoulement*, effective access to the international protection system and adequate guarantees during the examination of asylum claims. Moreover, in the context of migration, the procedural arguments developed by the Court concerning the prohibition of collective expulsion of aliens (Article 4 of Protocol 4) also gain special prominence.[20]

In terms of the typology of domestic proceedings which are subject to the ECtHR's procedural reviews, this chapter primarily refers to administrative procedures. This is due to the importance of establishing positive procedural obligations or assessing the quality of procedures regarding the human rights scrutiny conducted by administrative decision-makers in the migration field, such as border or coast guards, police officers, and authorities assessing asylum claims. States' shortcomings at these stages of the migration journey can in fact significantly impact the 'life-changing' stage of safeguarding individual substantive rights. Furthermore, whilst the Court's procedural control in migration jurisprudence generally does not involve the quality of national parliamentary proceedings and their outcomes,[21] the effectiveness of the contracting parties' judicial systems may instead play an essential part, especially with regard to fair trail guarantees and the obligation to conduct official criminal investigations.[22]

---

[19] ECtHR's Organising Committee for the opening of the judicial year 2015, *op. cit.*, p. 9.

[20] The wording of Article 4 of Protocol 4 ECHR 'only' prescribes that "Collective expulsion of aliens is prohibited". Hence, as the corresponding assurance in unwritten universal human rights law is largely seen as a substantive right granted to a collective of individuals, the ECtHR had to devise implicit procedural safeguards to protect individual migrants. In this regard, see J. Bast, F. von Harbou, J. Wessels, *op. cit.*, p. 84.

ECtHR, *Ilias and Ahmed v. Hungary* [GC], n. 47287/15, 21 November 2019.

[21] In this respect, see ECtHR, *Ribcheva and others v. Bulgaria*, n. 37801/16, 30 March 2021, §139 and ECtHR, *Anna Todorova v. Bulgaria*, n. 23302/03, 24 May 2011, § 74. For further details, see V. Stoyanova, *Positive Obligations under the European Convention on Human Rights,* cit., p. 123.

[22] *Ibidem*.

3.1. Forced removals and summary returns of migrants

In asylum-related removal cases, the Court's 'proceduralisation' is especially relevant with regard to the procedural aspects of Articles 2 and 3 ECHR.

Firstly, with regard to cases involving the expulsion of asylum seekers and their return to their country of origin, it is well established that the Court is not itself required to examine the actual asylum applications or verify how the states meet their obligations under the Geneva Convention. However, domestic authorities have a procedural duty under Article 3 ECHR to examine any alleged risk of ill-treatment[23] before removing applicants who had lodged asylum applications. Moreover, in cases of removing asylum seekers to third countries, the Court's interpretation of the procedural part of Article 3 ECHR is built upon the concept of *chain refoulement*, as it entails an obligation to assess whether asylum procedures in a given third state are adequate to protect individuals against direct or indirect expulsion to their country of origin without a proper evaluation of the risk of ill-treatment.[24]

Secondly, a considerable line of ECtHR's case-law deals with the procedural duty of state authorities to thoroughly investigate complaints from applicants regarding alleged ill-treatment during deportation or fatal incidents during removal processes, as derived from Articles 2 and 3 ECHR. This obligation should be understood as a broad requirement that does not mandate the state to perform a specific type of investigation, as any form of proceedings (criminal, civil, administrative, disciplinary, or a combination thereof) can potentially comply with it.[25] Moreover, Strasbourg judges, on the one hand, have elaborated on general principles that must be satisfied by state agents in conducting investigations.[26] On the other hand, the Court has assessed in detail the shortcomings of national authorities in in-

[23] Regarding the assessment of evidence, the Court ruled that "the existence of the risk must be assessed primarily with reference to those facts which were known or ought to have been known to the contracting state at the time of expulsion" (ECtHR, *Khasanov and Rakhmanov v. Russia* [GC], nn. 28492/15 and 49975/15, 29 April 2022, § 113; ECtHR, *F.G. v. Sweden* [GC], n. 43611/11, 23 March 2016, § 115). Moreover, contracting states have the obligation to take into account not only the evidence submitted by the applicant but also all other facts which are relevant in the case under examination (ECtHR, *J.K. and Others v. Sweden* [GC], n. 59166/12, 23 August 2016, § 87).

[24] ECtHR, *Ilias and Ahmed v. Hungary* [GC], n. 47287/15, 21 November 2019.

[25] In this respect, see ECtHR, *Ribcheva and others v. Bulgaria*, n. 37801/ 16, 30 March 2021, §139 and ECtHR, *Anna Todorova v. Bulgaria*, n. 23302/ 03, 24 May 2011, § 74. For further details, see V. Stoyanova, *Positive Obligations under the European Convention on Human Rights*, cit., p. 123.

[26] ECtHR, *Bouyid v. Belgium* [GC], n. 23380/09, 28 September 2015, §§ 114-123.

vestigating complaints of individuals ill-treated by state authorities[27] or forced removals of migrants that lead to their death.[28] Consequently, the Court typically reviews such procedural aspects of the Convention's provisions when a state has failed to investigate, either completely or in an adequate manner, its own actions, which could have potentially prevented harm either intentionally or unintentionally caused by the conduct of a public authority.

Therefore, in this line of cases, both procedural methods of the Strasbourg Court, as discussed in Section 2, are used concurrently and they appear to be strictly interrelated in reinforcing the substantive advancement of human rights. In this respect, the judgment of *Alhowais v. Hungary*[29] is illustrative. In particular, the Court found that Hungary violated the procedural and substantive aspects of Article 2 ECHR and the procedural aspect of Article 3 ECHR when expelling applicants to Serbia, which ultimately led to the death of one of them. In its reasoning, the Court evaluated the quality of national proceedings by employing the general principles previously developed on the effectiveness of a criminal investigation, as the reading of Articles 2 and 3 ECHR:

> *must be guided by the knowledge that the object and purpose of the Convention as an instrument for the protection of individual human beings requires that its provisions be interpreted and applied so as to make its safeguards practical and effective* (§ 76).

The review of the procedural human rights assessment performed by Hungarian authorities resulted then unsatisfactory, as the criminal investigation's outcome was determined to a significant extent by the impartial taking of oral testimonies and the collection of evidence was scarce due to state delays (§§ 90-92).

Nonetheless, the assessment of such positive procedural obligations can also have independent significance in the Court's scrutiny. This implies that violations of substantive aspects of Articles 2 or 3 ECHR are not necessarily required to establish states' breach of the procedural duty to investigate. But it also means that the failure of national authorities to carry out a thorough and effective investigation may be considered insufficient as a stand-

---

[27] ECtHR, *Thuo v. Cyprus*, n. 3869/07, 4 April 2017, § 125-140.

[28] ECtHR, *Mocanu and others v. Romania* [GC], nn. 10865/09 and 10 others, 5 May 2022, § 314; ECtHR, *M.H. and others v. Croatia*, nn. 15670/18 and 43115/18, 18 November 2021, §§ 127-131, 148-166.

[29] ECtHR, *Alhowais v. Hungary*, n. 59435/17, 2 February 2023.

ard of proof when assessing evidence to meet the minimum level of severity for a violation of the substantive aspect of Article 3 ECHR.[30]

To explore this argument further, we can refer to the decision of *Safi and others v. Greece*,[31] which concerned the ineffective investigation into a fatal accident involving migrants intercepted at sea in which the Strasbourg judges found a breach of both the procedural requirements and the positive obligations of Article 2 ECHR. Nevertheless, while examining the facts related to the violation of the substantive aspect of Article 2 ECHR, the Court emphasized that the applicants' complaint of attempted *refoulement* could not be proven 'beyond reasonable doubt' due to the lack of an effective investigation by the national authorities into the accident (§ 155). One may thus question whether the ECtHR, by resorting to such a procedural review, could generate a sort of 'reverse effect' against fair access to the international protection system, namely if ineffective investigations could be used as a means to evade states' responsibility for push-backs at sea and regarding the burden of proof about the risk of *refoulement.*[32] In addition, from a more general perspective, the procedural limitation in verifying the *ratione materiae* compatibility of the applicant's complaints may outweigh the necessity to rule on the merits of the case and, ultimately, to fulfil its mandate to safeguard the rights enshrined in the Convention.[33]

Finally, the ECtHR attaches value to procedural arguments in cases involving push-backs at borders or collective removals shortly after the entry of migrants into the territory of contracting parties. Regarding the more substantive aspect of the Court's procedural method, the scope of Article 4 of Protocol 4 ECHR has been progressively broadened, to the point that this provision can now be seen as a 'general due process clause' for migrants in Europe.[34] Based on the laconic formula of prohibiting the collective expulsion of aliens, the Court has indeed inferred the right to an individualized, independent, and rigorous examination of asylum claims,[35] as

[30] Such criterion was exemplified for the first time by the ECtHR in the case *Ireland v. United Kingdom*, n. 5310/71, 8 January 1978, § 162.

[31] ECtHR, *Safi and others v. Greece*, n. 5418/15, July 7, 2022.

[32] K. Spyridoula, "How to Get Away with Refoulement: Some Thoughts on Safi and Others v. Greece", *Strasbourg Observers*, 2022.

[33] On this regard, see V. Stoyanova, *Positive Obligations under the European Convention on Human Rights*, cit., p. 124, who questions whether, within the context of procedural obligations, the Court should avoid the phase in which it assesses whether the harm invoked by the applicant falls within the definitional scope of the relevant right, and instead proceed directly to reviewing compliance with the obligation to investigate.

[34] J. Bast, F. von Harbou, J. Wessels, *op. cit.*, p. 85.

[35] See, *inter alia*, ECtHR, *Čonka v. Belgium*, n. 51564/99, 5 February 2002, § 59.

well as the concrete possibility to submit arguments against expulsion orders and their appropriate examination by state authorities.[36] Such interpretation of Article 4 of Protocol 4 ECHR has been lately reaffirmed in the decision of *J.A. and others v. Italy*,[37] referring to the collective removal of four migrants fleeing Tunisia. More specifically, after being detained in the Lampedusa hotspot in inhuman and degrading conditions, they were transferred to the airport where they were asked to sign refusal-of-entry orders without proper consideration of their individual circumstances and without being given a 'genuine and effective' opportunity to present arguments against their deportation. The Chamber's ruling found, among others, a violation of Article 4 of Protocol 4 ECHR and provides further clarification on the requirements for avoiding collective expulsion (§§ 110-112). The reasoning of the Court in effect expands the substantive protection afforded to migrants, as it is argued that they must be granted sufficient time before signing their orders to have a realistic opportunity to understand the content of the order and to appeal against these measures, and must be provided with a comprehensive and understandable information sheet regarding the refusal-of-entry orders (§ 113).

By contrast, the controversial landmark judgement of *N.D. and N.T. v. Spain*,[38] which concerned the collective returns of migrants attempting unauthorized entry at land borders, highlighted weaknesses in the effectiveness of individual human rights in relation to the more formalistic aspect of the Court's procedural review. Particularly, the Court, addressing the systemic issue of 'hot returns' of migrants at the borders of the enclave of Melilla by the *Guardia Civil*, employed a 'culpable conduct test' based on two main conditions to assess the state's compliance with Article 4 of Protocol 4 ECHR: the presence of "genuine and effective access to means of legal entry, in particular border procedure"[39] and the ab-

---

[36] ECtHR, *Khlaifia and others v. Italy*, n. 16483/12, 1 September 2015, §§ 238, p. 248.

[37] ECtHR, *J.A. and others v. Italy*, n. 21329/18, 30 March 2023.

[38] ECtHR, *N.D. and N.T. v. Spain*, nn. 8675/15 e 8697/15, 13 February 2020. The same reasoning has been subsequently applied in all cases presenting the same scenario, namely *Shahzad v. Hungary*, n. 12625/17, 8 July 2021, §§ 59 ff.; *M.H. and others v. Croatia*, nn. 15670/18 and 43115/18, 18 November 2021, §§ 294 ff.; *A.A. and others v. North Macedonia*, nn. 55798/16 and 4 others, 5 April 2022, §§ 112-123.

[39] On the criterion of "genuine and effective access to means of legal entry" as a relevant factor in the assessment of whether contracting parties have complied with Article 4 of Protocol 4 ECHR, see E. Bratanova van Harten, "Complementary Pathways as 'Genuine and Effective Access to Means of Legal Entry' in the Reasoning of the European Court of Human Rights. Legal and Practical Implications", *European Journal of Migration and Law*, 25, 2023, p. 200 ff.

sence of valid reasons for not using official means of legal entry and procedures for assessing asylum claims, in combination with the unauthorized entry and 'forceful' crossing of migrants posing a threat to public safety (§§ 201, 209-211). More concretely, according to the Strasbourg judges, in the present case, the applicants crossed the Melilla fence in an illegal manner, deliberately taking advantage of their large numbers and using force, "*such as to create a clearly disruptive situation which is difficult to control and endangers public safety*" (§ 201). However, the Court overlooked significant third party' observations shedding light on the discriminatory practices of Spanish authorities towards migrants from sub-Saharan Africa, who did not have *de facto* access to immigration and asylum procedures at the official border checkpoint of Beni Enzar nearby Melilla, as they were systematically prevented from reaching the border on the Moroccan side (§§ 142-143, 152-163). This approach therefore raises concerns as it seems to prioritize formalistic compliance with the mere existence of acceptable legal checkpoints and asylum procedures over actual accessibility to the international protection system. This reasoning also risks widening the margin of appreciation to allow states to balance factors like public safety threats with the absolute provision of Article 3 ECHR when expelling migrants, potentially leading to inconsistent interpretations. Additionally, it appears to modulate the principle of *non-refoulement* based on migrants' entry mode (i.e., regular or irregular),[40] exacerbating inequalities among 'categories of individuals' in accessing international protection.

Notably, the argument of the culpable conduct of applicants carries some significance even in cases of summary and systematic removals of migrants who have been prevented from lodging asylum applications or, in instances where they did submit such applications, border guards have refused to accept them and initiate asylum proceedings. For instance, in the case of *M.K. and others v. Poland*,[41] and in subsequent judgments reflecting similar reasoning,[42] the Court found violations of Articles 3, 13, and 4 of Protocol 4 due to the collective expulsion of Russian nationals of Chechen origin who faced repeated refusals by Polish authorities at the Belarus border. According to the ECtHR, these violations principally stemmed from

---

[40] In this respect, see Article 31 of the Geneva Convention which compromises a clause of non-penalization of refugees for unlawful entry and presence.

[41] ECtHR, *M.K. and others v. Poland*, nn. 40503/17, 42902/17, and 43643/17, 23 July 2020.

[42] ECtHR, *T. and others v. Poland*, n. 41764/17, 13 October 2022; ECtHR, *A.B. and others v. Poland*, n. 42907/17, 30 June 2022; ECtHR, *A.I. and others v. Poland*, 39028/17, 30 June 2022.

irregularities in national asylum proceedings, characterized by a corroborated systematic practice of misrepresenting the statements given by asylum-seekers of Chechen origin by border guards (§ 174). Yet, the Court is also (unnecessarily) at pains to emphasize that the applicants attempted to cross the border legally by using an official checkpoint and submitting to border checks as required by relevant law (§ 207).

3.2. Access to international protection procedures and examination of asylum claims

Specific observations on the use of procedural arguments by the Strasbourg judges can be also drawn from the case-law involving shortcomings in migrants' access to domestic asylum procedures and examination processes of applications for international protection. It is in fact undisputed that the Court has entrenched further self-standing procedural safeguards concerning asylum seekers on the basis of the living instrument doctrine, such as access to adequate information about the international protection procedure in a language they understand, a reliable communication system with authorities offering interpreter services, legal aid, and the prohibition of arbitrary removals [43]. In particular, as affirmed in the leading *Hirsi Jamaa and others v. Italy case*, [44] states' practices which do not provide applicants with an effective remedy against arbitrary returns to countries where they could be predictability exposed to practices of ill-treatment amount to a violation of Article 13 ECHR in conjunction with Articles 3 and 4 of Protocol 4 ECHR. Furthermore, the duty to establish an effective and accessible procedure within a reasonable time is also recognized as a positive procedural obligation under Article 8 ECHR with the aim of protecting the right to privacy by means of appropriate regulations and ensuring that an applicant's situation of insecurity is as short-lived as possible. [45] Conversely, expediting the processing of an applicant's asylum claim should not replace the need for robust procedural safeguards to protect against arbitrary removal. Imposing unreasonably short time limits for submitting a claim, especially in accelerated asylum procedures, or for appealing a removal decision, can in fact "*render a*

---

[43] See, in particular, ECtHR, *M.S.S. v. Belgium and Greece* [GC], n. 30696/09, § 223, 21 January 2011, §§ 300-302, 304.

[44] ECtHR, *Hirsi Jamaa and others v. Italy* case [GC], n. 27765/09, 23 February 2012, §§ 123-136.

[45] See *B.A.C. v. Greece*, n. 11981/15, 13 October 2016; §§ 36-46, *A.J. v. Greece* (dec.), n. 34298/18, 26 April 2022, §§ 73-74.

remedy practically ineffective, contrary to the requirements of Article 13 taken together with Article 3 of the Convention".[46]

In addition to the development of positive procedural obligations, the ECtHR has recently placed stronger emphasis on the procedural aspects of age assessment processes for migrants seeking international protection who claim to be unaccompanied minors, as seen in the case of *Darboe and Camara v. Italy*.[47] This decision marks a significant jurisprudential development as it is the first time the Court has examined the issue of age assessment of asylum seekers under Article 8 ECHR. In previous migration-related cases, the Court had in effect already broadened the scope of Article 8 ECHR with reference to the profile of private life.[48] However, in *Darboe and Camara v. Italy*, the ECtHR also acknowledged the profound impact of the procedures and the outcome of age assessment on the development of the personality of applicants and, possibly, the protection of further substantive rights. Specifically, one of the two applicants, who had been wrongly identified as an adult by national administrative authorities, was subsequently placed in a reception centre for adults for an extended period, where he faced treatment considered incompatible with the status of a minor, reaching a level of severity that constituted a violation of the principle of dignity and the prohibition of inhumane and degrading treatment. It thus follows that Italy was not merely required to not interfere with the applicant's right to privacy but was also obliged to actively implement a set of procedural guarantees, including using appropriate techniques in the age assessment process, appointing a legal representative or guardian, providing access to a lawyer, and ensuring the informed participation of the individuals whose age is in question (§§ 142-157). The failure of national administrative authorities to act with 'reasonable diligence' to fulfil such positive procedural obligations eventually resulted in ill-treatment. Therefore, states' compliance with Article 8 ECHR, particularly if closely related to absolute rights such as Article 3 ECHR, also covers the fairness and due care taken in domestic procedures. Finally, given that related cases have been brought before the Court,[49] it is reasonable to as-

---

[46] ECtHR, *Guide on the case-law of the European Convention on Human Rights. Immigration*, 31 August 2022, p. 30.

[47] ECtHR, *Darboe and Camara v. Italy*, n. 5797/1721, July 2022.

[48] See, *mutatis mutandis*, ECtHR, *Mubilanzila Mayeka and Kaniki Mitunga v. Belgium*, n. 13178/03, 12 October 2006, where the concept of private life is understood by the Court as "*the development, without outside interference, of the personality of each individual in his relation with other human beings*".

[49] See, in particular, ECtHR, *Trawalli and others v. Italy*, n. 47287/17, communicated case.

sume that the Strasbourg judges may recognize and seek to address national systemic deficiencies concerning age assessment procedures for migrants claiming asylum in Italy in the near future.

4. Conclusion

This chapter has aimed to explore the significance of the jurisprudence of the Strasbourg Court in the context of European migration policies. Beyond formalized instruments of 'direct intervention' such as pilot procedures, the ECtHR has shown it can broaden its assessment of individual rights and influence national decision-making through the use of complex interpretative techniques.[50] These techniques have been built upon an evolving and teleological reading of the Convention, even on highly sensitive issues such as immigration and asylum, as briefly exemplified in the matter of the protection *par ricochet*.

In particular, this chapter has examined the implications of the Court's 'proceduralisation' trend in relation to the use of the margin of appreciation in recent asylum-related case law. This hermeneutic tool has been analysed according to a two-fold approach identified by previous studies. From a theoretical perspective, the procedural-obligations review tends toward judicial activism by imposing additional derived obligations and granting less margin to states. Conversely, the use of the procedural quality review may reflect an inclination towards self-restraint by the Court, which takes a step back in its substantive assessment in the face of, occasionally presumed, 'genuine and effective' domestic procedures.

Yet, when the Court does not privilege a specific procedural-type review, it appears able to reinforce its assessment in light of the principle of effectiveness of human rights. In advancing human rights, extrapolating the procedural nature of Convention's substantive provisions and converting them into further positive duties for states can in fact be as crucial as identifying gaps in various proceedings carried out by domestic authorities. Consequently, both modes of 'proceduralisation' can influence domestic institutions' understanding of the procedural aspects of the Convention and incentivize changes to the structural arrangements that ensure the effectiveness of substantive human rights. In other words, by employing this hermeneutic tool, the Strasbourg Court can facilitate the adoption of a

[50] On the ECtHR's impact on national case-law, legislation and policy, see J. Gerards, "The Paradox of the European Convention on Human Rights and the European Court of Human Rights' Transformative Power", *Kutafin Law Review*, 4 (2), 2017, p. 319 ff.

shared responsibility among Contracting States and foster mutual reinforcement of international and domestic human rights law,[51] even in the context of migration policy.

Nonetheless, the Court's practice of 'proceduralising' the examination of alleged violations of the Convention highlights weaknesses in its coherence and consistency. Namely, it is not always clear on the basis of which criteria the Court gives more weight to the formalistic elements of procedures instead of the positive procedural obligations in migration cases. Such unpredictability related to the use of the procedural-type reviews recalls the criticisms that have been also raised with reference to the application of the doctrine of the margin of appreciation, which often seems not be determined *a priori* but according to the solution that the Court aspires to reach in a given case.[52]

The analysis of the case-law in this chapter in fact suggests that the Court expands the scope of substantive guarantees for asylum seekers by inferring positive procedural states' obligations in judgments involving less controversial issues at the European level, such as national structural deficiencies in asylum procedures or in border procedures affecting migrants who have tried to enter a state through official border checkpoints. But it mainly, or almost exclusively, employs a formalistic approach focused on the mere existence of functioning legal procedures and the culpable conduct of migrants in cases related to the irregular crossing of a land border and collective expulsions, as in the leading decision of *N.D. and N.T. v. Spain*. It has been thus emphasized how this modality risks prioritising human rights protection of 'regular' migrants over 'irregular' migrants before the risk of *refoulement*, without considering the presence of *de facto* discrimination based on individuals' country of origin in accessing legal immigration and asylum procedures.

Moreover, in developing these tests, the Court does not sufficiently consider that asylum seekers as such are members of a particularly underprivileged and vulnerable group in need of special protection, in line with the broad consensus at the international and EU levels on this matter.[53] This may also be attributed to the Court's tendency to refrain from substantial

---

[51] In this vein, see also T. Kleinlein, "The procedural approach of the European Court of Human Rights", cit., pp. 106-107.

[52] B. Mac Crorie, G. Santomauro, "The Margin of Appreciation of States in the European Convention on Human Rights and Additional Protocol n. 15", in D. Moya, G. Milios, *Aliens before the European Court of Human Rights. Ensuring Minimum Standards of Human Rights Protection*, Leiden 2021, p. 275.

[53] ECtHR, *M.S.S. v. Belgium and Greece* [GC], § 251.

review or expressing normative preferences in highly sensitive matters, such as the management of irregular migration at national borders, especially if states are less likely to implement a certain judicial outcome.[54]

Whilst the enhancement of human rights cannot be automatically equated with judicial activism or the width of the margin of appreciation granted,[55] allowing excessive discretion to states based almost entirely on the quality of domestic-level processes is clearly contentious in judgments involving absolute rights such as Articles 2 and 3. Additionally, although the procedural requirements that states must comply with in cases of summary returns are well-established, the threshold used by Strasbourg judges to evaluate whether the quality of a certain national procedure is sufficient to avoid violating a substantive provision of the Convention has varied recently based on controversial decisive factors, such as the culpable conduct of migrants.

Therefore, when formalistic procedural fairness essentially replaces substantive scrutiny, the value of the procedural requirements put in place by contracting states to give concrete meaning to the Convention's provisions may be undermined. In other words, procedural control can actually influence the better protection of migrants' guarantees and contribute to shaping a stronger European responsibility in this respect, if it is seen as instrumental for the substantive outcome of the national proceedings under scrutiny, while the ECtHR also genuinely maintains its role as court of last resort in the assessment of human rights.

---

[54] In this regard, see S. Dothan, "Judicial Tactics in European Court of Human Rights", *Chicago Journal of International Law*, 12 (1), 2011, p. 115 ff., who claims that the ECtHR tends to adopt self-restraint when facing issues involving Western European states, which can damage its reputation by failing to comply with or severely criticize their judgments.

[55] F. Tulkens, "Judicial Activism v Judicial Restraint: Practical Experience of This (False) Dilemma at the European Court of Human Rights", *European Convention on Human Rights Law Review*, 3, 2022, pp. 297-298.

Chapter 14

FUNDAMENTAL RIGHTS PROTECTION AND JUDICIAL REASONING OF THE ITALIAN CONSTITUTIONAL COURT: OPENING UP TO SUPRANATIONAL MODELS THROUGH THE PROPORTIONALITY TEST AND THE USE OF COMPARATIVE ARGUMENTS

Giulia Vasino

ABSTRACT: *In the current stage of Italian Constitutional justice, the guardian of the Constitution has evolved into a highly interventionist political actor, thereby reshaping some of its traditional procedural standards. By focusing on recent case law and the Court's reasoning, this paper aims to highlight how the Court's conduct seems to show the intention to reconsider the constitutive elements of its decision-making style without renouncing a jurisdictional modus operandi. In this perspective, we will examine how the Court is now part of a well-established transnational judiciary network, which has contributed to building a permanent and mutually enriching dialogue between different constitutional systems and judicial models. In particular, the use of the proportionality test, which is the cornerstone of the protection of constitutionally protected rights in global neo-constitutionalism, as well as the increasing use of comparative arguments, both play a significant role. This rhetorical strategy is now frequently used not only with the aim of homogenizing and increasing fundamental rights protection, but to support the utilization of sophisticated judicial solutions implemented by European counterparts.*

SUMMARY: 1. Introduction. – 2. Theoretical arguments underpinning the construction of well-structured reasoning in fundamental rights decision-making. – 3. The harmonization of procedural standards in the European multilevel system. – 3.1. The proportionality doctrine and the Italian Constitutional Court's judicial reasoning. Towards the enucleation of a more 'structured' test? – 3.2. The increasing utilization of comparative law arguments in the current stage of Italian judicial review of legislation. – 4. Final remarks.

1. Introduction

The current evolution of the judicial review of legislation in Italy has activist features which have resulted in the strengthening of the role of the Constitutional Court. Therefore, despite the complexity of the issue highlighted by legal doctrine, academic debate agrees in affirming the advent of a new stage of Italian constitutional justice. In this perspective, the activity of the jurisdictional body has entered a new phase characterized by self-empowerment on the part of the Court. [1] Scholars have indeed highlighted how the Court has progressively emancipated itself from its original deferential attitude. [2]

Several expressions of this innovative path are widely perceived to be developing in the different areas of the architecture of judicial review. Upon observation of the Court's decision-making, it appears that its decisions have been increasingly inspired by the intention to provide more effective guarantees. A diachronic analysis of the Constitutional Court's decision-making process suggests that its approach is driven by the need to ensure a prompt restoration of constitutional legality. The Court is striving to maintain a balance between functional constraints and procedural rules while providing immediate relief to fundamental rights. This trend has taken several forms, including 1. the Court's claim to be the primary guardian of fundamental rights even in supranational contexts. Despite recognising several levels of guarantees, the Court has stated the priority of its own jurisdiction when an issue affects both constitutional principles and provisions of the EU Charter of Fundamental Rights (Judgment n. 269/2017). Furthermore, the development of the counter limits theory (see Judgement n. 24/2017) also adopts an activist approach within the multilevel system; 2. the less orthodox application of the procedural rule that requires national judges to identify an interpretation of a legislative provision in compliance with the constitution before promoting an issue of unconstitutionality (the so-called *interpretazione conforme*). In recent years, the Court has adopted a less strict approach to the requirement of intensifying its own role, as highlighted in Judgments n. 221 of 2015 and n. 42 of 2017. Additionally,

---

[1] D. Tega, *La Corte nel contesto. Percorsi di ri-accentramento della giustizia costituzionale in Italia*, Bologna 2020; A. Morrone, "Suprematismo giudiziario. Su sconfinamenti e legittimazione politica della Corte costituzionale", *Quaderni costituzionali*, 2/2019; T. Groppi, "Il ri-accentramento nell'epoca della ri-centralizzazione. Recenti tendenze dei rapporti tra Corte costituzionale e giudici comuni", *www.federalismi.it*, 3/2021, p. 129; A. Ruggeri, "Rapporti interordinamentali e rapporti istituzionali in circolo (scenari, disfunzioni, rimedi)", *Freedom, Security & Justice: European Legal Studies*, 2/2019.

[2] A. Von Bogdandy, D. Paris, *Building Judicial Authority: A Comparison Between the Italian Constitutional Court and the German Federal Constitutional Court*, Max Planck Institute for Comparative Public Law & International Law (MPIL) Research Paper, n. 1, 2019, available at SSRN: https://ssrn.com/abstract=3313641 or http://dx.doi.org/10.2139/ssrn.3313641.

there has been an innovative direction in constitutional jurisprudence regarding the direct system (*giudizio in via principale*). This includes reviewing legislation referring to extra-competential issues involving constitutionally protected rights (the so-called *ridondanza allargata*).

However, the most significant changes have arisen from the new activist attitude towards the indirect control. This has been observed in different sub-areas of the legal system, from ethical issues to criminal law. This evolution of judicial review of legislation has become a topic of concern. For many years, the Constitutional Court exercised caution in matters of constitutionality involving the political discretion of Parliament, however, the Court is now being criticized for questionable interventionism. As a result, some commentators have argued that these changes will have significant consequences. The aim of enhancing the effectiveness of its guaranteeing function may be considered to overshadow the procedural rules to which the Court must adhere. According to this view, even the institutional balance underlying the relationship between the Court and the Parliament has been significantly reshaped.[3]

However, this paper argues that the fractures in the legal framework may not be as significant as claimed and emphasizes that the judicial body's decision-making is demonstrating an effort to maintain self-imposed limitations and build a more structured legal reasoning. By analysing key factors of the Court's reasoning from an internal perspective, we will argue that the Court intends to reconsider some constitutive elements of its decision-making style while maintaining its jurisdictional *modus operandi*. In particular, we will explore the Court's openness to supranational judicial models. It will be noted that the Court is now part of a well-established transnational judiciary network, which has contributed to building a permanent and mutually enriching dialogue between different constitutional systems. Before analysing this scenario, we will highlight how legal doctrine has identified the importance of well-structured and persuasive reasoning when fundamental rights and core principles are at stake. According to a long-standing theoretical perspective, the consistency of a logical path has always been considered one of the most important requirements to support the Court's interventionism.

---

[3] R. Pinardi, "La Corte e il suo processo: alcune preoccupate riflessioni su un tema di rinnovato interesse", *Giurisprudenza costituzionale*, 3/2019.

2. Theoretical arguments underpinning the construction of well-structured reasoning in fundamental rights decision-making

The protection of core constitutional principles and values is the driving force behind the Court's recent and unprecedented jurisprudential development. However, this factor is also highly controversial and subject to severe disapproval. Some legal scholars argue that the reasoning lacks coherence, which could result in the protection of fundamental rights being subject to the arbitrariness of the constitutional judge.[4] This would make the guarantee dependent on a fragile, case-by-case approach. The recent jurisprudence of the Court has adopted new arguments to support its action, but this negative analysis also suggests that these arguments are slippery. Indeed, the reasoning has received sharp criticism for its emphasis on promptly safeguarding 'values of primary importance'.

This reception highlights the unresolved theoretical dilemma of whether a clear hierarchy can be identified among fundamental principles and rights. Despite reassurances from the constitutional jurisprudence itself, this remains a delicate issue. However, the main concern is the potential risks associated with rebuilding procedural standards based on vague assumptions presented in the Court's reasoning to justify intervention, such as 'unsustainable gaps of legal guarantees' and 'irreparable damages to individual rights'.[5] By highlighting the shortcomings of a new interventionism based on vague concepts such as 'values of primary importance', some authors caution that this could lead to an ethical-philosophical interpretation of the Constitution, which would weaken its juridical nature.[6] They refer to this as a 'hermeneutical slope'.

In this context, it is essential to seek clear, predefined direction and criteria and it is therefore necessary to form a coherent canon of intervention in the face of new upheavals in constitutional jurisprudence regarding decision-making techniques. This alternative approach has been strongly supported by legal doctrine. Throughout the long-standing debate on the modulation of temporal effects, which resurfaced after the publication of Judgment n. 10/2015, the importance of a clear and transparent motivational path with

---

[4] A. Morrone, "Suprematismo giudiziario. Su sconfinamenti e legittimazione politica della Corte costituzionale", *Quaderni costituzionali*, 2/2019, p. 251 ff.; A. Ruggeri, "Sliding doors per la incidentalità nel processo costituzionale", *Quaderni costituzionali*, 3/2015, p. 643.

[5] A. Spadaro, "Involuzione – o evoluzione? – del rapporto fra corte costituzionale e legislatore (notazioni ricostruttive)", *Rivista AIC*, 2/2023

[6] M. Luciani, *Ogni cosa al suo posto*, Milano 2023, p. 221.

well-defined parameters was highlighted.[7] Although the specific nature of constitutional jurisdiction prevents other constitutional bodies and individuals from appealing against the Court's decisions (Article 137, para. 3 It. Const.), a well-structured reasoning would play an 'external' function. In other words, despite the reasoning lacking any endo-processual value, the rationalization of the Court's decision-making process and its legitimacy are based on the enunciation of stable and transparent criteria.[8]

As noted with regard to the unprecedented outcome of the decision on the so-called *Robin Tax*, the Court's standards aim to provide transparency and clarity in justifying the balancing act. More precisely, it is important not only to justify the exercise of a function but also to take responsibility for the intervention by reaching an explicit and adequately motivated conclusion. With regard to the modulation of temporal effects, a well-founded reasoning would make it possible to assess whether a more extensive interpretation of Article 136 of the Constitution and Section 30 of Law 87/1953, which rules on temporal effects, is congruous with the protected value.

Throughout the long-standing doctrinal discussion on the effects of the Court's decisions, the importance of sound argumentation has been authoritatively emphasized in order to 'test' the strength of the principle at stake in relation to other relevant principles.[9] All these issues have been presented as a 'balancing problem' and an issue concerning substantive constitutional law.[10]

The effectiveness of the latter was entirely dependent on the persuasiveness of the reasoning. Despite the various issues at stake, the importance of strengthening the argument and developing a structured procedure based on clear standards had already been established. The need for this was highlighted in the 2015 abovementioned judgment, where the Court imposed a radical *pro futuro* application on its declaration of unconstitutionality. However, the Court did consider the criterion of proportionality (in a narrow sense) when making its decision. The Court affirmed that

---

[7] C. Colapietro, "La trasparenza del percorso motivazionale seguito dalla Corte costituzionale nella teorizzazione del potere di modulazione degli effetti temporali delle proprie sentenze di accoglimento", in A.A.V.V., *Liber amicorum in onore di Augusto Cerri*, Napoli 2016, p. 263 ff.

[8] E. Bindi, *La garanzia della Costituzione. Chi custodisce il custode?,* Torino 2010, p. 142.

[9] C. Mezzanotte, "Il contenimento della retroattività degli effetti delle sentenze di accoglimento come questione di diritto costituzionale sostanziale", in AA.VV., *Effetti temporali delle sentenze della Corte costituzionale anche con riferimento alle esperienze straniere*, Milano 1989, p. 44.

[10] *Ibidem.*

the modulation of constitutional provisions concerning temporal effectiveness is subject to the compelling need to protect one or more constitutional principles and limited to what is strictly necessary to ensure the safeguard of the values at stake.

This theoretical framework remains unchanged when applied to the current stage of Italian constitutional justice. Furthermore, it appears to gain further importance. Although the issue of temporal effects highlights the risks associated with rule reinterpretation, the need to anchor the reshaping of the provision that directly sets the functional boundaries of the guaranteeing body to solid argumentative parameters has become even more urgent.

3. The harmonization of judicial procedural standards in the European multilevel system

In this situation, the longstanding interaction between courts positively impacts the development of a new convincing procedural framework. Beyond mere institutional exchange, judicial discourse has gradually forged a meaningful connection, serving as a crucial arena for mutual enrichment between the constitutional systems involved.[11] Through this reciprocal influence, a shared 'plural sensitivity' has become ingrained in the Court's decision-making process.[12] Notably, the integration of a comparative viewpoint often proves pivotal in the Court's rulings. This rhetorical tactic is now frequently employed not only to standardize and bolster the safeguarding of fundamental rights but also to endorse the adoption of sophisticated judicial approaches akin to those of European counterparts. In this context, the increasing interconnection between jurisdictional models serves as an additional reassuring factor to address concerns regarding the Court's purported activism. The ongoing exchange of constitutional experiences can further enhance the coherence and transparency of this evolving judicial reasoning. Indeed, it represents a valuable resource for assimilating new procedural norms and refining existing ones still in their primary stages within the Court's judicial deliberations.

Beneath this perspective lies the overarching theory that the *rationale* presented by courts serves as a vital tool for ensuring transparency in judi-

---

[11] D. De Lungo, "Comparazione e legittimazione. Considerazioni sull'uso dell'argomento comparatistico nella giurisprudenza costituzionale recente, a partire dal caso Cappato", in F.S. Marini, C. Cupelli (eds.), *Il caso Cappato*, cit., p. 97.

[12] T. Groppi, "Il ri-accentramento nell'epoca della ri-centralizzazione", cit., p. 141.

cial review. [13] Contrary to aiming to sway the audience with persuasive arguments, the goal of constitutional reasoning is to furnish clear, substantial, and plausible justifications to rationally validate court rulings. According to this stance, the Court's deliberations should eschew a mere 'justification theory,' rhetorical persuasion, or a simple manifestation of the collective will of the bench. [14] Instead, judicial reasoning should strive to provide comprehensive "information on the substance of the decision and the facts and reasoning underlying it," thereby upholding what is defined as "transparency *in rationale*". [15]

Nevertheless, as authoritatively emphasized, transparency in constitutional reasoning can also have an 'internal' impact. [16] Specifically, a logical and robust judicial path can influence the judiciary itself by potentially setting a precedent for future judgments. [17] In this context, the Court's discretion would inherently impose self-restraint.

3.1. The proportionality doctrine and the Italian Constitutional Court's judicial reasoning. Towards the enucleation of a more 'structured' test?

The proportionality test is a significant criterion stemming from the multilevel system. As is widely recognized, it serves as a fundamental argumentative framework available to constitutional judges for decision-making through a methodical assessment process. Thus, the intricate equilibrium of fundamental rights relies firmly on clearly delineated logical stages arranged in sequence. [18]

Adherence to this sequential process is imperative for the permissible limitation of a specific fundamental right. Scholars employ the term 'structured analysis' to identify the soundness of the proportionality frame-

---

[13] F. Falorni, "Giudice costituzionale e trasparenza: un binomio sempre più ricorrente", *www.federalismi.it*, 30/2020, p. 84 ff.

[14] See M. Taruffo, *La motivazione della sentenza civile*, Padova 1975, pp. 118-126.

[15] J. de Fine Licht, D. Naurin, P. Esaiasson, M. Gilljam, "When Does Transparency Generate Legitimacy? Experimenting on a Context-Bound Relationship", 27 *Governance: An International Journal of Policy, Administration, and Institution*, 1, 2014, p. 113.

[16] R. Romboli, "La mancanza o l'insufficienza della motivazione come criterio di selezione dei giudizi", in A. Ruggeri (ed.), *La motivazione delle decisioni della Corte costituzionale*, Torino 1994, p. 339 ff.

[17] F. Falorni, "Giudice costituzionale e trasparenza", cit., p. 96 ff.

[18] R. Alexy, "Constitutional Rights, Balancing, and Rationality", *Ratio Juris*, 16, 2, 2003, pp. 133-134.

work.[19] The test was initially formulated by the German Constitutional Court however, due to its esteemed reputation, it has since been integrated into international legal culture.[20] Currently, it undeniably serves as a fundamental tool for both the ECtHR and the CJEU.[21]

Moreover, the concept of 'constitutionalism of rights' strives to establish a universal constitutional justice based on the concept of human dignity. However, this goal has long clashed with the deeply fragmented and conflicting nature of modern pluralistic societies.[22] In the context of structural and ideological disputes revolving around the core tenets of the legal system, the proportionality test, owing to its inherently procedural nature, offers an approach that can mitigate their wide-ranging impacts. Through a methodical process that dissects an issue into its constituent components, judicial review can arrive at an appropriate solution. The underlying assumption behind the three or four-step analysis is that binary responses are inadequate for the delicate balancing of constitutional rights. Particularly with regard to the third stage of assessment (the narrow application of the proportionality test), the objective of judicial scrutiny is not to establish a hierarchical ranking of values.[23]

As a significant component of Europe's shared legal heritage, proportionality holds considerable sway in the reasoning of the Italian constitutional court. Nevertheless, despite its impact, it is only implicitly alluded to and does not align with the sophistication characteristic of the European model. Consequently, scholars claim the presence of a 'de-structured' proportionality in the Italian judicial review process.[24]

First, there is ambiguity at the terminological level. Rationality, proportionality, and reasonableness frequently overlap in the judicial reasoning of

---

[19] See A. Barak, *Proportionality. Constitutional Rights and their Limitations*, Cambridge 2012, pp. 460-462; V.C. Jackson, "Constitutional Law in an Age of Proportionality", *The Yale Law Journal*, 124, 8, 2015, p. 3098.

[20] See A. Stone Sweet, J. Mathews, "Proportionality Balancing and Global Constitutionalism", *Columbia Journal of Transnational Law*, 47, 2008, p. 73.

[21] A.L. Bandor, T. Sela, "How proportional is proportionality?", *International Journal of Constitutional Law*, 13, 2, 2015, p. 530 ff.

[22] See R. Nania, "Sui diritti fondamentali nella vicenda evolutiva del costituzionalismo", *Nomos-Le attualità nel diritto*, 1/2020, p. 3.

[23] G. Scaccia, "Proportionality and the Balancing of Rights in the Case-law of European Courts", *www.federalismi.it*, 4/2019, p. 4.

[24] M. Cartabia, *I principi di ragionevolezza e proporzionalità nella giurisprudenza costituzionale italiana*. Intervento presentato a Incontro trilaterale tra la Corte costituzionale italiana, la Corte costituzionale spagnola e il Tribunale costituzionale portoghese, Roma, Palazzo della Consulta, 2013, available at *www.cortecostituzionale.it*.

the Court, alongside principles such as adequacy, consistency, appropriateness, and non-arbitrariness. On one particular occasion, the CC explicitly asserted that proportionality directly reflects the broader principle of reasonableness.[25]

Furthermore, these two pivotal criteria are frequently referenced together as hendiadys, in contrast to other jurisdictional systems where their nature and significance vary considerably in terms of intensity.[26] Conversely, within the Anglo-American legal tradition, reasonableness is considered a 'minimal' judicial standard, typically invoked when the examined provision seems overtly absurd upon initial examination.[27] As per the renowned Wednesbury test,[28] the reasonableness assessment represents the most lenient scrutiny and often embodies judicial deference to legislative authority. Furthermore, given its residual nature, the reasonableness analysis serves as an open-ended standard, operating intuitively: judges aren't required to follow a strict logical framework when the statute's irrationality is blatantly evident.[29] Hence, the meticulously organized European proportionality, marked by a growingly pervasive oversight, diverges from the Italian judicial review.[30]

However, it could be argued that each phase of the proportionality test is extensively utilized by the Court on a regular basis. In particular, there is a recurring focus on assessing the adequacy of the relationship between means and objectives. Additionally, the necessity for legislative interventions to strictly align with safeguarding constitutional interests is frequently scrutinized by the collegium. Most importantly, the balancing of rights, sharing fundamental similarities with the strict sense of the proportionality test, has also been incorporated into the toolkit of the Italian constitutional Court.

---

[25] See Judgement n. 220/1995.

[26] For example, as has been pointed out in M. Cartabia, *I principi di ragionevolezza e proporzionalità*, cit., p. 2, in Judgement n. 2/1999 the Court stated that the automatism in the disciplinary measure under examination was «irreasonable, since it does not comply with proportionality, which is the foundation of rationality that informs the principle of equality».

[27] M. Cartabia, *I principi di ragionevolezza e proporzionalità*, cit., p. 3.

[28] See J. Law, E. Martin, *A Dictionary of Law*, 7th ed., Oxford 2014.

[29] See G. Bognetti, "Il principio di ragionevolezza e la giurisprudenza della Corte suprema americana", in *Il principio di ragionevolezza nella giurisprudenza della Corte costituzionale*, Atti del seminario svoltosi in Roma, Palazzo della Consulta, 13-14 ottobre 1992, Milano 1994, p. 43 ff.

[30] F. Falorni, "Verso una compiuta elaborazione del "test di proporzionalità"? La Corte Costituzionale italiana al passo con le altre esperienze di giustizia costituzionale", *DPCE online*, 4/2020, p. 5308 ff.

It might be argued that there is no need to transform naturally evolved standards into a more structured framework, as the various steps have already become ingrained in constitutional reasoning. However, it should be noted that since the last decade, the Court itself has displayed an intention to move beyond the de-structured approach to proportionality. Notably, with decision n. 1/2014 – which also marked the starting point of the current phase of Italian constitutional justice – the various stages of the test have been articulated with greater precision by the CC.[31] While timidly referenced in prior judgments, the three fundamental stages of proportionality – suitability, necessity, and proportionality (in its narrow sense) – were all met in this decision on electoral affairs. On closer scrutiny, legitimacy was also encompassed, as the Court indicated that the legislative provision aimed to promote the formation of a stable parliamentary majority.

Additionally, proportionality was cited in decision n. 10/2015 as a benchmark for modulating temporal effects.[32] More precisely, the *stricto sensu* proportionality analysis was utilized to justify the decision to depart from the usual retroactive application of its judgment, stipulating that it would only have prospective effects.[33] In that ruling, the CC articulated that a sophisticated judicial intervention must adhere to the following criteria: 1. the urgent need to safeguard one or more constitutional principles, which would otherwise suffer irreparable harm; 2. any deviation from the normal retroactive effect must be limited to what is strictly necessary. In this context, it becomes increasingly apparent that proportionality functions primarily as a guiding principle for the Court itself.

Indeed, the Court's inclination toward a more structured and intricate application of proportionality has been evidenced and subsequently implemented in subsequent rulings (Cases 275/2015, 20/2019, 170/2019, and 119/2020)[34]. Therefore, this suggests a partial achievement that merits a positive reception and is likely to progress further.

---

[31] G. Scaccia, "Proportionality and the Balancing of Rights", cit., pp. 5-6.

[32] See F. Falorni, "Verso una compiuta elaborazione del "test di proporzionalità"?", cit., p. 5317 ff.

[33] C. Mainardis, "Limiti agli effetti retroattivi delle sentenze costituzionali e principio di proporzionalità (un'osservazione a C. cost. n. 10/2015)", *Forum di Quaderni costituzionali*, 9/2015, p. 4 ff.

[34] F. Falorni, "Verso una compiuta elaborazione del "test di proporzionalità"?", cit., p. 5320 ff.

3.2. The increasing utilization of comparative law arguments in the current stage of Italian judicial review of legislation

Along with the changes concerning the proportionality test, the use of comparative arguments also seems to be acquiring an increasingly central role.[35] The reference to supranational case-law and foreign legal systems have always been a custom in judicial reasoning. Besides, even the analysis of the utilization of legal comparative references is not a new issue, as it too was extensively examined in the Italian doctrinal debate in the 1980s.[36]

In general, under the institutional perspective, there are two main systemic reasons underlying the utilization of comparative references. First, it is once again the main effect of the constitutional state's evolutionary dynamics toward open and cooperative models, characterized by the attenuation of national sovereignty. In this context, fundamental rights have benefited from such cosmopolitan dimension, fulfilling their inner nature toward universalization. This evolution has contributed to the establishment of stable legal and judicial interdependence between systems. But, most importantly, the reference to authoritative supranational case-law also has an internal effect. It supports the constitutional judge as well in recalibrating precisely their role within the form of government, in its relations with the other apex constitutional subjects. Thanks to the natural comparative attitude of fundamental rights, the Court implicitly invokes *ius alii loci* to legitimize its goals to strengthen its position in the constitutional scenario.

Furthermore, in relation to the depicted phenomena of homogenization and comparison, a biunivocal cause-and-effect relationship can be identified. More clearly, as the degree of legal and cultural assimilability of different systems increases, so does the congruence of comparative interpretative approaches. Therefore, the constitutional judge attempts, at the same time, to find an equilibrium between the 'centrifugal' forces that over time have marginalized its role and to legitimize its decisions through foreign experience as well. Among various doctrinal stances, it was also pointed out that the influence of comparative jurisprudence on the reasoning was

---

[35] Among less recent studies on this matter, see L. Pegoraro, P. Damiani, "Il diritto comparato nella giurisprudenza di alcune Corti costituzionali", *DPCE*, 1999, p. 411 ff.; A. Sperti, "Il dialogo tra le Corti costituzionali ed il ricorso alla comparazione giuridica nella esperienza più recente", *Rivista di diritto costituzionale*, 2006, p. 125 ff.; A. Baldassarre, "La Corte costituzionale italiana e il metodo comparativo", *Diritto pubblico comparato ed europeo*, 2006, p. 983 ff.

[36] L. Pegoraro, "La Corte costituzionale e il diritto comparato nelle sentenze degli anni '80", *Quaderni costituzionali*, 1987, p. 601 ff.

not expressly evident, since it played a 'magmatic' and multi-faceted function.[37]

Since the current stage of constitutional justice, the inclusion of comparative arguments in the reasoning is a more recurring feature, albeit not relevant if compared to other constitutional jurisdictions. Empirical analysis has shown that 2010 represented a turning point, with a further increment from 2017 onwards. Since that time, the number of foreign and comparative references have increased to 2.20% if compared with the previous decade.[38]

Based on the aforementioned premises, the Court's increased use of comparative arguments can be attributed to its progressive self-positioning within multilevel constitutionalism. The Court is aiming to assert itself in the multilevel system of rights by referencing decisions made by supranational and European jurisdictional bodies involving similar individual claims.

The increased acceptance of supranational case law can be seen as a natural result of the expansion of constitutional courts and guaranteeing forums. Over the years, a common heritage of principles has been established, and constitutional experiences have been integrated. Judgments are enhanced by cross-references and comparisons to be shared and validated, thus legitimising themselves. These conclusions are no longer placed in a self-referential, closed system, but in a network of legal 'communicating vessels'.[39] The recourse to comparison when fundamental rights are at stake is therefore a recurring trend of the last decade.

In various legal areas, the Court has relied on supranational jurisprudence and foreign legal systems to support its judgments on fundamental rights. This judicial direction was already evident in decision n. 10/2015, as mentioned previously. In that Judgement, the Court not only applied the proportionality test but also established a direct link between the objective of adequately preserving fundamental rights and the Court's right to reshape the rules of the constitutional proceedings. The Court offered several comparative references to support its decision.

---

[37] D. De Lungo, "Comparazione e legittimazione. Considerazioni sull'uso dell'argomento comparatistico nella giurisprudenza costituzionale recente, a partire dal caso Cappato", *www.federalismi.it*, 17/2019, p. 21.

[38] P. Passaglia, "The Italian Constitutional Court and the Use of Comparative Law: An Empirical Analysis", *The Italian review of International and comparative law*, 2/2022, p. 99.

[39] D. De Lungo, "Comparazione e legittimazione. Considerazioni sull'uso dell'argomento comparatistico nella giurisprudenza costituzionale recente, a partire dal caso Cappato", *www.federalismi.it*, 17/2019, p. 21.

At present, its approach has been further applied from ethical issues to criminal law. In the well-known 2010 judgment n. 138, which dealt with same-sex marriages, the Court included two references. However, it can be observed that at that time, the comparison was still moderate and less explicit. The Court generally affirmed that other countries have adopted solutions to identify adequate legal protection for homosexual couples. These solutions include extending the legislation in force for civil marriages or alternative forms of protection.[40] Again, the Court appeared to make a clear reference to the legislation of another country when addressing the issue of unconstitutionality related to the so-called 'automatic divorce' in the event of one spouse undergoing gender reassignment (Judgement n. 170/2014). In that case, the Court adopted an innovative solution that had been widely debated by legal scholars and cited similar decisions made by the Austrian and German Constitutional Courts.[41] In its decisions on medical assisted reproduction and Law n. 40/2004, the Court made several references to supranational case law. In its legal reasoning for decision n. 84/2016, the Court extensively referenced the *Parrillo v. Italy* Judgment of the Grand Chamber of the Court of Strasbourg.[42] Comparative arguments were used to demonstrate the lack of consensus among the Member States of the Council of Europe. Due to the lack of uniformity on this matter, the Court was able to support its decision to defer the issue to political discretion.

However, after examining case law from the past five years, it appears that comparative references have become an even more prominent feature in legal reasoning, regardless of their role. For instance, in Judgement n. 141/2019, the Court's extensive use of comparisons made them a crucial aspect of the decision.[43] The Court dismissed the constitutional issues raised concerning provisions that criminalize recruitment, aiding, and abetting of prostitution by using comparative arguments as a pivotal point to elucidate the overall framework of the legislation.

In Judgement n. 207/2018, also known as the Cappato decision, the

---

[40] R. Romboli, "Il diritto «consentito» al matrimonio ed il diritto «garantito» alla vita familiare per le coppie omosessuali in una pronuncia in cui la Corte dice «troppo» e «troppo poco»", *Giurisprudenza costituzionale*, 2010, p. 1629 ff.

[41] F. Biondi, "La sentenza additiva di principio sul c.d. divorzio "imposto": un caso di accertamento, ma non di tutela, della violazione di un diritto", *Forum di Quaderni costituzionali*, 2014, p. 2 e P. Veronesi, "Un'anomala additiva di principio in materia di "divorzio imposto": il "caso Bernaroli" nella sentenza n. 170/2014", *Forum di Quaderni costituzionali*, 2014, p. 2 ff.

[42] P. Passaglia, "The Italian Constitutional Court and the Use of Comparative Law", cit., p. 114.

[43] *Ivi*, p. 116

Court used comparative arguments in two ways. Firstly, the judicial body employed a decision-making approach that was implicitly inspired by the toolkit of the German Federal Court. Furthermore, the Court frequently referred to foreign case law (the Supreme Court of Canada's *Carter v. Canada*, 2015 and the Supreme Court of the United Kingdom's Judgment *Nicklinson and another*, 2014) as well as *ECtHR* decisions, to justify its decision to partially declare the provision of the criminal code unconstitutional without completely striking it down.[44] This was indeed in line with supranational and foreign cases. From this perspective, the comparison serves as additional argumentative reinforcement for the Court's decision to cooperate with the legislative branch on the delicate subject of assisted suicide. The Court affirmed that it would be institutionally inappropriate for a constitutional court to declare something unconstitutional without giving Parliament the opportunity to rule on the issue. Based on the argumentative path used, the Court appeared to be further emphasizing the importance of case law, creating a horizontal system of precedents with a key persuasive effect. This is similar to decision n. 1/2014, which marked the beginning of the Court's activism.

Judgments nn. 32 and 33 of 2021, which concern the formal recognition of the parent-child relationship and medically assisted reproduction for homosexual couples, also refer to the French legal system.[45] This was in relation to a request for an advisory opinion made by the French Court of Cassation to the Court of Strasbourg, which fell under the application of Protocol n. 16 to the European Convention on Human Rights.[46]

The use of comparative arguments referring to rulings of other courts is currently becoming more common, and the Court of Strasbourg is often used as the main reference point. For instance, in order n. 132/2020, the Constitutional Court examined two referral orders concerning the constitutionality of provisions imposing detention as a penalty for crimi-

---

[44] D. De Lungo, "Comparazione e legittimazione. Considerazioni sull'uso dell'argomento comparatistico nella giurisprudenza costituzionale recente, a partire dal caso Cappato", *www.federalismi.it*, 17/2019, p. 2 ff.

[45] On the controversial ethical issue of surrogacy and on the dialogue between Courts on such matter see M.G. Rodomonte, "The Controversial Issue of the Status of those Born Abroad through Surrogacy. The 'Dialogue' between the Italian Constitutional Court and the European Court of Human Rights, and the Role of the National Legislator", in this volume.

[46] See A. Ruggeri, "La PMA alla Consulta e l'uso discrezionale della discrezionalità del legislatore (Nota minima a Corte cost. nn. 32 e 33 del 2021)", *www.Consulta online.org*, 1/2021 and F. Mannella, "Oltre un serio avvertimento al legislatore? La Corte costituzionale e la nuova categoria di "nati non riconoscibili" Nota alla sentenza n. 32 del 2021 della Corte costituzionale", *Nomos-Le attualità nel diritto*, 2/2021, p. 7 ff.

nal defamation. Although the comparative reference was made due to the alleged violation of Article 117.1 of the Italian Constitution, the decision-making process was supported not only by the ECtHR jurisprudential precedents but also by the Resolution of the Venice Commission.[47] These were used to support the substantive profile of the adopted solution, which foresees unconstitutionality. The Court confirmed that the questions raised required a complex balancing act between freedom of expression and the protection of reputation, both of which are key rights within the constitutional order.

The criminal law sphere has increasingly recognized the importance of the role of ECHR case law. For instance, recent developments in prison law, particularly those related to life sentences, have been significantly influenced by the Court of Strasbourg, as evidenced by the landmark *Viola* decision. While the role of comparative arguments is primarily legal, as it deals with alleged violations of Article 117.1, it has also played a crucial function in legitimising the decisions made by the Court, from Decision n. 253 to 97 of 2021.[48] The role of comparison in these decisions is not the traditional argument *ad abundantiam*, but rather part of the *ratio decidendi* adopted by the court.

4. Final remarks

In recent years, the Italian Constitutional Court has undergone significant changes in its judicial approach, challenging key standards of constitutional review. The Court is currently engaged in a significant process of rewriting the legal framework with the aim of enhancing the effectiveness of its guaranteeing function.

On the one hand, the Court's activism appears to be firmly grounded in a jurisprudential modus operandi. Despite its evolving proactive approach, it still complies with an inherently coherent procedural framework. In the Court's self-empowerment phase, the aim of judicial reasoning is to blend the Court's 'renewed sensitivity' with the maintenance of procedural constraints. This innovative attitude, though marked by less restrictive inter-

---

[47] M. Cuniberti, "La pena detentiva per la diffamazione tra Corte costituzionale e Corte europea dei diritti dell'uomo: l'ordinanza della Corte costituzionale n. 132 del 2020", *Osservatorio costituzionale*, 5/2020, p. 123 ff.

[48] Among many, see M. Ruotolo, "Reati ostativi e permessi premio. Le conseguenze della sentenza n. 253 del 2019 della Corte costituzionale", *Sistema penale*, 12 December 2019, par. 3; M. Massa, "La terza incostituzionalità «prospettata» e la questione dell'ergastolo ostativo", *Nomos-Le attualità nel diritto*, 2/2021, p. 9.

ventions, still finds its fundamental rules and primary legitimization in adherence to institutional limitations and the principles of transparency and solid standards, as emphasized by legal doctrine over the years. In the ongoing effort to establish clear procedural standards that align with the objective of effectively safeguarding fundamental rights while maintaining the judicial nature of the body, transnational dialogue between courts provides valuable inspiration and assurance. The driving force and standardization influence from supranational and European models positively contribute to the fairness and transparency of constitutional reasoning.

The utilization of the proportionality test is crucial to protecting constitutionally guaranteed rights in global neo-constitutionalism. It holds significant potential within this enriching endeavour as it delineates the criteria for limiting fundamental rights. The proportionality test is a crucial procedural standard that should be further embraced by the Italian Court. The author affirmed that this is linked to the renewed approach of the Constitution's guardian to the essence of indirect proceedings. This text appears to discuss the impact of safeguarding individual rights on the alteration of the Constitutional Court's functional boundaries however the significance of this factor is more nuanced upon closer scrutiny. The need to amplify the influence of individual instances within the hybrid system of judicial review cannot be the only reason for this. Instead, it has a specific 'individualizing' significance, as it aims to preserve and strengthen individual claims as they arise in the original judgment.[49]

Improving the specificity of judicial review means that the reinstatement of constitutional values cannot be delayed indefinitely. In this evolving context, where the judiciary's scrutiny of legislation is increasingly susceptible to the significant impact of factual circumstances, the proportionality test can be effective. Factual considerations hold a crucial position within the framework of proportionality reasoning. This approach offers evaluations based on specific circumstances and is therefore subject to change and inherently precarious.[50] Principles, rights, and values are intertwined with reality, including its evolving conditions, influences, and constraints.

However, the increasing use of comparative arguments may be framed differently from proportionality. Despite the available evidence offered by recent case law, comparative argumentation appears to have gained increased significance in constitutional case law in recent years, at least in quantitative terms, as empirical studies demonstrate. When safeguarding fundamental rights is urgent, the Court's reasoning relies on comparative

[49] G. Repetto, *Recenti orientamenti*, cit., p. 5 ff.

[50] G. Scaccia, "Proportionality and the Balancing of Rights", cit., p. 4.

references as a crucial supportive argument. Nonetheless, it has been noted that this trend does not fully reflect the overall influence of comparative law on the Constitutional Court's decision-making. Upon examination of the Court's use of comparative arguments, it is evident that supranational and foreign case law is seldom the primary basis for a decision.[51] Comparative references primarily play a complementary role, reinforcing a decision that could have been reached even without such justifying logic, albeit possibly with a less robust argumentative foundation. Only in limited cases is comparison decisive for the outcome.[52] As empirical data confirms, it often takes on a more neutral and recognitive formulation, and only in limited cases does it prove persuasive. Therefore, there is still a lack of a useful standard that would require a rationalization process for the use of this element in reasoning. Instead, an episodic approach seems to emerge, which appears to be related to the choices of individual judges rather than being proportionate to the centrality of the value at stake or the degree of 'universalization' that the constitutional principle involved acquires.

Considering these elements, it can be argued that in a context where the Constitutional Court plays an increasingly central role in guaranteeing fundamental rights, openness to the supranational dimension and judicial dialogue can be seen as a factor of rationalization with different tendencies and nuances.

Positive effects arise in relation to supranational decision-making models, such as the proportionality test. This argumentative model is well-established in Italian court decision-making however the continuous intermingling process appears to be gaining strength. Comparative arguments also involve the 'substantive dimension' of the Court's case law, but only in a logic of comparison between models. In this regard, although comparative supportive arguments are increasingly used in decisions concerning fundamental rights, the Court appears to be proceeding cautiously and with less linearity. This less coherent and less intelligible use can be seen as a result of the need to protect national jurisprudential tradition regarding the essence of fundamental rights. From this perspective, supranational references can only provide support in framing and identifying the potential expansion of fundamental rights. However, the core binding effect of the decision-making process still prioritises the preservation of robust jurisprudential traditions and unique interpretations on substantive matters, preventing the establishment of more structured standards.

---

[51] P. Passaglia, "The Italian Constitutional Court and the Use of Comparative Law", cit., pp. 120-121.

[52] *Ibidem.*

Chapter 15

THE CONTROVERSIAL ISSUE OF THE STATUS OF THE CHILD BORN ABROAD THROUGH SURROGACY. THE 'DIALOGUE' BETWEEN THE ITALIAN CONSTITUTIONAL COURT AND THE EUROPEAN COURT OF HUMAN RIGHTS AND THE ROLE OF THE NATIONAL LEGISLATOR

Maria Grazia Rodomonte

ABSTRACT: *The chapter aims to explore the issue of the recognition of a child born abroad through surrogacy, despite the prohibition against this practice by Italian law. In particular, an attempt is made to understand the role of the Italian judges, the Constitutional Court and the European Court of Human Rights in this regard, while there is also an exploration of the national policy-maker's role in defining this delicate issue that requires a balance between the 'best interest of the child' and the ban on surrogacy in Italy. Over the years, in fact, the complex interweaving of the jurisprudence of the Constitutional Court in dialogue with the European Court of Human Rights, has resulted in a sufficiently articulated and broad framework of protections that today leads to questions about the residual extent of legislative discretion.*

1. Introduction

The evolution of science and technology and the changes that have affected customs and social conscience have led to the emergence of ever-new claims (which cannot always be considered rights) and the related difficulty of governing and resolving the contradictions and conflicts arising from the demand for protection of new individual needs. This phenomenon can be described as the "'normativization' of desire";[1] a concise expression which nevertheless captures the problematic crux of an evolution also related to the role of judges and legislators in a context not always characterized by a shared *ethos*. The crisis of the legitimization of political representatives and "the crisis of the represented"[2] have revealed a framework in which the legislator often prefers to remain silent, leaving room for the judge. The regulatory 'vacuum' thus translates into space for a substitute role of the judge, with the result, however, of simultaneously reducing the space for political decision-making, jeopardizing legal certainty and the principle of the separation of powers.

The issues concerning the definition of the status of a child born abroad through surrogacy, despite the prohibition expressly established by Italian law, are certainly emblematic of the situation described above. The silence of the Italian legislature and the 'dialogue' between national judges, the Italian Constitutional Court and the European Court of Human Rights have certainly contributed to the recognition of new individual requests and have given a central role to the Strasbourg Court within the multi-level protection system.

2. Surrogacy: definition and legislative provisions in Italy

Surrogacy is a particular assisted reproductive technology (ART) in which a woman agrees to carry a child for another party on the basis of an agreement with a commissioning individual or couple (heterosexual or homosexual). At the end of the pregnancy, the gestational mother delivers the baby to the 'clients' either free of charge or, as is more often the case, for a fee. Surrogacy may involve a genetic mother, who is the one who – usually for a fee – provides her own eggs, which are fertilized by the biological father of the unborn child, who may be a member of the couple or a donor. The child is carried by the birth mother who will not, however, also be the 'intended' mother since her relationship with the child will necessarily end at the time of its birth and delivery to the commissioning parents. Both members of the couple may then be so-called 'intended' parents or one of them may be the biological father and the other the intended parent.

---

[1] L. Antonini, "Autodeterminazione nel sistema dei diritti costituzionali", in F. D'agostino, *Autodeterminazione. Un diritto di spessore costituzionale?*, Atti del Convegno nazionale dell'UGCI, Pavia, 5-7 dicembre 2009, Milano 2012, p. 12.

[2] M. Luciani, "Il paradigma della rappresentanza di fronte alla crisi del rappresentato", in *Percorsi e vicende attuali della rappresentanza politica*, ed. by N. Zanon, F. Biondi, Milano 2001, p. 109 ss.

As is clear, this is a multifaceted practice, not least because an extremely variable number of subjects can be involved[3]. However, all possible combinations of surrogacy result in a diversion from the fundamental principle of the Italian legal order, according to which *mater semper certa est*. In fact:

> the woman who gives birth (and who may participate in part or be totally unrelated to the genetic heritage of the born child) would not be considered a mother within the meaning of Article 269 of the Civil Code by virtue of an agreement made for free or for a fee and by which two other persons assume the parentage of the child born, sharing its genetic heritage or resulting as such in the forms of intentional parenthood[4].

Surrogacy is therefore a practice that raises a number of questions, both of an ethical and legal nature.

The 'fragmentation' of the parental figures, and specifically the maternal one, is evident. Not only is it possible to have two fathers, one biological and the other intended or social, but even three distinct 'mothers': the genetic mother, the uterine or biological mother and the intended or social mother. In this case, the damage caused in particular to the child must be highlighted, both as a consequence of the immediate interruption of the deep symbiotic bond that was created with the biological mother during the nine months of gestation and for the:

> substantial 'deconstruction' of the maternal identity and, consequently, the identity of the child, which sooner or later will have to ask himself/herself of which maternal figure to take as a reference among the many involved in the generative process.[5]

The legal aspect of the importance of the connection between motherhood, pregnancy and childbirth is represented by the acceptance in the Italian legal system of the principle that *mater semper certa est*. This is a principle that guarantees the child "to immediately be the holder of a relational and legal identity" and therefore represents the "necessary condition

[3] As pointed out by R. Bin, "Maternità surrogata: ragioni di una riflessione", *BioLaw Journal*, 2/2016, who identifies as many as 11 different possible surrogacy scenarios of which 5 relate to heterosexual couples and 6 relate to same-sex couples.

[4] L. Conte, *La famiglia. Istituti e istituzione nella prospettiva costituzionale,* Napoli 2020, p. 130.

[5] B. Salone, "La maternità surrogata in Italia: profili di diritto interno e risvolti internazionalprivatistici", *BioLaw Journal – Rivista di BioDiritto,* 2/2016, p. 42.

for the child to be the subject of a right rather than the object of the rights of others" [6].

In addition to the 'fragmentation' of parental figures, particularly the maternal one, and the consequent fragmentation of the child's identity, the 'contractualisation' of motherhood, with all that this entails, should also be taken into consideration. On the one hand, the exploitation of women and their probable condition of need is evident. Surrogacy is a true commodification of the female body and its maternal function, which can only lead to the violation of dignity, which must be understood:

> even before being a fundamental right – as a principle that permeates the entire constitutional pact based on the centrality of the human person, considered, as such and in his relational life, always an end and never a means, a principle which inheres, by integrating, with the fundamental rights from which it becomes inseparable [7].

While all this implies numerous easily imaginable consequences and raises multiple questions, it seems difficult to deny the violation of dignity of the child [8] who is considered a mere product of a contract entered into between the gestational mother and the commissioner. It is very difficult to find an analogy between the situation of a child 'commissioned' through surrogacy and an adopted child. As has been keenly noted:

> In the surrogacy, commissioning parents scrupulously choose a woman who (often due to economic needs) is willing (often forced) to leave the future born child with them and then plan the fate of a human being, who [...] does not exist yet, by planning his/her removal, at the moment of (future) birth, from its mother [...]. The baby is predestined

---

[6] F. Angelini, *Bilanciare insieme verità di parto e interesse del minore,* cit., p. 162.

[7] Thus the Milan Court of Appeals in its order of referral to the Constitutional Court July 25, 2016, n. 273, para. n. 11 in relation to the issue later decided by Judgment 162 of 2014.

[8] F. Angelini, *op. cit.*, p. 155, points out all the doubts relating to the lack of reference to this profile by the referring court in the case decided with Judgement n. 162 of 2014. She states, in fact, that: "In the practice of surrogacy of motherhood, the violation of dignity, understood precisely as the founding principle of the constitutional order and prerequisite to the protection of the human being, clearly also involves the child, whose birth is nothing more than a 'means', an 'instrument' to realize the desires of others, so much so that its appearance in the world coincides with the immediate loss of the most important relationship for him precisely because it is the only one he knows, as well as the most natural, as the maternal one; the absence of that relationship means, moreover, to make his first experience of life, his baptism to the world coincide with the experience of abandonment".

> for maternal abandonment even before its conception [...] without the possibility of pursuing that exclusive relational continuity already developed with the mother during the nine months of pregnancy.

It seems indisputable that there is:

> a profound difference from what happens in adoption, where the child already exists and is in a current state of abandonment (or in a situation of severe parental inadequacy).[9]

All this, as mentioned, is only made possible by the fact that the child, as a result of the 'contractualisation' of motherhood, is not considered as the subject of a right but as the object of an alleged right "to have a child"[10].

All this therefore explains the Italian legislator's decision to ban this practice in 2004, also considering that from a comparative point of view the legislation currently in force in Italy is among the most restrictive on the subject. According to the provisions of Article 12, para. 6, Law n. 40 from 2004, the law by which medically assisted procreation was belatedly regulated in Italy:

> Anyone who, in any form, carries out, organizes or publicizes the commercialization of gametes or embryos or surrogacy shall be punished by imprisonment from three months to two years and a fine of 600,000 to one million euros.

This provision, as is well known, was upheld by the Italian Constitutional Court, which, through its jurisprudence, did not hesitate instead to declare the unconstitutionality of many other provisions originally set out in Law n. 40/2004.

3. Surrogacy in the age of the "network" protection of rights

The provision of the offence of surrogacy in Italy is part of a varied and

---

[9] A. Bianchini, "Maternità surrogata e diritti umani dei minori", in *diritto.it,* 1/2021, pp. 5-6.

[10] See Judgement n. 162 of 2014 of the Constitutional Court, which however recalls an "incontrovertible right to become parents". See the critical comments of A. Morrone, "Ubi scientia ibi ura. A prima lettura sull'eterologa", *forumcostituzionale.it,* 11 June 2014; C. Tripodina, "Il "diritto" a procreare artificialmente in Italia: una storia emblematica, tra legislatore, giudici e Corti", *BioLaw Journal – Rivista di BioDiritto*, 2/2014.

composite framework of international and European regulatory provisions[11]. This variety of approaches, often at odds with the radical ban in Italy, has proved to be a fertile ground for so-called 'procreative tourism' thus opening up new uncertainties in the domestic legal system. Those uncertainties have arisen precisely because the Italian legislature, in this case, perhaps, short-sightedly, has failed to regulate the status of children born abroad through surrogacy.

'Procreative tourism' refers to that phenomenon whereby potential clients travel to countries where surrogacy is permitted, conclude an agreement with the surrogate mother and obtain a birth certificate. The birth certificate obtained abroad designates one or both members of the couple as 'intended' parents, depending on whether or not one of the couple shares genetic heritage with the unborn child and is thus recognized as the biological parent. Once back in Italy, the question arises as to the status of the child born from surrogacy.

In this uncertain context, the rulings of the Italian Constitutional Court and of the Court of Cassation, together with the jurisprudence of the European Court of Human Rights, have defined a regulatory framework on the status of children born abroad from this practice, which is now sufficiently consolidated, although not without some clear contradictions.

3.1. The jurisprudential trends of the European Court of Human Rights

It seems useful to recall, first, the case law of the European Court of Human Rights[12]. The court has repeatedly reiterated that the child's right to an identity, as established by Article 8 of the ECHR, is violated if ties with both members of the couple, who have voluntarily assumed responsibility for becoming parents, are not recognized. This is the position taken by the Court as early as 2014 with the *Mennesson v. France* and *Labassée v. France* rulings[13] on two similar cases involving French

---

[11] See J.M. Scherpe, C. Fenton-Glynn, T. Kaan (eds.), *Eastern and Western perspective on surrogacy*, Cambridge 2019; S. Penasa, "Tra legge e corti: la gestazione per altri in prospettiva comparata e multidimensionale", in *Riproduzione e relazioni. La surrogazione di maternità al centro della questione di genere,* ed. by M. Caielli, B. Pezzini, A. Schillaci, Torino 2019, pp. 82-105; G. Luccioli, "La maternità surrogata e l'interesse del minore", in M. Bianca (ed.), *The best interest of the child,* Roma 2021, p. 70.

[12] See C. Fenton-Glynn, "International surrogacy before the European Court of Human Rights", *Journal of Private International Law*, 13/3, 2017, pp. 546-567.

[13] *Mennesson v. France* (ECtHR, Section V – 65192/11 – 26 June 2014); *Labassée v. France* (ECtHR, Section V – 65941/11 – 26 June 2014).

couples who resorted to surrogacy in the United States. In both cases, only the intended father was the biological parent of the children born through surrogacy. The *status filiationis*, recognized in both cases in the United States, was denied in France, where surrogacy is a prohibited and sanctioned practice, preventing the transcription of the birth certificates in the relevant French civil status registers and denying recognition of the judgments that in the United States had granted this status, deeming them contrary to international public policy. In the two judgments, which came within a few months of each other, the Strasbourg Court simply recorded a different regulation in the States belonging to the Council of Europe with reference to the practice of surrogacy, thereby recognizing a wide margin of appreciation on ethical issues. At the same time, however, the Court specified that this margin of appreciation must be limited when Article 8 of the Convention is violated with respect to children born of surrogacy. For the Court there was no violation of the right of the children or intended parents to respect of family life. Considering the practical implications for the family life of the applicants of the lack of recognition in French law of the parent-child relationship, and the respondent State's margin of appreciation, the situation resulting from the Court of Cassation's findings struck a fair balance between the interests of the applicants and those of the State as regards the applicants' right to respect for their family life. Indeed, the non-recognition of the parent-child relationship has affected the private life of the children resulting in a situation of legal uncertainty that has undermined their identity within French society [14]. For the ECtHR there was therefore a

---

[14] See also the Decision of the Grand Chamber of ECtHR, *Paradiso and Campanelli v. Italia* (n. 25358/12, 24 January 2017). In this case, however, the Court considered that there had been no violation of Article 8 of the Convention as there was no biological tie between the applicants and the child. Besides, as for the duration of the relationship with the child, the Court noted its short duration and specified that such a factor is "a key factor in the Court's recognition of the existence of a family life" (§ 153). The Grand Chamber thus estimated that the conditions leading to conclude that family life existed de facto were not met and concluded that there was no family life. Finally the Court (§ 215): "does not underestimate the impact which the immediate and irreversible separation from the child must have had on the applicants' private life. While the Convention does not recognise a right to become a parent, the Court cannot ignore the emotional hardship suffered by those whose desire to become parents has not been or cannot be fulfilled. However, the public interests at stake weigh heavily in the balance, while comparatively less weight is to be attached to the applicants' interest in their personal development by continuing their relationship with the child. Agreeing to let the child stay with the applicants, possibly with a view to becoming his adoptive parents, would have been tantamount to legalising the situation created by them in breach of important rules of Italian law. The Court ac-

serious issue as to the compatibility of that situation with the children's best interests, which must guide any decision concerning them. In the subsequent advisory opinion (10 April 2019) requested to the Grand Chamber on the basis of Protocol n. 16, by the French Court of Cassation, the European Court reiterated that in the case of surrogacy abroad carried out with the genetic contribution of the male of the couple, upon return to the country of origin, the family tie with the intended mother must also be recognized in the interest of the child. It therefore reiterated that it is within the margin of appreciation of the States to choose how to recognize family ties, specifying, however, that the solution chosen must be able to guarantee immediate and effective protection for the child [15]. For the Court:

> "What is important is that at the latest when, according to the assessment of the circumstances of each case, the relationship between the child and the intended mother has become a practical reality [...], an effective mechanism should exist enabling that relationship to be recognised. Adoption may satisfy this requirement provided that the conditions which govern it are appropriate and the procedure enables a decision to be taken rapidly, so that the child is not kept for a lengthy period in a position of legal uncertainty as regards the relationship. It is self-evident that these conditions must include an assessment by the courts of the child's best interests in the light of the circumstances of the case".

3.2. Decisions of the Italian Constitutional Court

As far as the Italian Constitutional Court is concerned, it is necessary first of all to point out that it has not hesitated, on several occasions, to define the practice of surrogacy as deeply damaging to women's dignity and such as to undermine the roots of human relationships. The Italian Constitutional Court did so in an *obiter dicta* in Decision n. 162/2014 and n. 272/2017. In particular, with the latter decision, the Court fully addressed the issue of the status of the surrogate birth saying in fact "more

---

cepts that the Italian Courts, having assessed that the child would not suffer grave or irreparable harm from the separation, struck a fair balance between the different interests at stake, while remaining within the wide margin of appreciation available to them in the present case".

[15] The Court also relied on this opinion to decide subsequent cases such as *D. v. France* of 2022. Finally, a decision which seems to go against the case-law cited. It is the case of the *K.K. v. Denmark* ruling for which see note n. 34.

than what was asked" [16], thus abandoning the "prudent demeanor" [17] that in matters of surrogacy had marked its jurisprudence up to that point. The Court firstly condemned surrogacy as it "intolerably offends the dignity of women and deeply undermines human relationships" before recalling "the high degree of disvalue that our legal system attaches to surrogacy of motherhood, which is prohibited by special criminal provision" [18]. Even within the clearly stated limits of the prohibition of surrogacy, the Court found it necessary to balance the opposing interests represented by the preservation of the *mater semper certa* principle, on the one hand, and the *best interests of the child*, on the other. The need to strike a balance between different interests, with the exclusion of any unreasonable decisional automatism, stemmed from the observation that "while the system's accentuated favor for the conformity of the status to the reality of procreation should be recognized," nevertheless, the ascertainment of the biological and genetic truth of the individual does not constitute a value of absolute constitutional importance. The Court recalled how in its previous jurisprudence the biological truth of procreation was "an essential component" of the child's personal identity, which nevertheless contributed, along with other components, to defining its content [19]. In accordance with the evolution of the legislative provisions relating to the *status filiationis* and in line, therefore, with its past jurisprudence, the truth of the status can no longer be assumed as an absolute and prevailing value, but it is the "interest of the child" that has progres-

[16] F. Angelini, "Bilanciare insieme verità di parto e interesse del minore la Corte costituzionale in materia di maternità surrogata mostra al giudice come non buttare il bambino con l'acqua sporca", *costituzionalismo.it,* 1/2018, p. 151.

[17] S. Agosta, "In fuga dai divieti: una riflessione sulla proibizione italiana alla gestazione per altri", *Quaderni costituzionali*, 1/2018, p. 90.

[18] This practice, already in the judgment n. 162/2014, was also distinguished from heterologous fertilization, admitted instead under certain conditions. In particular, the aforementioned judgment states that the heterologous PMA practice: "must be strictly limited to the donation of gametes and kept distinct from other and different methods, such as the so-called «surrogacy of motherhood», expressly prohibited by Article 12, para. 6, of Law n. 40/2004, with uncensored prescription and that in no way and at no point is engraved by this pronunciation, thus preserving its validity and effectiveness".

By this decision, the Court came to the conclusion that the prohibition on recourse to the practice of heterologous PMA provided for by Law n. 40/2004 is unlawful, "only in reference to the case in which it has been ascertained the existence of a pathology that is irreversible cause of sterility or absolute infertility".

[19] The Constitutional Court recalls in para. 4.2 of the Decision, *ex plurimis*, the Judgments n. 7/2013; n. 31/2012, n. 283/1999, n. 303/1996, n. 148/1992 and n. 11/1981.

sively become the guiding criterion of the Court's action, in the absence of solutions predetermined by the legislature. The best interests of the child, also in light of the most recent case law of the European Court of Human Rights, expressly referred to by the Constitutional Court, would thus entail the need to ensure the maintenance of the child's bonds of care and affection also with the intending parent. This should not entail the automatic transcription of the birth certificate, as this interest must be balanced against the ban on surrogacy established by Italian law. Thus, the path indicated by the constitutional judge is that of the procedure known as "adoption in special cases" [20] at the outcome of the screening carried out in individual cases, by the judge.

After decisions n. 221/2019 and n. 230/2020 [21], both referring to the different issue of the recognition of children born to same-sex female couples and in which the limit of the prohibition of surrogacy was again reaffirmed in a series of *obiter dicta*, the next stage of the Constitutional Court's jurisprudence on surrogacy was represented by Judgement n. 33/2021. This latest decision appeared to represent a significant *overruling* on the part of the Constitutional Court, perhaps implicitly prompted by the changed framework of the ECtHR's post-2017 jurisprudence. On this occasion, the Constitutional Court examined the legal status of children born through surrogacy. According to the Constitutional Court, an alleged 'right to parent-hood' was not at issue, but the perspective appeared reversed, as it was now considered 'paedocentric'. Indeed, it is precisely the perspective of duties, rather than that of rights, that enables the Court to envisage certain solutions as an unfailing path that can no longer be postponed by the legislator. This path is represented by the need for social ties to be maintained with the child by both the biological and intended parents, who have freely assumed responsibility for the parental project and any family unit, whether heterosexual or homosexual, created through a consciously and voluntarily assumed choice. According to the Constitutional Court, therefore, it is not a matter of recognizing a 'right to parenthood', which has already been ruled out by its previous jurisprudence, but rather of maintaining a responsibility assumed to safeguard the best interests of the child. Indeed, these interests, even in light of the most recent jurisprudence of the European Court of Human Rights, can only be the maintenance and strengthening of ties of affection and care

[20] The "adoption in special cases" (or "adoption under special circumstances") is provided for by Article 44(1)(d) of Law n. 184 of 1983.

[21] In line with Judgement n. 272/2017 these decisions have both considered that the solution to maintaining family-ties with the non-biological parent is represented by adoption in particular cases.

that have been determined over time between the child and its caregivers. According to the Constitutional Court:

> there is no doubt that the interest of a child who has been cared for from birth by two people (for almost six years, in the case before the Court) who had jointly decided to bring him or her into the world, is to obtain legal recognition of the ties which already exist in respect of both of them, without prejudice to the possible establishment of a legal relationship with the surrogate mother.

This interest is also relevant with respect to the fact that such ties, as stated by the European Court of Human Rights, are an essential part of the child's identity:

> It is unquestionable that the child has an interest in having these ties recognized not only on the social but also on the legal level, with regard to all the fundamental aspects of his or her life – as healthcare, education, and inheritance rights. Even more importantly, he or she has a clear interest to be legally identified as a member of that family or household, which includes all the persons who are actually part of it. This is also the case when the household in question is structured around a same-sex couple, as the couple's sexual orientation does not in itself affect their suitability to assume parental responsibility (Judgment n. 221/2019; Supreme Court of Cassation, First Civil Division, Judgment n. 12962 of 22 June 2016; First Civil Division, Judgment n. 601/11 January 2013).

The Constitutional Court also pointed out that there is a perfect correspondence between the balance reached by the ECtHR and the set of principles enshrined in the Constitution on the matter and mentioned by the referring court. While that balancing point does not impact on the non-transcribability of the birth certificate, it does however require that the:

> protection of the child's interest in the legal recognition of his or her relationship with both members of the couple who not only willed his or her birth in a foreign country in accordance with the *lex loci*, but who then cared for him or her by exercising *de facto* parental responsibility should [be ensured. Such protection, moreover, should] be ensured through an effective and expeditious adoption procedure that recognizes the fullness of the filial bond between adopter and adoptee, when it has been ascertained in practice that it is in the best interests of the child. [Moreover] any solution that were to offer the child no chance of such recognition, albeit ex post and as a result of a concrete

> verification by the judge, would end up instrumentalizing the person of the child in the name of the albeit legitimate goal of discouraging the use of surrogacy.

Precisely in light of what has been observed, according to the Constitutional Court, as was correctly argued by the appellant, the use of adoption in special cases therefore no longer seems feasible. The institution in question lacks those features deemed indispensable by the ECtHR, in particular the effectiveness and speed of the adoption measure and the fullness of the filial relationship between adoptee and adopter. Adoption in special cases is in fact:

> a form of protection of the interests of the child that is certainly significant, but still not fully adequate to the standard of the constitutional and supranational principles recalled.

Compared to the precedent established by Judgment n. 272/2017, this is therefore a real *revirement* with reference in particular to whether the best interests of the child can be safeguarded through non-legitimating adoption. In this new direction taken by the Court a clear echo of the most recent case law of the European Court of Human Rights is evident, not only the one referring to the best-known decisions but also the one deriving from the opinion, referred to in the judgment of the Constitutional Court, rendered under Protocol n. 16, although not ratified by Italy. In this circumstance, unlike the well-known case-law on end-of-life judgements, the Constitutional Court with a rejection but monitory decision thus did not establish a *dies a quo* for Parliament's intervention, a choice that would have been far more challenging for the Court itself. Faced with a range of possible options "all compatible with the Constitution and all involving intervention in matters of great systemic complexity" (Judgement n. 33/2021), the Court recognized that it was Parliament's primary responsibility to intervene. Moreover, the latter could intervene with a margin of choice that the Court considered significant in identifying a solution that takes into account all the rights and principles at stake. Parliament's intervention, however, was considered 'unavoidable,' and this does not, therefore, exclude the possibility for the Court to intervene should the legislature remains culpably inert, in a 'game of remittance' that it therefore reserves for itself and that clearly shows that it considers the legislature's role to be perfectly fungible with its own role of 'supply.' In other words, the national legislature's discretionary power is *sub condicione* and, as has been rightly stated, there is as a result a "structural yielding of the principle of the separation of powers, liable to be set aside at the discretion of the constitutional judge and according to occasion".[22]

A recent Decision of the Constitutional Court, n. 79/2022, contributes to completing the framework we have just outlined with reference to the status of a child born through surrogacy. With this decision, the Constitutional Court, following its previous jurisprudence, did not hesitate to remove one of the obstacles that prevented adoption in special cases from being considered as adoption that could ensure "fullness of the filiation bond between adoptee and adopter". In fact, with this ruling, the Constitutional Court provided for the declaration of the constitutional illegitimacy of Article 55 of Law n. 184/1983 on the "Right of the child to a family," in the part in which this legislation provides that the institution of adoption in special cases does not establish any civil relationship between the adoptee and the adopter's family, recalling the application of Article 300 of the Civil Code, relating to the regulation of the adoption of persons of full age.

3.3. Surrogacy and the judges: a path with "lights and shadows".

As is clear from the rapid reconstruction of the jurisprudential framework, the solution accepted by the Constitutional Court and also by the Court of Cassation itself[23], in relation to the definition of the status of child born abroad through surrogacy, is represented by the balance between the public interest in maintaining the ban on surrogacy and the best interests of the child. While the former is defined by the law and appears to be in accordance with constitutional principle of human dignity, the latter is instead

---

[22] A. Ruggeri, "La PMA alla Consulta e l'uso discrezionale della discrezionalità del legislatore (nota minima a Corte cost. nn 32 e 33 del 2021)", *Consultaonline,* 1/2021.

[23] In the reconstruction of the jurisprudential framework in Italy that has led to the definition of the status of a child born despite of prohibition, it is also necessary to consider the most recent intervention of the Supreme Court of Cassation, United Sections, with Decision n. 38162 of 30 December 2022. On this occasion, the Court reiterated what was already stated in Decision n. 12193/2019, that the prohibition of surrogacy represented a limit of international public policy; moreover, the balance between the need to maintain this limit and the need to ensure the best interest of the child, i.e., the need to safeguard the ties of care and affection with those who have concretely taken care of the child, is represented by adoption in special cases. According to the United Sections, it seems indisputable that "mild adoption", as adoption is called in special cases, following the Constitutional Court's Decision n. 79/2022, allows the criteria identified by the European Court of Human Rights to be met, particularly those referred to in the opinion given under Protocol 16 and in more recent decisions.

considered a container without a predefined content, a general clause, which, over time has taken on different meanings, conditioned by various factors. These include precisely the aforementioned jurisprudential evolution that has significantly narrowed the scope of application of the absoluteness of the principle of truth of birth by valuing the relational continuity of the child with those who have over time established family ties with him or her. This is on the basis of the clearly expressed directions of the jurisprudence of the European Court of Human Rights 'conveyed' by Constitutional and Supreme Court of Cassation jurisprudence.

Even before the decisions of the Supreme Court of Cassation and the Constitutional Court, the ECtHR had given a well-defined content to the best interests of the child: as has already been highlighted, in several well-known judgements, it has in fact "definitively sanctioned", and peremptorily[24], that the best interest of the child is traceable to the need not to interrupt those ties of care and affection that have been created with the intended parent, and thus to recognize a right to the certainty of the filiation relationship regardless of the existence of a biological tie, holding that the child should not be forced to pay for the faults of others[25]. This implies that, precisely by appealing to the best interest of the child, once a tie has been established between the child and the couple, the legal parents in the foreign country specially chosen for the birth, they claim the consolidation of the status quo, that is, the continuity of those affective ties that were, in any case, determined due to the violation of the child's rights, his/her dignity and the dignity of the surrogate mother. The ban on surrogacy placed by the Italian legislator, in the context of the network protection of rights and in the era of the centrality of the judge, thus risks fading into the background, particularly when set against the context of the considerable economic means available to some. With its "healing" effect[26], the child's best interest becomes the instrument that can guarantee the desire for parenthood of couples who go abroad to resort to the practice of surrogacy, thus becoming a sort of tool to meet the needs of the adult couple rather than those of the child.

---

[24] See F. Paruzzo, "Status filiationis e assenza di legame genetico. La Corte d'Appello di Trento riconosce la validità del certificato di nascita di due gemelli nati in seguito al ricorso alla maternità surrogata da parte di due uomini", *Osservatorio costituzionale,* 2/2017, p. 617.

[25] Often in Italy the question of incestuous relationship is also referred to in this perspective, with reference to the well-known ruling on the subject of the Constitutional Court, n. 494 of 2002 – a ruling also recalled by the Court of Cassation in 2016 – in analogy with the case of those born from surrogacy.

[26] I. Massa Pinto, "Unione omosessuale e adozione: chi decide?", *Rivista AIC,* 4/2016.

Furthermore, it is evident that the scope of individual States' effective discretion in matters of surrogacy has been significantly reduced. Even if the ECtHR recognized a margin of appreciation in their favour, today this margin is actually limited only to the definition of the method with which individual States will be able to guarantee that best interest, while the definition of that best interest remains excluded.

4. Conclusions: who must intercept the evolution of the "social conscience"?

The context in which the issue of the status of the child born of surrogacy is set is that of the 'bewilderment' that characterizes family law more generally. The 'bewilderment' of law is indeed:

> a lemma that, evoking both disorientation and a-territoriality, particularly effectively describes the contemporary phenomenon of the spread of a de-territorialized normativity[27].

In the same perspective, it is also possible to refer to that trend described as *cross-fertilization*, a reciprocal contamination between the individual national and supranational or international legal systems. With respect to this phenomenon, the role played by the jurisprudence of the European Court of Human Rights is clear, particularly when referring to the transformations that have been 'shaking' family law for some time. In this context, the role of the ECtHR should result in a dialectical form of conditioning, characterized by the fact that the Court's influence, with respect to individual national legal systems, should not result in a simple homologation of each legislation. This result, as is well known, should be achieved through the 'margin of appreciation', a means of preserving the identities of each national system while ensuring a uniform level of protection of the specific good involved. It is indisputable, however, that when it comes to the family and its rights, the cultural humus of reference of ECtHR, by appealing to the right to private and family life in Article 8 of the Treaty and the right to marry and to establish a family, traceable to Article 12, leads:

> to the emergence of a protection of the family built on the emphasis given to the sphere of autonomy and self-determination of the person,

[27] L. Carota, "Corte EDU e tutela del rapporto con il genitore "d'intenzione" nelle coppie dello stesso sesso", *federalismi.it*, 20/2023, p. 24.

focused on the protection of individual members of the family unit rather than of the family unit itself.[28]

In other words, the Convention's special emphasis on the principle of self-determination has contributed to an "eminently individualistic conception of the family"[29], typical of European family law, and therefore to the "destandardization"[30] of the concept of family by the ECtHR. However, the progressive jurisprudential recognition of new couple and parenting models has inevitably contributed to undermining the coherence of the regulatory framework outlined by the national legislator which is instead inspired by the *ad instar natura* family model attributable to Article 29 of the Constitution.

This is a transformation that has taken place in all case law, as we have seen with regard to the status of the child born through surrogacy. An evolution often justified by the reference made by the constitutional judge and by the same judge of legitimacy, in 'conveying' the directions of the ECtHR[31], to a supposed evolution of social conscience. However, not only it is necessary to underline that it should be up to the legislator and not the judge to intercept such an evolution, but it also seems very difficult to affirm how much the evolution of social conscience is actually the prerequisite for the all-jurisprudential path that has led to the valorisation of the *de facto* ties between the child and the intended parent; or how much this path is rather the result of expressed guidelines of the European Court of Human Rights, sometimes far too homologizing and not very dialogic, as the technique of margin of appreciation would require. The result is thus likely to be represented not only by a reduction in the space of legislative discretion but also by the attribution to the judge of a role other than the one he is entitled to[32]. The judge, in fact, through his interpretative activity, sometimes in a context that is still uncertain and char-

---

[28] *Ivi,* p. 26

[29] *Ibidem.*

[30] *Ibidem.*

[31] In this respect, with special regard to the Italian Constitutional Court, see G. Vasino, "Fundamental Rights Protection and Judicial Reasoning of the Italian Constitutional Court: opening up to Supranational model trough the Proportionality Test and the Use of comparative Arguments", in this volume.

[32] The DDL S. 245 *Amendment to Article 12 of Law No. 40 of 19 February 2004, concerning the prosecution of the crime of surrogacy committed abroad by an Italian citizen*, was finally approved by the Senate on 16 October 2024. This bill is certainly an attempt by the legislator to regain a space for intervention strengthening the ban on the practice of surrogacy by providing for the prosecution of the offence even if committed abroad by an Italian citizen.

acterized by the lack of a common framework of principles, ends up helping to support some trends that have not fully emerged and consolidated, thus becoming an active player in public discourse. However, in contemporary democracies, unless the principle of the separation of powers is questioned, it is the political representatives who have to perform this delicate and inevitable task of balancing opposing interests, especially in controversial cases [33] and within the framework of respect for constitutional values such as human dignity. Moreover, it is clear that all the different problematic aspects of surrogacy must be addressed through organic choices of legislative policy: only in this way will it be possible to avoid the risk related to the variability of the judicial solution taken on the basis of the individual case, and therefore not suitable to provide stable and certain protection of the different interests at stake [34].

---

[33] N. Zanon, "I rapporti tra la Corte costituzionale e il legislatore alla luce di alcune recenti tendenze giurisprudenziali", *federalismi.it*, 3/2021, p. 86 ss. On the relationship between politics and democratic processes with judicial decisions, see also M. Nettesheim, "EU Rule of Law or Rule of Lawyers?" in this volume.

[34] In this perspective a new direction, in comparison with the previous jurisprudence, seems to emerge in the Decision *KK and Others v. Denmark* (ECtHR, Section II, n. 25212/21, 6 December 2022). In this decision, the Court recognises that the intended mother's exclusion of the adoption of a child born by surrogacy abroad, on the basis of Danish legislation, has also led to the infringement of the right to private and family life of parents. Indeed, there are those who rightly wonder about the further reduction of the margin of appreciation of the Member States and therefore about the compatibility of the solution adopted in Italian living law of adoption in particular cases as a suitable solution in the light of the latter jurisprudence. M. Caielli, "La Corte EDU Torna sulla maternità surrogata e conferma la sua giurisprudenza in materia: no news good news?", *DPCE online,* 1/2023, p. 1495 ss.

INDEX